W9-BKM-343

Praise for *How to Work for an Idiot*

"If you have the unhappy experience of working for someone you think is a real jerk, Dr. John Hoover says there is hope."
—Bloomberg Television

"How to Work for an Idiot is so cleverly disguised, you might think you're reading Norman Vincent Peale."
—Bloomberg Radio

"...an irreverent and realistic look at what people must deal with every day at work."
—CNNfn

How to Work for an Idiot

Revised & Expanded
With More Idiots, More
Insanity, and More

Incompetency

Survive & Thrive Without Killing Your Boss

By John Hoover, PhD
With illustrations by Steve Lait

The Career Press, Inc.
Pompton Plains, NJ

Copyright © 2011 by John Hoover

All rights reserved under the Pan-American and International Copyright Conventions. This book may not be reproduced, in whole or in part, in any form or by any means electronic or mechanical, including photocopying, recording, or by any information storage and retrieval system now known or hereafter invented, without written permission from the publisher, The Career Press.

HOW TO WORK FOR AN IDIOT, REVISED & EXPANDED
EDITED BY KIRSTEN DALLEY
TYPESET BY NICOLE DEFELICE
Cover design by Howard Grossman/12E Design
Printed in the U.S.A.

Cartoons used with permission of Steve Lait.

To order this title, please call toll-free 1-800-CAREER-1 (NJ and Canada: 201-848-0310) to order using VISA or MasterCard, or for further information on books from Career Press.

The Career Press, Inc.
220 West Parkway, Unit 12
Pompton Plains, NJ 07444
www.careerpress.com

Library of Congress Cataloging-in-Publication Data
Hoover, John, 1952-
    How to work for an idiot : revised and expanded with more idiots, more insanity, and more incompetency : survive and
thrive without killing your boss / by John Hoover. -- Rev. and expanded.
        p. cm.
    Rev. ed. of: How to work for an idiot : survive & thrive -- without killing your boss. c2004.
    Includes index.
    ISBN 978-1-60163-191-6 -- ISBN 978-1-60163-635-5 (ebook) 1. Managing your boss. 2. Executives--Psychology. 3. Office
politics. 4. Interpersonal relations. 5. Psychology, Industrial. I. Title.

HF5548.83.H66 2012
650.1'3--dc23
                                                            2011026934

Dedication & Acknowledgments

At this stage of my life I'm grateful that my boss is not an idiot. In fact, Amy Friedman, CEO and founder of Partners in Human Resources International, where I direct the executive coaching practice, is a most caring and compassionate business leader, well known for her endearing and enduring relationship skills. My other two bosses at Partners International from 2006 through today, Paul Gorrell and Trish Kyle, are talented, resourceful, and engaged corporate learning professionals, as well. I therefore send half of this dedication to all of the Good Bosses out there, like Amy, Trish, and Paul, who are cutting edge enough to understand that a key ingredient to success is the ability to make the first laugh of the day at one's own expense. The other half of the dedication I send to those who suffer under the yoke of working for one of the other boss types. Keep the faith.

This second edition would not be going to print if not for the confidence and leadership demonstrated by my publisher, Ron Fry, who had the prescience to back this title with public relations and creative marketing. Laurie Kelly-Pye and Michael Pye of Career Press have also been at the vanguard of this book's success since its original release in 2003. Kirsten Dalley edited this second edition brilliantly, giving my mother, Ruth Schultz Hoover, the gifted writer and über-editor of the first edition, a chance to simply wave appreciatively as this edition went to press.

Many thanks to my legal eagles, Mark Merriman and Andy Tavel, at Frankfurt Kurnit Klein and Selz PC in New York.

Other acknowledgments could be legion if space allowed. For example, I send heartfelt thanks to my dearest friend, Paula Hammond, who is always eager to give helpful advice to this recovering idiot. My sister, Ann Bourke, is an ally in my mission to rescue people from their inner idiots, beginning with my own. I am also grateful for the experience of working with talented colleagues throughout the executive coaching industry, at Fielding Graduate University, at City University of New York, and at the American Management Association. Most of all, I thank a loving God who has forgotten as far as the east is from the west what a nincompoop I have been at times in my personal and professional affairs. I am blessed.

Contents

Introduction

This book contains the debris they scraped off the walls after my head exploded. For years I wrote books on leadership, creativity, and organizational performance, traveling far and wide while extolling the virtues of innovation, flattened organizations, collaborative leadership, and shared responsibility in the workplace. My clients welcomed me and nodded approvingly as I taught the principles of teamwork and open communication. They even waited politely until I had finished and left the building before ignoring my advice.

How to Work for an Idiot is my revenge.

Regardless of what you're thinking, the Idiot I am most worried about is not the one in the corner or penthouse office—it's the one in the mirror. Accepting my personal powerlessness over stupidity and how my life had become unmanageable, I joined a recovery program for clueless creatures and found idiot-free serenity. Not a world without Idiots, but a peaceful perspective from which they could no longer perturb me.

By studying the evolutionary hiccup that resulted in Idiot Bosses (I-Bosses), I discovered why the females of some species eat their young rather than allowing them to grow into bosses who impose their ignorance on others with less institutional authority. Many direct reports from my early days as a boss might have wished my mother had had a healthier postpartum appetite.

Publishing a book such as this is not without consequences. I'm an executive coach, I supervise an executive coaching practice at Partners International in New York City, and I even helped launch a coaching certificate program at City University of New York, where I teach Coaching in the Context of the Organization. Certain people are shocked to hear the word *idiot* in my lexicon. It is not generally considered a term of endearment in polite company. Some people, especially those in human resources departments who might otherwise hire me to coach and consult, find it pejorative, even offensive. As a recovering Idiot Boss, I find that using language that aptly describes my history is a terrific reminder to me as well as a bridge to others who use such language—in their heads or aloud—when they describe their employers to friends, colleagues, family members, and coaches.

The Anger Is Out of Control

Where such language exists, there is work to be done. Many people out there are angry and self-destructive and blame it on their bosses. They need help from someone who will press pause on the Polite Machine, roll up his sleeves, engage with them, laugh with them, and cry with them on the journey to becoming a changed person who is truly appreciative of others and dedicated to the success of the organization that employs them.

If you don't believe there is an underlying current of anger and resentment running beneath the surface of all the contemporary boss humor— from Scott Adams's eternally popular *Dilbert* and *The Office* on NBC to *The Devil Wears Prada* from Fox 2000 Pictures and *Horrible Bosses* from New Line Cinema—you're not paying attention. Since the first edition of *How to Work for an Idiot* was released in 2003, the tsunami of boss bashing has risen to new heights. Whether you are the boss or the bossed, it's time to take this boss satire seriously.

I authored the original edition of this book mostly for comic relief, only to find that many people were buying it out of sheer desperation. The reader reviews posted on Amazon.com from the first edition became a curious debate between readers with a healthy sense of humor versus those who nursed homicidal fantasies about their bosses. There were those who purchased the book expecting humor, and who got humor and raved about it. Five stars. There were also those who expected the first edition to contain previously unpublished secret methods and techniques for taking the boss down without detection. Some readers thought I was going to share powerful ways to take on the boss, stomp him into a pulp, and be rewarded handsomely by the corporate Kahunas with pay raises and all-expense-paid trips to Philadelphia, or perhaps cheered with standing ovations and cornered for autographs as they walked into meetings, the employee cafeteria, or industry trade shows.

These latter readers were seriously disappointed and said so in their scathing reviews, calling me a fraud for promising to teach them how to work for an Idiot only to teach them the most successful way to work for an Idiot is to *not to be the Idiot*. Some Amazon.com reviewers who liked the book began critiquing the reviewers who hated the book, pointing out that they missed the point, thus turning the Amazon.com review page into a forum.

Sadly, both sides of the debate missed at least part of the point, which leaves the responsibility squarely on my shoulders as a less-than-stellar communicator. Those who read the first edition and split a gut laughing (which led to a few Transportation Security Administration incidents) appreciated the satire and sacrilege, but skipped over the substantive messages about materially transforming how one deals with one's boss. Those who bought the book and read between the lines in search of invisible ink and secret, clandestine instructions for a foolproof bosscide—the perfect crime that no jury in the land would hold against them—found nothing between the lines and felt cheated.

The greatest heartbreak of all came in e-mail after e-mail from all over the world (the first edition was published in 19 languages) to *www. howtoworkforanidiot.com* informing me that people had purchased the book, loved the book, laughed with friends over the book, even left the book on their worst enemies' desks while their worst enemies were at lunch and the boss was sure to see it, yet failed to appreciate that the boss management information on those pages was legit. After some of them lost their jobs or were passed over for promotions, they wrote to me describing the epiphanic moment when they realized, *Oh, there really is an art and science to boss management and I was supposed to actually* do *this stuff*. It happened to a talented journalist who ran a popular feature on the book, then turned and defied his new, younger editor and got a pink slip for his efforts. Ouch.

MAKING MONKEYS OUT OF YOU AND ME

The tone in this book is decidedly irreverent because other than outright waste, fraud, negligence, or stupidity, nothing will consume an organization's precious resources faster (with no return whatsoever) than a sacred cow. Sacred cows graze on sacred ground in nearly every for-profit or against-profit organization I've ever been exposed to. Sacred cows and sacred ground are part of the undocumented culture that no one is allowed to acknowledge, let alone challenge. Only a few corporate leaders bought copies of the first edition of *How to Work for an Idiot* in bulk for their employees to read because most Kahunas felt that it expressly violated the "hear no evil, see no evil, speak no evil" corporate code. They were correct. It did.

But just because people aren't walking around the company calling their bosses Idiots to their faces doesn't mean they're not thinking it. Just because people aren't coming to blows doesn't mean they're working well together. There is more power and thereby more potential danger in what people seal in their hearts than in what they choose to show. Anyone with an ounce of tenure in an organization is aware that the organization operates on unspoken rules and follows an unpublished org chart. Pretending otherwise is to become one of those cute little monkeys who neither hears, sees, nor speaks any evil.

CHEESEBURGERS IN PARADISE

As Mark Twain (or Abbie Hoffman, depending on which camp you subscribe to) once said, "Sacred cows make the tastiest burgers." I feel it is my mission from On High to harvest the livestock, feed the beef to the poor, and clothe them with leather pants, jackets, belts, shoes, hats, and gloves that were once sacred cattle grazing on sacred real estate. But don't be surprised if it's your personal real estate that's at stake. Here's the truth: *No one ever advanced his or her career by making the boss look stupid.* (Bosses usually don't need your help in that department anyway.) Your shining comes from helping your I-Boss shine, not in outshining him. *Your next promotion or termination will be determined in a conversation that will take place when you are nowhere around.* Everything you're thinking, saying, and doing, even when you think no one is paying attention, is scripting that conversation.

This book contains real answers to real issues, including:

☐ Idiot-speak: How to speak and understand your Idiot Boss's language.

☐ Idiot-eat: What to do at lunch when your I-Boss gets lettuce stuck in his teeth.

☐ Banishing talent: How to appear dumber than your boss and save your job.

☐ Competency-based punishment: When you pay the price for doing things right.

☐ Re-purposing anger: Because harboring resentment against your boss is like drinking a cup of poison and expecting your boss to die.

☐ Situational stupidity: Because not every boss is an Idiot and not every Idiot is a boss; flexibility is essential in the land of the clueless.

This new edition contains two new boss types: the Reluctant Boss and the Unprepared Boss, as well as new material on how all the boss types line up on a matrix of 10 leadership characteristics and competencies. As you will see, some of the scores are pretty frightening. This new edition deals with situational stupidity in an edgier and more contemporary manner that is more likely to get me sued than the first edition. There is also more trans-generational conversation in this edition. Millennials meet Old School and vice versa as they seek common ground.

LEGAL DISCLAIMER

Reading this book in a meeting when you are supposed to be paying attention is not recommended because laughing can be grounds for termination. (You may be laughing at yourself, but your clueless I-Boss won't know the difference.) Reading this book during commencement speeches, sermons, or funerals is not recommended if you ever want your spouse or children to speak to you again. Use caution when reading this book on an airplane. Many pilots now carry weapons. If you're lucky enough to not get shot, you might be ushered off the aircraft by local authorities and placed on 72-hour hold at a facility in your destination city. Caveat emptor.

Maybe we'll get the opportunity to work together in a coaching engagement or a workshop and examine your boss situation through a truly edgy lens that can reveal the hardest of truths about your boss and about you. Believe it or not, we'll have a blast, just as you will reading this new edition. Maybe you'll get to take a whack at me with the Boss Bat. As the John Nash character in the 2001 film *A Beautiful Mind* said, "There's no point in being nuts if you can't have a little fun with it."

You are welcome to contact me at *www.howtoworkforanidiot.com* and vent your spleen about your Idiot Boss, nominate an Idiot of the Month, or even vent your spleen about this book. If you're going to complain, however, I doubt you'll be telling me anything I haven't already heard. Writing this book isn't the first mistake I've ever made.

Read slowly, chew thoroughly, and swallow carefully.

1

Confessions of a Recovering Idiot

This is not a business fable featuring the exploits of Barry, Larry, Frederica, or Ferdinand as they navigate the treacherous waters of leadership or cultivate the perfect high-performing team. The stable of fables that has accumulated in business publishing is remarkable. Fables and parables are divine teaching tools and have been immensely helpful to many. I might try one for my next book. However, *How to Work for an Idiot* is an urgent and edgy warning to reach people poised on the ledge outside their office windows, ready to jump to their deaths because they thought they had life at the office all figured out only to wake up one day and discover they had been looking through the wrong lens. For them, the thought of doing this work, for this Idiot Boss, for the rest of their careers feels like staring into the abyss. Hopeless.

That would be me through most of my working life and, if you are still thinking that your boss is solely to blame for the misery and misfortune in *your* working life, it might be you, too. I specify "working life" because everything else is pretty much dealt with in *How to Live With an Idiot;* same principles and rules of engagement for the most part, different venue, set of expectations, and parameters on conduct.

This is a book about me and it is a book about you. It's about real issues and real people. It's about being alive versus being dead. More specifically, it is a book for the living dead who died to the joy they once found in working, but still show up at the office every day and collect the check. It's also for people so angry with what they perceive to be their boss's failures that they are dead to many people and things around them that could otherwise make them feel alive and energized. Anger is such a huge factor in workplace dissatisfaction that I've devoted the final chapter to the topic and titled it "Recalibrating Expectations and Repurposing Anger."

There is a point of impact where our boatload of expectations as to how our boss should treat us is dashed and splintered against the rocks of reality. Most everything you're about to read going forward deals with wave after wave of expectations crashing against those rocks of reality and rolling harmlessly back in to the surf.

The promise of this book is that you and I can live out our lives, especially our careers and the work we do, with a sense of peace and contentment that comes from accepting and skillfully playing the hand we've been dealt. Playing the hand we've been dealt requires mastery of the game; mastery and dignity that does not include complaining, kvetching, and generally seething in resentment as we grit our teeth, stay in the game, and desperately hope someone or something will change the rules in our favor.

The rules are the rules. If I could change them I would have done so a thousand times already. Those rules I can change, I do. But, human behavior is human behavior and the role of work has essentially remained unchanged since Adam and Eve bit off more than they could chew, had to get dressed, go out, and get real jobs. It is trying to white-knuckle our way past the world of work as it truly is and pretending it is the way we want it to be that gets most of us in trouble.

None of this is to say that our working lives are hopeless. On the contrary, there is enormous reason for rejoicing and hope for a better tomorrow. As long as we cling tightly to a twisted, distorted, misaligned perception of working relationships *as we feel they ought to be*, we essentially cancel the rejoicing and snuff out the candle of hope. As Theodore Roosevelt once said, it's about starting where we are, using what we have, and doing what we can.

Reality Rant

Getting clear about how the human condition impacts working conditions is step one. It begins with surrender to the notion that there might be another explanation than the one we've been trying to force on the world. Fancy that. There are other ways to go about working and functioning in workplace relationships than the ones we've been married to all these years. Moreover, there is a larger truth governed by a Higher Power and said Higher Power has been trying to entice, lure, or otherwise persuade us to implant said truth in our brains for a long, long time. Our Higher Power knows how subscription to reality is in our individual and collective best interest. Hopefully, we will exercise our precious free will to turn away from denial and toward the light of reality.

If you are anything like me, you have set and re-set world records for stubbornness while resisting the wisdom your Higher Power has been trying to impart to you. As an executive coach, I do everything I can to avoid imposing my ignorance on my clients, because that's not a skillful approach to helping someone solve problems and/or overcome personal and professional challenges. Instead, I do my best to simply establish a safe environment in which my clients can access the wisdom they already possess or can tap into vis-à-vis that larger truth. As my clients allow, I try to facilitate, through powerful questions, alignment between what works best for them and what works best for the organization that employs them. In short, I try to align what people do best with what their organizations need most. A healthy partnership between the employer and the employed and between the boss and the bossed is nirvana to the working person and the person he or she works for.

But it is not easy. No relationship worth having is easy, except perhaps in the honeymoon stage when reality has nothing to do with anything. Fast-forward to the point where the rose-colored glasses come off, the laundry hamper begins to fill with dirty socks and underwear, and unrealistically optimistic initial expectations between people in both personal and professional relationships begin to churn like troubled waters. Before you know it, a once-harmonious personal or working relationship has become the perfect storm, and chances of surviving the storm fully intact are slim to none. More likely, the storm will change you forever. You come out bruised, battered, and, worst of all, cynical and eternally resentful that your once-lofty expectations for the perfect career are at the bottom of the sea with SpongeBob SquarePants.

It takes two to dance with the stars. That is, one star plus one real dancer equal one act. Nobody dances alone. In our book, *The Coaching Connection,* Paul J. Gorrell and I wrote about treating the individual executive being coached and the organization sponsoring the coaching as co-clients. It's part and parcel of Paul's concept of Contextual Coaching. Similarly, when I was in graduate school at Azusa Pacific University earning a master's degree in marriage and family therapy, I learned that the husband coming into the clinic isn't my client. Neither is the wife. It is the relationship between them—their marriage, in fact—that I am treating.

As you will see, boss bashing is one of the most traditional and, for many, satisfying indulgences you and I need to abandon if we really hope to restore a reasonably complete sense of fulfillment in the work we do. When you and I experience difficulty or disruption with the person we report to at work, the universal solution of bashing the boss doesn't make any sense, any more than it makes sense for our bosses to bash us anytime they're unhappy. It takes two people to cause a hiccup or misalignment between what are probably two opposing sets of expectations. True resolution (write this on the palm of your hand and etch it forever on the inside of your forehead) will only come when you master the art of acceptance and appreciation.

Sounds all warm and fuzzy, doesn't it? Forgetaboutit. Learning how to work with, for, and around Idiots requires real behavioral change *on our part.* But the experience of that enlightenment doesn't need to be all bad. Just ask my readers who enjoyed the humor in this book and wrote it off as a joke the first time around and now write to me from all over the world saying, had they applied the knowledge, regardless of how funny, they would have not "unexpectedly" lost their jobs. Some of the reader reviews on Amazon.com reflect as much. To my knowledge, *How to Work for an Idiot* made virtually every bestseller list a business book can make. People loved the humor and the biting satire. Appearances on NBC's *Today,* CNN, *Fox and Friends*, more than 100 other broadcast interviews, and a half page in the *New York Times* Sunday Business section all became part of the joke. Neil Cavuto had me on *Your World* twice, so amused was he with the satire. But despite the incredible coverage the first edition of this book enjoyed, people all too often missed the all-too-obvious point: to successfully work for an Idiot (or any other boss), *don't be the Idiot.*

As you read on in this new edition, I will sometimes reference the hackneyed notion of embracing your inner child. Admittedly, the inner child stuff feels like 1980s touchy-feely gobbledygook. Be that as it may,

I for one have an *Inner Idiot* that wreaks havoc on my career aspirations. Forget my inner child. At any point in my career, when I was not getting along with my boss or when I was not getting along with peers or people reporting to me, my Inner Idiot had invariably slipped off its leash and was pridefully ignoring any greater truth or Higher Power as it tried to impose what I considered to be my sovereign, immutable, and intractable wisdom on others—with disastrous effects.

I want to embrace my Inner Idiot, all right. I want to hold him close. Hold him tight. Get a firm grip around his neck and choke the life out of him. I don't think a day goes by that he doesn't embarrass me in one way or another. I guarantee that a week won't go by in which he doesn't threaten a friendship or a client relationship. He's a nasty little gargoyle. And he knows the precise moment, usually when I'm under stress, anxious, or scared, to rear his ugly little head and pop off with some lunatic

remark. If you find me in a meeting babbling like an Idiot, saying things I'll later wish I'd never uttered, it's my mini-me, my Inner Idiot, out of his cage and trying to help me yak my way out of a tense situation. Just find something to hit us with— me and my Idiot alter ego. I don't mean to advocate violence; in fact, I can't really do much more than joke about my Inner Idiot because violence against him would be violence against me. I just need to keep him feeling content, involved, safe, and confident. Then and only then will he be reasonably well behaved. Sort of like your Idiot Boss, eh?

I don't need to couch this stuff in parable or fable. Admittedly the truth is hard to digest when told straight out, but we can chew carefully and swallow before taking another mouthful. Real-life business scenarios are crazy enough without my fictionalizing them. Having said that, however, there are some composite characters in the book and some I just made up to bridge gaps in an otherwise-factual story. So take me off the high and mighty list. I'm just an author, corporate educator, and executive coach who supervises the executive coaching practice at Partners International in New York City. But, in all those things, I have a powerfully compelling and transformational subject to address. So buckle up. My Inner Idiot is real. And so is yours. They are not likely to behave themselves on the trip we're about to take.

KNOW THYSELF

Author John Irving advises aspiring writers to write about what they know. I published five business books before I realized I had yet to write from my personal ground zero. That was more than 10 books/new editions ago. Now, as then, standing in a pile of shards where a glass house once stood, I can't remember who threw the first stone. Maybe it was me. Maybe not. It doesn't matter. The stone throwing got so intense that I forgot why they were being thrown in the first place. Oh, yeah. I remember. I was pointing my finger at others and accusing them of things of which I was equally, if not more, guilty. For every stone I threw, a bigger one came back at me. I felt justified in my accusations and victimized by the criticism of others. Dishing it out came naturally and felt righteous. Taking it seemed unnatural and unfair. Just because I lived in a glass house didn't mean I wanted others to see through me. Or did I?

MI CASA ES SU CASA

Are you living in a glass house? Are you accusing your Idiot Boss of things that you can just as easily be convicted of yourself? These are not easy questions. Nor are they questions we routinely ask ourselves. That's why I'm asking you now. The things that annoy us about others are often the same annoying characteristics we possess. Our own flaws are irritating when they show up in someone else's words and actions, and they are almost indescribably irritating when they show up in the words and actions of someone with power and authority over us.

Now that my glass house has been shattered, I'm able to write about false confidence, false security, and false pride. I know them all. Somewhere in the beginning, my wires were crossed. If not at birth, then soon thereafter. Was it nature or nurture? Genetics or environment? It doesn't matter. Now I pray daily for the serenity to accept the nature and the courage to change the nurture. As the Reinhold Niebuhr prayer implies, wisdom is the ability to distinguish between the two. All self-actualization aside, I can't help but be a little disturbed and perturbed that nobody explained these distinctions to me until I had already messed up a major portion of my life. But, that, too, is blaming. I might as well bend over and pick up another rock.

Be Not a Victim to Your Triggers

When you think of the word *trigger*, do you think of Roy Rogers's horse, or that event or moment in time when pent up hostility and resentments are detonated, exploding and caking the walls of the conference room with all kinds of toxic detritus? Who or what pulls your trigger or tends to set you off? If you pause and think about your pet peeves, idiosyncracies, or other things that cause you discomfort, you are compiling a laundry list of personal issues that need addressing. This is especially true in your professional affairs. Your chances of stopping people in positions of power and authority from doing things that typically pull your trigger are next to nil. Things other people do and say are usually beyond anything you can control or change.

However, you have a great deal of control when it comes to removing or disarming your internal triggers, thereby diminishing the likelihood that your I-Boss or coworkers will upset you. This exercise of control on your part will change the whole dynamic between you and your boss, Idiot or otherwise. Consciously disarming your triggers is the best way to build immunity against aggravation, tension, and anxiety. You'll still experience aggravation, tension, and anxiety, but they will no longer eat your lunch. Why should you care how much power an Idiot has, as long as he or she can't use it to annoy you? Reducing your I-Boss's ability to annoy you, whether he or she does so intentionally or unintentionally, is a tremendous, dare I say *phenomenal*, form of self-empowerment. And, like your dignity, no one can take it away from you.

Dealing with a trigger-puller

"My name is John and I'm an Idiot," I tell the group in the big tile-floored room in the church basement every Wednesday evening at 7 p.m.

"Hi, John," the chorus responds between swigs of coffee. Some say it clearly, as if to welcome me. Others mumble, as if speaking unintelligibly will mask the fact that they're present.

"I used to think my glass house was the perfect place to live," I continue.

"Speak up," one of the mumblers interjects, suddenly very articulate. "We can't hear you."

Annoyed by the interruption, my instincts tell me to attack him with a toxic mixture of sarcasm and innuendo, impugning his intelligence and, should I be sufficiently irritated, his ancestry. That's what we do, those of us who consider ourselves super-smart, orbiting high above the stupidity. We impugn other people's intelligence—especially after we've been caught doing something stupid. But that would be my disease talking. That's why it's called recovery. At least now I can catch myself before I throw the stone. Most of the time anyway.

I still instinctively bend over to pick up stones and formulate a poison blow-dart question like "Did someone forget his medication this morning?" But now I can regain control before opening my mouth and letting it fly. In that moment, when the stone would have been en route to its target, the truth floods over me like acid rain, eating away my pretenses. I *was* mumbling. Guilty as charged. If I'm at a meeting of recovering Idiots, trying to get beyond the thoughts and behaviors that have imprisoned my personal and professional potential all of these years, why am I mumbling? The acid burns away another layer and I decide to share my stream of consciousness with the group. "I learned that living in a glass house is not a good idea if you're going to throw stones."

"How original," Mr. Mumbles says, *sotto voce*.

I quickly pick up another stone and suck in some additional oxygen, not to calm myself, but to have enough breath support to achieve maximum volume. That's when I notice the others are glaring at him. "Don't interrupt," a woman scolds. "You know the rules."

Yeah, I think to myself. *What she said*. I feel relieved, comforted, and protected. Somebody stood up for me. Somebody cared. Instantly the anger begins to drain from my body and I feel a tinge of compassion for Mr. Mumbles. He slumps back in his metal folding chair and picks at the edge of his Styrofoam coffee cup. When I feel that someone is on my side and cares about my right to occupy space in the universe, toxic thoughts dissipate, and in their place are curiosities about how others came to be the way they are. I even begin to wonder how I came to be the way I am.

Your Idiot Boss needs to feel that someone is on her side, in her corner, and has her back. Never forget that you and your Idiot Boss are both human beings. She will have the same basic responses to feelings and situations that you have. This is important because when you feel unsupported or even undermined, you tend to become more suspicious, grasp more tightly, and fight more intensely. Your Idiot Boss does the same thing.

Find ways to support your Idiot Boss, especially in her times of uncertainty and doubt. When you do, she will feel as I did when the woman spoke up against my mumbling detractor. I had a new best friend. Recall how you felt the last time someone spoke up or took up for you. You can engender the same feeling within your boss toward you. Try it and feel the tension evaporate. Send an encouraging e-mail, mention in the hallway how well you thought she handled a situation. Keep it all in the context of the department's goals and objectives so as not to sound syrupy.

THE KILLER B'S

The four killer B's—boss bashing, boss blaming, boss bickering, or boss baiting—are best abandoned in the pursuit of positive relations with your I-Boss. Turning these four alliterative behaviors loose on your boss might seem like fun—and ultimately a fair thing to do, in light of what said boss has forced you to suffer. But in the end, you'll be the one who gets stung. Perhaps literally and figuratively *in the end.* Delayed gratification is the operative thought here. Delayed to the point that you replace these righteously indignant fantasies of wielding a sword of justice with a solid plan to engender and sustain a relational environment wherein you can serenely sail through whatever tropical disturbance your boss stirs up.

Killer B #1: boss bashing

Many people are conditioned from early childhood to detest and defy authority. Be honest: How many of you had parents who truly taught graciousness, tolerance, and respect for authority as positive virtues? Even if your parents talked the talk, did they walk the walk? Or did strife with the boss make it home to the dinner table? Was there an unspoken subtext of revenge and revolution that was never uttered aloud but nevertheless understood?

We're a society that turns songs like "Take This Job and Shove It" into legendary hits. How well would a song titled "I Love My Job and I Will Do Anything to Keep It" sell? Where is the resonance with the beleaguered and bullied spirit of the employee in that? No matter what color one's collar is (those who still wear collars), we carry within us a legacy that pops up in our culture from time to time in the form of a movie like *Office Space,* a television series like *The Office*, or a comic strip like *Dilbert*. If this weren't true, you would have already put this book back on the shelf or posted it on eBay.

Don't ever be part of a conversation that your boss couldn't walk into unexpectedly without your needing to do some damage control. When you find yourself headed toward the "B" topic with friends, family, coworkers, or perfect strangers, turn around 180 degrees and walk away from that evil place as quickly as possible. Keep yourself and your reputation on the high road by:

1. Changing the subject from the boss to a bigger challenge you're facing in the marketplace. It's easy to fall into your pre-programmed habit of boss bashing instead of looking at who gets out of bed every morning with the expressed purpose of dis-employing you—your competition.

2. Making a bigger play. Refocusing the discussion on the state of the domestic and global economy and how to best swim in those waters is a far more important conversation and relevant to your long-term future. In other words, go big picture.

3. Acknowledging that many aspects of life are challenging. So what else is new? Politely decline the invitation to bash your boss (or anybody else's) and disconnect from the boss bashing by saying that you're committed as a general life principle to finding ways in which everybody can win. Then turn the conversation back to someone else in the conversation.

That's a mirror, not a window

Before I stepped across that line between active idiocy and recovery, I didn't understand that seeing other people as nincompoops was actually a self-indictment. I didn't necessarily want my boss to stop being an Idiot: I wanted to be the Alpha Idiot. I didn't really want to stop him or her from antagonizing me with impunity: I wanted the power to antagonize him and others with impunity. I wasn't on a mission to create a kinder, gentler workplace: I coveted the power to make other people's lives miserable.

When I finally realized that other people could see me for the Idiot I was (and still am), I felt naked. Worse, I felt as if I had been living a naked dream for most of my life without knowing it. It is embarrassing, but what can I do about it now? Get comfortable with my nakedness, I guess.

That, or stitch together some fig leaves. Building another glass house with thicker walls won't help. There will always be bigger, heavier rocks to shatter them.

I can now write about being an Idiot from a position of knowledge, as John Irving suggests, because I fell into the trap. More accurately, I skipped down the road to ultimate idiocy by following my best intentions to succeed. Back then, success meant having the freedom to do whatever I wanted to do, whenever I wanted to do it, and having unlimited resources. I also wanted complete anonymity on demand, no accountability for anything I chose to do, and I wanted all of it without lifting a finger to make it all possible. I wanted to be a hybrid of William Randolph Hearst, Jr., Howard Hughes, Donald Trump, and any and all of the Kennedys. Make me Prince Charles, please. At least Mark Zuckerberg wrote the code to make his fortune with Facebook. In my heart of hearts I don't even want to do that. I want to make a big fortune the old-fashioned way—by inheriting a small one. Give me the proverbial silver spoon. Oops, too late.

Just because I'm a recovering Idiot Boss doesn't mean I don't still secretly want all of those things. The sirens never stop singing, and I never stop fantasizing. What *is* changing is my attitude toward the objects of my desire and conditions under which I want to live and work. I can now accept that I will never live like any of the aforementioned silver spooners and that this book will never put me in Zuckerberg's league. Nevertheless and better yet, I can be grateful for the things I have. If I ever achieve anything remotely close to the financial status these guys enjoy(ed), it will result from my efforts and the grace of my Higher Power. I could always win the lottery. But that's my disease butting in again. As a recovering Idiot, I live a happier, more peaceful, and more satisfied life. Despite how messed up I allowed my past to be, I still have time to live large and enlightened.

Idiots, idiots everywhere, and not a thought worth keeping

Part of a large and enlightened life is accepting there will always be 1.) Idiots, 2.) recovering Idiots like me, and 3.) those who remain oblivious to the fact that they are Idiots. Idiocy is sometimes defined as a permanent state of stupidity. I disagree with this definition. As a recovering Idiot, I know I'll always be vulnerable to stupid thoughts, stupid words, and stupid deeds. But I can reduce the frequency of their occurrence. This might sound stupid, but by the grace of my Higher Power, I've lived in spite of my stupidity my whole life. I can exercise control, minimize the debilitating effects of stupidity, and be less annoying to or annoyed by others.

We can watch Jim Carrey and Jeff Daniels depicting Idiots in a film like *Dumb and Dumber* and laugh. Same thing for Owen Wilson and Jason Sudeikis in *Hall Pass* or Jack Black in *Year One*. But when dumb and dumber are running organizations, corporations, and government agencies, it's not funny anymore. The ugly truth is that active Idiots are lurking all around us. The tentacles of their stupidity reach deep into the lives of millions. Their power is seemingly without bounds. Fortunately, Idiots are largely unaware of how much power they wield. If I-Bosses knew how many bullets they had in their chambers, things could really get scary. Why is there such power in stupidity? The answer will roll out in front of you like a red carpet as you read on. It's too much to capture in a single sentence or clever phrase. Contexts must be built. Paradigms must be shifted. Thoughts must be moved outside the box.

Killer B #2: blaming the boss

Who hasn't blamed the boss for a screw-up that was really one's own? Yes, that's my hand in the air. This is about responsibility and accepting blame when it belongs to us and (swallow hard here) oftentimes when it does not. Paul Watzlawick wrote a great book titled *The Pragmatics of Human Communication*. His thesis: "One can never not communicate." This clever use of the double negative drives home the message that being a blame-thrower at work sends a strong message that you have no interest in being part of the team, part of the solution, or part of the future. Remember, everything you say or do—sometimes things that you merely think—makes a statement about you. Everyone you encounter, in person, on the telephone, on-line, wherever or however, will read what you're communicating in their own unique way. Be aware that everything you do communicates *something*.

If and when you are tempted to transfer responsibility to your boss to avoid being tarnished by failure, think more broadly. Regardless of the boss's ineptitude, you are part of a team. More than likely, the Kahunas up the organizational food chain identify you as a member of "[insert boss's name]'s team." They're not going to see you as an innocent bystander if the team fails, so look at responsibility as a team effort.

A few salient facts about boss blaming:

1. It is self-incriminating to blame others for problems. Why even go there? Pointing the proverbial finger at my boss leaves three more equally proverbial fingers pointing back at me.

2. Any time there is accountability to be absorbed, jump on it as an opportunity. When you say "I'll take responsibility for my part in that" or "I'll be accountable for this or that part of the program," you're sending a solid message that you aren't going to stink up the room by stepping in the small stuff. You're invested in your success and everybody's success.

3. Blaming is about the person, not the problem. When the search for a scapegoat begins, aim high and lead the conversation quickly back to the problem you're trying to solve. What is the larger agenda and how do you break it down to produce a better outcome next time? If it's not clear by now, John Hoover is all about focusing on solutions and getting disentangled from blaming and personality disputes as quickly as possible, lest we get sucked into that black hole of blaming.

Cosmic questions

All of us who are committed to Idiot-proofing the universe need to make a pact to pray hard. In addition to the care and feeding of my better angels, I have a list of questions for God that, if not voiced in answer to prayer, will hopefully be answered when I meet him. I suggest you keep floating your questions, as well. The faster we get answers from the Almighty, the sooner we'll know that we're asking the right questions, and the sooner we can begin crafting sustainable solutions to the I-Boss pandemic. Here are some sample questions for your Higher Power:

- ☐ Why did You create Idiots in the first place?
- ☐ Why must intelligent people suffer from worry, fear, and anxiety while Idiots sleep well at night and awake refreshed?
- ☐ What purpose is served by keeping Idiots oblivious to the carnage they create?
- ☐ What is the purpose of Idiots, anyway?
- ☐ How do Idiots fit into the big picture?

The question on the mind of every working person the world over is: "Why does God allow Idiots to become bosses?" In a world where basketball players are paid more than scientists working to cure cancer (and that's just in college sports) and where people actually care what Hollywood actors and multi-millionaire musicians think about global politics, the fact that Idiots become bosses seems like the cruelest trick of all.

Testing the theory

You can clearly see why such profound questions must be addressed incrementally. Shamu the whale couldn't swallow such a big pill in a single gulp. An important initial question to ask, albeit one you might not *want* to ask, is "Am I an Idiot?" The following quiz can help determine whether or not you fall into that category. If it makes you too nervous to consider yourself a potential blockhead, go ahead and use the quiz to assess your boss. Answer the questions honestly. You'll decide whether the test is accurate after you determine if the results jive with your preconceived notions.

1. When something goes wrong at the office I...

    a. Automatically blame it on someone else.

    b. Drop important work and focus on damage control.

    c. Send out for pizza.

    d. All of the above.

2. When I receive orders to cut my staff I...

    a. Check the batting averages of everyone on the department softball team.

    b. Cut the people who challenge me the most to think and innovate.

    c. Send out for pizza.

    d. All of the above.

3. When I receive orders to increase production I...

    a. Threaten to fire the people who challenge me to think and innovate.

    b. Start a list of employees to blame for low production.

    c. Send out for pizza.

    d. All of the above.

4. When I receive orders to cut costs I...

a. Cancel the holiday party.

b. Force employees to provide their own office supplies.

c. Force employees to pay for their own pizza.

d. All of the above.

5. When I'm ordered to reward employees for good performance I...

a. Check the batting averages of everyone on the department softball team.

b. Allow employees to order extra office supplies.

c. Order extra pizza.

d. All of the above.

We really don't need to go any further. If you tried taking the quiz for yourself and you threw your pencil across the room before you finished, there is still hope. If you took the quiz with your boss in mind, here's how the scoring goes:

Each (a) answer is worth one point, each (b) answer is worth two points, each (c) answer is worth three points, and each (d) answer is worth four points. Four points: Just Plain Stupid; five to 12 points: A Real Idiot; 13 to 19 points: A Complete Idiot; 20 points: A Colossal Idiot. How did your boss do?

Killer B #3: bickering with the boss

This "B" is often a killer because many I-Bosses are legendary for making horrendously bad decisions and forcing you to comply or even carry out the dirty deed yourself. Inasmuch as you can influence your boss to make a better decision, use your energy accordingly. In the chapters to come, you will find techniques for exerting influence where you have limited authority. For now, consider when it's best to go ahead and get the work done that will promote your boss's agenda.

I'm not suggesting and I would not coach anyone to believe that resistance is futile, especially when working with a clueless boss. That would be abdicating the control you have to make informed choices regarding your life and work. But it's up to you to be judicious and decide when it's best to go with the flow, tread water, or actually row upstream. The amount of risk you're willing to take is your decision alone. No one can take that *or* your dignity from you.

Bickering with your boss means backing away from the responsibility to either 1.) do what you're asked to do and shut up about it, or 2.) not do what you're asked to do and shut up about it. No, I don't mean that you should literally clam up and be passive aggressive. What I do mean is that you shouldn't mumble your displeasure under your breath, nag, whine, call people or ideas "stupid," or argue clumsily and/or pointlessly. When you find yourself wanting to nit-pick at your boss, reconsider. Like boss bashing, bickering with your boss will forge you a reputation for being more of an annoyance than someone with generative ideas and sound judgment. Is it really that important to win approval among disgruntled employees? Where do you want your picture in the dictionary—beside "annoyance," or "good ideas and sound judgment"?

A few pointers to help you avoid the temptation to bicker:

1. No matter what you're asked to do, carry it out with dignity. I'm not suggesting you walk around singing "The Greatest Love of All." Unless you want to. I am saying that even if your I-Boss compels you to do some crappy things, it doesn't mean you need to conduct yourself in a crappy way. Whatever you do, conduct yourself in a way that sends a clear message as to what you're all about.

2. If you want to argue a point with your boss, practice the proverbial "Yes, and" instead of launching with "Yes, but" or just plain "But...." Say, "If we're going to follow that path, I think we should keep our eyes open and be prepared to flex and accommodate whatever unexpected responses we might receive." Okay, you said it. Nobody can argue with that. You're being strategic and the boss will feel like you have his back.

3. When your peers or your own subordinates try to engage you in bickering behavior or encourage you to bicker with the boss, steer the conversation to the higher principle you're now operating under. Say, "I know, I know," because you do know. You get it. But immediately follow that with "The problem we're solving for here is...."

The imitation myth

Most people are promoted into boss-hood without the benefit of leadership training or formalized personal development. As such, it is common for Idiot Bosses to merely imitate the leadership styles and practices of their predecessors. That's how we learn to be parents, isn't it? We either do what our parents did or we do the opposite, neither one of which is likely to be the best choice. Because virtually no I-Bosses are prepared, trained, or otherwise acclimated to the best practices of effective leadership, it's up to you to train them. You can't let your I-Boss know you're training him. That's your little secret. Just prepare your lesson plan and be consistent.

Pretend you're a CSI detective. Observe what pictures your I-Boss hangs on his office walls, and what artifacts he proudly displays around his office. What animals are pictured on his wall calendar? Listen to the words and phrases he uses. Is your I-Boss literate? Can he operate a computer? Can he build a computer? Can he write software? Can he *spell* software? Is the child in the picture on his desk indescribably ugly? Can you bring yourself to compliment your I-Boss on all of the things he so obviously holds dear, including the (not-so-cute) child that only a mother could love? Be patient. It doesn't happen overnight. If nothing else, it will give you something to look forward to at work. You can also feel smug satisfaction that you are improving the working environment for all of your peers. Don't feel dirty or guilty for brightening the relationship between you and your boss. It's survival. Think of yourself as a missionary to the clueless. You're cleaning the tank water for every single fish swimming in that aquarium. You're one of the good guys.

AN UNSPOKEN RULE OF WORKPLACE SUCCESS: YOU'RE NOT INVISIBLE

Remember that you are never not communicating. You're also likely being watched more often than you realize. This unspoken rule of workplace success amazes most people when they first learn it because it should be so obvious. Your future will be determined in conversations that take place when you aren't around. Decisions about whether or not you get a raise or a promotion, get terminated or laid off, will be made at times when you are not in the room, on the golf course, in the hotel, at the restaurant, or anywhere else the decision might be made. By the time someone sits down and tells you about it, the decision is old news to those who made it. You and I need to learn how to not only script those conversations that take place in our absence to the best of our abilities, but also make sure we make it into the conversation in the first place.

If you feel invisible or ignored, it's likely that what you're doing isn't sufficiently impressive or important to those around or above you. But they're just pretending you don't exist. Put your detective skills to work again and note what types of behavior they approve of, and start behaving accordingly. As an executive coach, I often point out that adopting someone's metaphorical language, framing ideas in the context you know resonates with that person, and then feeding back to them their exact language from a meeting or an e-mail two weeks old will produce near immediate and positive results in your favor. Even if you don't plan to alter your personal style or work habits over the long term, the experiment will prove that what you do and say are noticed more often than you think.

Please people and you'll get recognition. You need to distinguish between what your I-Boss perceives as positive and negative behavior. In sufficient quantity, both positive and negative behaviors will make those who feel invisible, visible. If you don't elicit much attention from your I-Boss, you know whatever it is you're doing falls into his or her dead zone.

Idiot Bosses usually lack imagination, or, if they have it, are imagining themselves as more grand and glorious than they truly are. That deficiency, coupled with the tunnel vision Idiot Bosses are famous for, means the ship will be submerged before they realize it hit an iceberg. If you want attention, you not only need to say or do things that warrant attention in the Idiot's eyes, but you also need to exaggerate them so much that she can't possibly fail to notice. If you're trying to impress your I-Boss by watering the plants around the office, drag in the fire hose from next to the elevator. If you want your boss to notice you're vacuuming the carpet, remove the muffler from the vacuum cleaner so the noise will deafen people two floors away; then, run a couple of circles around her desk.

Become an influencer

A former CEO of the equally former Maytag Company told me he couldn't drink coffee at work when he was a newly hired young manager because his office was down the hall from Fred Maytag, Jr. To reach the restroom he had to pass Fred's office, and he didn't want the grandson of the founder (who was president at the time) to see him making multiple trips to the john. So he gave up drinking coffee in the morning. How far are you willing to go to improve your situation? The ex-coffee drinker was trying to avoid making a negative impression. I'm suggesting you develop and employ some tactics of your own to intentionally and systematically engineer the desired impression. Consider the following:

☐ If you're willing to help look after the office plant life, do it when and where the boss will see you, but only if that's a behavior that will garner favor in your boss's eyes.

☐ If you see trash on the floor, pick it up. You never know who's looking. If you have a chance to police the area when your boss is present, make a reasonable and believable demonstration. Don't audition for the custodial crew, but demonstrate that you're into what Disney calls "Good Show."

☐ If an opportunity arises to lend the boss a hand with something, from carrying a large box to helping reboot the computer, graciously offer to help. Remember, the Killer B's and do the opposite. *Don't* bash, blame, bicker with, or bait (as in antagonize) the boss.

☐ Bring the donuts once in a while. When you do, don't just drop them in the coffee area. Walk past the boss's office, display the box, and say, "You can have first choice before I put these out for the masses."

☐ If your boss articulates frustration with a situation to which you can bring a reasonable solution, offer to help. Don't get pushy and aggravate her insecurities—make suggestions in the form of questions: "Would it help if...?" or "What if we tried...?"

☐ In all things and at all times, *be positive.* Not over-the-top, make-everyone-want-to-vomit giddy. Positive. This means finding ways to get along with difficult people, greeting your boss's directives with a can-do attitude, and making sure the boss knows you're a team player.

☐ Arrive early and leave late. If you don't want your family life to suffer, drop into conversations that you polished up that proposal last night at home or got up early to work on it before coming to the office.

Your success when working with difficult peers and difficult people in positions of power all comes down to attitude—yours. "But, Dr. Hoover," you complain, "I have serious problems and I need serious solutions." I agree. I've been there, done that, and have the mouse pad to prove it. No matter how miserable your situation, your solution starts in your head and works its way out through your hands. Brainstorm how you can be a positive influence in your working environment. But, as Jack Welch said, have fun with it.

If you think it sounds cheesy to tidy up the coffee area within your boss's view or to offer first dibs at the donuts, you don't understand how a boss's brain functions. Henry Ford said he was willing to pay more for a person's ability to get along with others than any other quality in a manager. If you think shedding resentment and hostility and replacing them with a positive and helpful demeanor is for Boy Scouts and Girl Scouts, you're not really serious about improving your working atmosphere (read: career). There is no more powerful way to impress a boss than to be a supporter. There is nothing more miserable to a boss than a detractor. Even an Idiot knows that.

Think this through to its logical conclusion. That's *your* office you're tidying up. You enjoy those plants along with everyone else. A happy boss, Idiot or no Idiot, is key to a pleasant working environment. Be honest and real about it. You are doing these things, as silly as some of them sound, and purposefully altering your attitude to improve your professional living conditions. Aren't you worth it?

Killer B #4: baiting the boss

Move over baseball—baiting the boss has become a national pastime for many people. Some folks are so stuck in the boss-as-enemy space, regardless of who it is or what the circumstances are, that the day won't be complete without a good dig at the person in charge. When you and I realize that the boss is in a cage—trapped between us and the problems we expect him to fix for us on one hand, and those above him on the organizational food chain and problems they expect him to fix for them on the other hand—we can go one of two ways with it.

The first direction is to spend otherwise-productive time poking sticks though the bars of our boss's cage in torment. Few people would do this overtly unless they had a powerful collective bargaining agreement in place. Even that isn't what it used to be. Of course, you're pretty safe if your boss works for Uncle Billy or, better yet, Dad. If "none of the above" applies to you, baiting can be risky business. The other direction is to realize that the vise-like pressure the boss is likely feeling is an opportunity for you to help ease the strain and do for the boss what you wish the boss would do for you. Even though an I-Boss probably won't help ease the strain on you the way you did for the I-Boss, don't forget that there are eyes on you and you are never not communicating. If you ever read Aesop's Fables, you'll remember that Androcles saved his own life by removing the thorn from the paw of his natural enemy, the lion. If you've been raised to believe the boss is your natural enemy, you can turn the tables by deliberately and systematically engaging in acts of kindness and helpfulness. Too warm and fuzzy for you? Try calling it enlightened self-interest.

Conversely, don't "forget" to copy the boss on important e-mails, "forget" to invite her to the right meetings, or "forget" to pass on important and relevant intelligence you collect in the course of your business— just to watch her squirm when she needs such information and doesn't have it because you suppressed it. The people I'm guessing you least want to be around are those who brown-nose the boss all day long, giving every appearance of removing the thorn from the boss's paw—perhaps even doing so—and then giggling maniacally as they strategically place the thorn where the boss is sure to sit on it. When the temptation is to bait and torment the boss, it might be a good time to rally the team and *carpe* the opportunity to position yourself for power sharing. It might be a stretch, but maybe not.

- ☐ If it becomes apparent that the boss is operating with one hand tied behind her back, be aware that she will be viewed with great sympathy by her peers. There is a simpatico at her level that you don't qualify for at your level. How you respond will be on display for numerous audiences: your boss's peers and superiors, your peers, and your subordinates. Make sure the behavior you adopt vis-à-vis your boss is the same behavior you display toward the other groups, especially your peers and subordinates.

- ☐ Schedule acts of kindness. Seriously. This stuff is too important to be left to chance. Don't wait for a good moment to arrive— make one. I'm not talking about fetching coffee. Unless you want to. I'm talking about managing by walking around. Dave Packard of (Bill) Hewlett & Packard fame is credited with this notion. If your boss isn't doing it, go do a drive-by with your boss and bring him a progress report about something important.

☐ Make your boss's cage more livable by keeping principles high and the personality stuff in check. If you know where her stress is coming from, take on one "stretch" task that will relieve some of the pressure. Not all of it—you have enough to do. But, the gesture is all that may be required to send the distinct message that you have "chosen into" the firm and not "chosen out." That might be all it takes to steer those critical conversations the way you want them to go when you're not around.

THE STUPID GENE

Be cautious with your Idiot diagnosis. Sometimes what appears to be an Idiot is just a regular person with idiot-syncrasies. We all have them. Idiot-syncrasies become exaggerated with exhaustion and dehydration. If a colleague arrives at the office wearing a different color sock on each foot, he might be a genius, a trend-setter, or just color-blind. Most likely, though, he's an Idiot.

Stupidity is different than alcoholism, drug addiction, or smoking. Well, maybe not entirely. But that's a different discussion. The analogy I'm about to make borrows liberally from 12-step recovery programs. I'm not disparaging 12-step programs, mind you. Just remember where I spend my Wednesday nights. The point is that stupidity is nearly as ubiquitous as oxygen. We have no control over stupidity in others. We didn't cause it, we can't cure it, and we can't control it. The only stupidity we can deal with is our own.

Steps to stop stupidity

Once you've become a self-realized, enlightened, transcendent (as in surpassing, going beyond the limits of ordinary experience) Idiot—one who can simultaneously reflect upon the past, present, and future of his or her personal condition and circumstances—you can no longer wander back into the Idiot population and disappear. Your intelligence, such as it is, will torment you night and day. You'll suffer from sleep deprivation (which will exaggerate your idiot-syncrasies), begin experiencing psychotic episodes, be involuntarily institutionalized, get sprung by an ACLU lawyer without your knowledge, put back on the street, and worry your family to death until your dog finds you sleeping in your garage.

The only reasonable alternative you have left is to accept the inevitability of stupidity in the form of Idiots. Welcome to the real world. You can sooner change the weather than have any effect whatsoever on the number and distribution of Idiots on this planet. Sometimes it seems as if alien Idiots in human bodies have invaded Earth. Maybe it's a cosmic conspiracy to keep us from extended space exploration beyond our own neighborhood, which the occupants of neighboring galaxies wrote off long ago as depressed real estate.

You're here. I'm here. Wherever they came from, Idiots are here. They're the only ones who don't know it. Can't we all just get along? I say yes...sort of. Our focus must be on our personal journeys toward recovery, enlightenment, and enrichment. Genuine Idiots probably won't be reading this book, so it's kind of like a private conversation between us. The good news is that we can live fulfilling lives and have rewarding careers in spite of the Idiots we work for. The bad news is we must do all of the work. Don't get mad at me. The active (as in not recovering) Idiots don't even know what's going on, so how could they help? But aren't a fulfilling life and a rewarding career worth the effort? I say yes—absolutely. With that, I take you to step one of our journey to Idiot-proof (so to speak) nirvana.

Did you notice that I tried to leave myself and my Inner Idiot out of that last rant? I can't in good conscience do that. I might as well be honest, take my Inner Idiot by the hand, launch off the stage into the mosh pit, and join the party. I am recovering, but I'm still an Idiot. I try to never forget that I've been an Idiot employee, an Idiot Boss, an Idiot spouse, an Idiot student, and an Idiot teacher. I've been an equal-opportunity aggravation to more people than I care to count. Therefore, I invite you to join me, come clean, experience the catharsis of speaking openly about your idiot-syncrasies, and begin your own journey toward an Idiot-resistant experience. Like all typical recovery programs, Idiots Anonymous has 12 steps.

STEP ONE: "I ADMIT THAT I AM POWERLESS OVER THE STUPIDITY OF OTHERS AND MY LIFE HAS BECOME TOO STUPID TO MANAGE."

Don't let this first step depress you too much. Stupidity might not be a disease, exactly, but it should at least be classified as a syndrome. We can't begin our journey of recovery until we first confess how much trouble we're in. Feeling, much less admitting, powerlessness is intolerable to most people. It implies a loss of control (which they never had anyway), and they just won't go there. Meet the living dead. These zombies walk around thinking that they can change the Idiots in their lives. I say we need to succeed in spite of the Idiots in our lives and the Idiots within.

Life will be unmanageable if you try to control stupidity other than your own. Do I need to say it again? It's too big. Let it go. Your Higher Power can handle it. You and I need to invest our resources in managing our own stupidity. *Now* we're talking manageable. Maybe. If we keep the whole universal Idiot thing in perspective and context, there is hope. Trying to manage our own stupidity issues without deference to the stupidity around us is like driving the wrong way down the freeway. You're asking for trouble. Conversely, driving in the right direction, minding your own business, and even driving defensively doesn't guarantee that some Idiot won't run into you. Each one of us is a car in heavy traffic. Keep one eye on your rearview mirror.

Confession is good for the soul. Even if the confession is somewhat of a stretch, go with the flow. It's easier to push off toward the surface from the bottom of the pool. Admitting powerlessness is the first step to recovery. Subsequent steps will reveal who has the power and how you can tap into it to achieve your own serenity. Think about what I've said in the context of managing yourself: You are ultimately your own boss, even if you report to someone else. Are you your own I-Boss, as I am? Can you be a recovering I-Boss, as I am? How effectively you interact with your boss is your choice. Will you be a monkey-see, monkey-do kind of person? Or will the monkey see bad boss behavior and think better of it?

In the chapters ahead, we'll get down to brass tacks and examine the whole Idiot issue and the roles we play in it. It makes dealing with your I-Boss at the office much easier if you can see the parallels to your own experience. I don't suggest the type of reflection that leads to regrets. But changing your thinking and behavior doesn't happen naturally or effortlessly. Contemplating your past will only serve to predict your future unless you decide to follow another road. Welcome to the journey.

STEP ONE EXERCISE

Consider what is troubling you most about your relationship with your boss and perhaps others in the workplace. Make a list with three columns. Label the first column "Things I can't change." Label the second column "Things I can change." Label the third column "The activities in which I will invest my energy." The exercise will organize your thinking and focus your efforts on the activities where you can make a difference. This exercise will help liberate you from the tyranny and oppression of things you cannot control. It will then challenge you to take ownership of and responsibility for the things you can control.

Just as we are never not communicating, people never do things for no reason. If you scratch your head at the end of this exercise and wonder why you worry and work so hard to control things over which you have no control, and avoid assuming active control over the things you *can* control, I've got an even more perplexing question for you. In the *Prairie Home Companion* motion picture, Jearlyn Steele sang, "Why do we work so hard to get what we don't even want?" If you figure that one out, please text me.

There is a reason why some of us behave this way. Solutions that depend on changing thought processes alone probably won't help much because it was illogical thinking that got us bollixed up in the first place. Only new behavior will effect the change you and I want. Just do the exercise. Don't try to over-think it. Investing in activities you *can* control will produce positive results.

Have fun.

2

Will the Real Idiot Please Stand Up?

If you think you are smarter, more talented, and more resourceful than your boss, and you resent your boss for it, who is the Idiot? If you truly are smarter, more talented, and more resourceful than your boss, here's your chance to prove it, if only for your own peace of mind. By proving it I refer to the fine art of successfully managing your physical, emotional, and spiritual well-being in spite of working for an Idiot.

Not every boss is an Idiot and not every Idiot is a boss. Some bosses rate far worse than an Idiot. Idiot Bosses are not all bad. Most of them are good at something. Even a broken clock is right twice a day. Even a blind squirrel stumbles over an acorn once in a while. You know the colloquialisms. Idiot Bosses are, as a rule, just not very good at being bosses. However, once you learn more about some of the other boss types, you might actually be grateful to have an Idiot Boss. It's time to fine-tune your radar so that you can distinguish between these boss blips. All bosses are *not* created equal, and they should not be dealt with as if they were.

It's a mistake, possibly a fatal mistake, to assume your boss is an Idiot if she is not. Using Idiot modification techniques on a non-Idiot will prove to be about as effective as snorting nasal spray to get rid of a kidney stone. Depending on the type of boss you work for, using the wrong approach might leave you wishing you were passing a kidney stone instead.

I have organized the entire world of bosses into 10 general categories:

☐ Good Bosses

☐ God Bosses

☐ Machiavellian Bosses

☐ Sadistic Bosses

☐ Masochistic Bosses

☐ Paranoid Bosses

☐ Reluctant Bosses

☐ Unprepared Bosses

☐ Buddy Bosses

☐ Idiot Bosses

EXERCISE

As we examine each boss type, place all of the bosses you have ever worked for, including your current boss, into their appropriate category. You might just list their names and make a note beside each one as to which type or types each one represents. It might be a good idea to wait until you've read this chapter to best understand each type. Reading Chapter 3 will provide even greater clarity after you see the 10 × 10 Matrix for All Boss Types. Once you've listed your current and former bosses and the types they represent, you might find that your boss history reveals a disturbing pattern. Having been both an Idiot Boss and an Idiot Employee, I have found if there are prominent boss patterns in your professional life, it could mean:

A. You are attracted to a certain type of boss to fulfill a subliminal desire for self-punishment.

B. There is a dominant type of boss in your industry.

C. You are chronically unlucky.

D. You are the Idiot.

E. All of the above.

As your coach, I remind you that there is one common denominator in every experience you have ever had with every boss type you have ever worked for: you. Do the math. You are the constant through it all. There are those who have succeeded with every boss type listed in this book or any other book. There are others who have ended badly with every boss type, even the Good Bosses. Whether you're at either end of the spectrum or somewhere in between, I ask you to reflect: Which kind of boss have you succeeded with the most? Which kind of boss have you struggled with the most? Most important, what was your role in the success or failure of each experience? Studying the boss types I've listed will help you chart the best possible course through the backwaters of boss management. When completing the first exercise from Chapter 1, take into account the type of boss you're dealing with. How would the exercise change if you changed the boss type? You might not be able to change the person, but you can change the nature of the relationship. That power is yours if you have the courage to own it—and use it.

GOOD BOSSES

As hard as it is for some to believe, there *are* Good Bosses out there. I start with this boss type because finding a Good Boss will likely be as rare as finding either a Millennial or a mosh pit (or both) at a Wayne Newton concert. Not impossible, but definitely not a sure bet. Having said that, if you see a coworker leaning back in her cubicle with her eyes closed and a silly grin on her face, chances are her thoughts have drifted back to a happier place and time when she was working for a Good Boss. Those who have worked for Good Bosses often wax nostalgic. Those who have never had that pleasure can only imagine. Throughout the balance of the chapters in this book, Good Bosses will generally be listed last because they simply aren't as likely to grab the headlines as the train-wreck bosses.

Shortly after the first edition of this book was published, the June 2004 issue of *CPA Journal* published survey findings that identified the top five reasons people leave their jobs. The same study also identified the top five reasons people stay at their jobs:

☐ Being paid well

☐ Liking their coworkers

☐ Having job security or building equity/seniority

☐ Having good benefits, such as medical/dental insurance and pension plans

☐ Being used to the job

According to the same study, the top five reasons people leave their jobs are:

☐ More money

☐ Better benefits

☐ More opportunity for career growth

☐ Less stress or pressure

☐ A change of pace

The main themes in successful employee engagement are all there: job satisfaction, social network support, compensation, and a promising future. I suspect that "not getting along with your boss" was not one of the options available in the study. A preponderance of research, coupled with my decades of experience as a corporate executive, an executive coach, and a leadership communications consultant indicate that management practices, more than any other factor, determine whether a person stays with an organization or leaves. I have seen people leave incredibly high-paying positions with no place to land because the relationship with their boss and the organization is too painful. People sometimes try to white-knuckle their way through fractured boss/subordinate relationships, only to have the organization ultimately send them off to seek their happiness elsewhere.

After conducting a employee-retention study titled "The Top Ten Reasons People Quit Their Jobs," Atlanta-based author and international business consultant Gregory P. Smith concluded that "[p]eople don't quit their companies, they quit their bosses." On the flip side of that coin, I have seen people stay in an organization that paid them poorly or turn down transfer and/or promotion opportunities within the same organiza-tion in order to stay with a boss they liked. I have seen people turn down bigger-money, loftier-title opportunities in dream companies for the same reason. Many people have the prescience to know when they have struck real gold.

It's surprisingly simple to be a Good Boss, which makes me wonder why more bosses don't get it. If a Good Boss is the most powerful factor in retaining quality people, why don't organizations pay more attention and invest more in promoting the bosses with the most popular authority (as in respect, admiration, and/or proven competence and ability to lead others earned over time)? I'll wager you know at least one I-Boss who hasn't done anything right since the Clinton administration and yet he or she is still in power. You probably also have known at least one terrific boss who crossed the wrong person, the wrong line, or the wrong wire, even by mistake, and was never heard from again.

Before I cast too many stones, I must confess it took me a long time to get it, and I still don't get it completely. The ways in which we think and act are like the tires on our car; we never give them any thought until one goes flat. For an Idiot Boss to change (and believe me, they can), some incident or series of incidents of sufficiently colossal magnitude needs to occur before he will know there is a problem. Sometimes this is a matter of introducing an executive coach and perhaps a 360-degree assessment into the equation to expose the blind spots. Once the Idiot Boss is aware that a problem exists and he is it, he can begin making the transformation from Idiot Boss to Good Boss by adopting the surprisingly simple yet profound golden rule of leadership: *Lead the way you like to be led. Duh.* Having said that, this is much easier said than done for any number of reasons that will be discussed in the pages ahead.

Simply put, Good Bosses lead the way they want to be led. In most human interactions, the simpler something is, the more effective it is. We all want simple answers, the easy road, and the easy money. If we are convicted, we want to do easy time. Have you ever heard an appliance advertisement that promised "...in just three difficult payments"? Staples, the office supply store, once built an advertising campaign around the slogan "That was easy." They still sell a big, red "Easy" button that will recite the slogan when you press it. Good Bosses have the self-awareness to understand how they like to be treated and the common sense to figure out that other people probably like to be treated the same way.

How we communicate with one another is a good place to start when you want to be a better boss or survive a bad one. Remember that one size never fits all, so read on with that in mind. Good Bosses provide a constant flow of clear and concise information and encourage you and the rest of your team to do the same. Good Bosses don't like to play 20 questions in order to figure out what you mean, and they don't want to read your mind in order to learn what you're withholding. Good Bosses typically won't do those things to you, particularly the mind-reading part.

Remove the mystery

If you make your boss play a round of Jeopardy in order to figure out what you're doing, you have a problem with her and vice versa. Making someone guess at what you want or what important information you hold in your little clutches is passive-aggressive behavior. It's resentment playing itself out. We tend to be passive-aggressive with people we want to punish. When was the last time you gave the silent treatment to someone you were happy with? The concept is easy to test—just reverse the situation and think about how you feel when your boss withholds information from you. Your imagination probably starts running wild. *Doesn't she trust me? Does she think I'm too stupid to be let in on the big secret? Is she afraid that I might do something I will get praised for?* All kinds of thoughts run through your mind—none of which produce warm and fuzzy feelings about your boss. If your boss is likewise filled with doubt, how warm and fuzzy can you expect her to feel about you?

Uncertainty always leads to uneasiness. How often do people go to lunch together and speculate about what's going on around the office? How often do you hear whispered conversations with hands cupped over the telephone mouthpiece? Have you ever found yourself sitting in a bathroom stall when your boss came in with someone else in management? You kept very still, hoping you might overhear some tidbit of information that would affect your job, didn't you? Are you aware of how often you strain to overhear what is being said in a conversation in the next cubicle or around the corner? Remember from Chapter 1, the conversation that will determine your next promotion—or termination—will be held when you are nowhere in sight.

Good Bosses are aware that sharing information in a thorough, timely manner makes people feel included, respected, and acknowledged for their ability to contribute—not to mention far more productive. Good Bosses make open communication a priority. They keep everybody informed all the time. And they are receptive to feedback. Not just when conducting MBWA drive-bys between 3 and 4 p.m. every third Tuesday, but all of the time. It's so remarkably easy that bosses who don't do it should undergo psychiatric examination and electroshock therapy if necessary. What benefits of engagement don't you understand? *Zap.*

The equitable treatment of all team members is nearly as important as communication. I say "nearly as important" because if people are going to be treated inequitably, it's better to be told up-front about it than to pretend it's not happening. The real sting from preferential treatment comes from the charade that everyone is being treated equally. People don't mind being Cinderella before her run of luck ran out as much as they hate being promised the whole prince and glass slipper thing with no follow-through.

Good Bosses are fair

Fairness in the office simply means applying the rules fairly, equally, and without regard for political alliances. Even if the rules are stuffy and cumbersome, applying them fairly across the board builds good relationships. Holding someone's feet to the fire while giving others a pass produces hostility, resentment, and even payback, if it goes far enough. Communicating openly and honestly with people and treating them fairly is really just a matter of treating them the way you like to be treated. Repeat after me: "Lead the way you like to be led." It might sound overly simple, but it works. It's not hard and it doesn't cost anything. It also works on everybody, regardless of where you are on the organizational food chain. Good Bosses treat those with more power the same way they treat those with less power. People are people. Yet, how often do you encounter a double standard? Worse, how often do you practice a double standard? I admit that I've been guilty of that.

Good employees tend to make Good Bosses, and Good Bosses tend to make good employees for those above and around them, because the same factors apply to both. Positive behaviors that produce good relationships work in all directions. Conversely, self-indulgent employees usually make self-indulgent bosses. People who screw the little person are just as likely to screw the big person, given the opportunity. If you're not a fair person or you don't communicate openly, you're not going to be the boss the cubicle daydreamer with the silly grin on her face is dreaming about. Managing in all directions is an important concept to comprehend because the implications are so far-reaching. If you have a Good Boss, chances are he is also a good employee. The values he demonstrates in your presence are likely to be the same values he demonstrates when you're not around.

Being a Good Boss is so easy, it makes you wonder why anyone would invest the extra effort and energy required to be a bad one. I guess it all could come down to not knowing any better, to monkey-see/monkey-do, or to choosing the wrong role model out of the available options. As much as go-along-to-get-along social butterflies around the office want to believe that animals and small children left to their own devices never hurt each other, there is always the ever-present hidden agenda and the ever-popular ulterior motive. When you have a bad boss, chances are somebody is up to no good.

Fairness is great, but don't be unrealistic in your expectations. As a recovering I-Boss, I learned in that church basement that fair is something that comes to town once per year and is overpriced. If you encounter true fairness in a boss/subordinate relationship, consider it icing on the cake.

Thicker than blood

When the owner's kid is working for the company, you'd be a dim bulb indeed to not figure out he is special rules material. You don't need to study much history to learn that blood is thicker than water and family money is thicker than blood. I've seen heads of families bypass talented, capable, loyal, dedicated, life-long employees to hand their businesses over to a son or a daughter whose mental faculties have been significantly reduced by generations of inbreeding. The diminished capacity often contributes to the demise of the enterprise. Typically, the first generation establishes the business, the second generation grows it, the third generation barely sustains it (maybe), and the fourth generation usually destroys whatever is left. Not just mom-and-pop shops, but big firms with hundreds of millions in revenues. Go figure.

There are exceptions. I know of several fourth-generation owners who are still growing their family business. I also know business founders who have run the entire lifecycle, from prosperity to driving the last nail in their corporate coffins, before their children had a shot. Like so many things I once rebelled against, nepotism is now on my "Get Over It and Get On With Your Life" list. In the first exercise at the end of Chapter 1, nepotism would definitely go on the list of things I cannot change or control. Even when nepotism is the order of the day, open and honest communication, along with fairness in everything else, can take away much of the sting. Working for a family-owned business can be a rewarding experience.

GOD BOSSES

There are people who think they're God. Call it narcissism with delusional overtones if you want, but no one is sure how or why some people come upon self-deification. It could be an extreme case of choosing a loftier-than-average role model. There is nothing wrong with emulating God-like qualities, but to imagine that you are the voice from the burning bush—now you're scaring me.

A God Boss is not an Idiot Boss in the classic sense. Thinking you're God actually transcends cluelessness—it's like believing you're Napoleon Bonaparte and then some. For their own safety and the safety of the population at large, God Bosses should be locked up and the key dropped in the deepest river. Of course, armies of ACLU lawyers would have them sprung before nightfall, so why bother? Ironically, God Bosses often appear in churches or missionary organizations where the real God is considered boss to begin with, so the whole thing winds up as a power struggle with you-know-who coming up short. The misguided mortal in such cases merely tries to usurp the authority. God probably doesn't consider God Bosses a threat as much as an annoyance and/or comic relief. You should take a deep breath and do the same—unless you work for one. If you have a God Boss, I hope and pray that he is a loving and gracious lord with a lowercase L, as fire and brimstone in the wrong hands can really ruin your day. Hopefully the megalomaniac doesn't expect you to wear sackcloth and sandals. Then again, the more institutional authority the God Boss possesses, the more important it is to find a way to peacefully coexist with him.

If you find it is expedient to appease a God Boss, pray for pardon from your real Higher Authority and then play church. Upon seeing your God Boss for the first time each morning, bow slightly. When he seems down or depressed, take up a collection around the office and deliver tithes and offerings unto him in the form of his favorite food, beverage, or gadget. If your God Boss indicates you have displeased him, don't argue. Beg for forgiveness. When your God Boss is angry, find something or someone to sacrifice on his desk. Johnson from Accounting would probably make a decent burnt offering. Just be careful not to grind the ashes into your boss's carpet.

Use your imagination. One of the many reasons God Bosses annoy you might be that you can't believe the real God would create such workplace piety. Believe it. Leave room for the possibility he is playing god to compensate for a tremendous lack of confidence. In either case, it pays to consider what will please him and deliver. Trying to subvert or compete with a God Boss will invariably leave you the loser.

A few pointers when dealing with a God Boss:

☐ Make sure you address your God Boss as he wants to be addressed. If he wants to be called Mr. Johnson instead of Joe, do it. Resistance will only cost you peace of mind and whatever influence over your working conditions you hope to preserve.

☐ Follow his rules. Even if his rules conflict with company policies, find the middle ground and present him with the illusion that you are doing things his way—from how to format your e-mails to the types of pictures you can hang in your cubicle.

☐ Lose the battles and win the war. God Bosses are about power because power sometimes hides incompetence. The God Boss, however, fully inhabits his delusion and doesn't believe for a minute that there is such a thing as incompetence as far as he is concerned. This fact works in your favor as you consider what it is you want to accomplish. The God Boss might well be in a position to help you if he is pleased with you. That's the war you want to win. Why get tangled up in little battles? Don't play at little games when you can play at big ones.

☐ Offer him sacrifices. Seriously. It might cost you less than you think. If he likes donuts, as I mentioned in Chapter 1, show up at his door and offer him first pick or the whole box. If he likes granola, bring him granola (and eat it yourself around him). These are silly little things, but God Bosses firmly believe that if you're not for them, you're against them. Stow your pride in the closet. If you're still hung up on that defiant "over my dead body" thing, the God Boss might be more than happy to accommodate you.

☐ Ask for forgiveness for having thoughts that did not emanate from the mind of the God Boss. It's not that hard. By saying things like "If it's okay with you..." or "Would you mind if...?" or "What do you think of...?" your God Boss will hear "You have the power to grant..." and, ultimately, "It's your will that matters most around here."

☐ Acknowledge his presence. God Bosses don't think of themselves as invisible. Don't make the mistake of ignoring him. When he comes into a meeting or enters the cafeteria, welcome him verbally. If you don't have the floor at the moment, make eye contact and nod your head to let him know you noticed his arrival.

If your God Boss had his way, there would be an announcement in the employee cafeteria every time he arrives that says, "Ladies and gentlemen, please stand to acknowledge the arrival of Boss Almighty"; when the elevator doors open, the "Fifth floor, going down" voice would be programmed to say, "Please stand aside for Boss Almighty." It sounds ridiculous to you and me, but to a God Boss, it's sweet music to his ears and a darned good idea, so somebody ought to make it so. God Bosses can be humorous to behold, but it's worth your while to respect the power he does have. Not to do so is to risk bringing a plague of locusts on yourself that will devour everything in the break room refrigerator.

MACHIAVELLIAN BOSSES

Machiavellian Bosses are fiercely intelligent, and they channel this formidable intellect not into fantasies of self-deification, but into a ruthless pursuit of power. Machiavellian Bosses view the universe as an enormous pyramid. There is one spot at the top and it belongs to them by divine right. Machiavellian Bosses have committed every ounce of their being to achieving that top spot. They don't care what or whom they must climb over to get there. They simply won't be denied. If you are run over or run through or otherwise become a casualty of a Machiavellian's race to the top, don't take it personally. It's not about you. It was never about you. And it will never be about you, except for the moment you are actually in her way. That moment is yours forever and will live on, over and over again, in your nightmares.

Machiavellian Bosses are too intelligent and shrewd to ever be considered Idiot Bosses. The only time they are ever clueless is over things that don't matter to them—like the health and well-being of other people or the goals and objectives of the organization. Machiavellian Bosses are highly focused, highly driven, and highly efficient. Translated, that means lean, mean killing machines. They remove obstacles from their path by whatever means necessary and readily available. Don't cross the street in front of a speeding Machiavellian, even if you have the "Walk" signal.

If you find yourself working for a Machiavellian, there are several ways to protect yourself. You can say things like "You know, boss, the carpet in the CEO's office matches your eyes." If the CEO of your company drives a Lexus 430 LS you can say, "You seem like a Lexus 430 LS kind of person to me." Or you can skip the symbolism and appeal directly to her insatiable appetite for power with "This organization would run like clockwork if you were in charge." Telling God Bosses and Machiavellian Bosses what they want to hear is always your best bet. Resistance is truly futile, and potentially lethal.

Like the God Boss, the Machiavellian is dead serious about her self-perception and has little or no genuine regard for you—unless she perceives you as a means to an end. Read that last thought as an opportunity. On the upside, demonstrating the proper attitude to your Machiavellian Boss will make your working environment more pleasant, and, just possibly, may keep you from getting run over.

Here are a few tips for dealing with a Machiavellian:

☐ Use the words *for you* often. Merely saying "I'll take care of it" can actually be interpreted by a Machiavellian as a threat to go over her head or steal the limelight. You probably have no such intention. But, if a Machiavellian Boss suspects that you're going over her head, she'll have yours served on a platter. To be truly safe around a Machiavellian, she must believe that what you do, you do in her name and to her credit only.

☐ Mirror her rhetoric. Because everything a Machiavellian says and does is strategically crafted to attain the top of the pyramid, it behooves you to use that language. If the Machiavellian believes that you are working on her behalf, even when you're out of sight, she is likely to begin sharing some of her institutional authority with you so that you can do more for her. You can then use the additional authority to make good things happen. As long as the Machiavellian is receiving the equity, you've found a way to potentially help others for fun and profit.

☐ Alert her to intelligence. When you find out something interesting, tell your Machiavellian Boss. Send an e-mail or mention it in passing. In constant competition with everyone (or so she thinks), the Machiavellian will appreciate any information that could be useful to her. The information might not mean much to you, but you're not engaged in her struggle for supremacy. This is a good way to build up your own "positive communications" muscle. Machiavellians are famous for killing messengers who deliver unpleasant news, no matter how factual that news is. So temper your bad news.

☐ Copy her first. Make sure your Machiavellian Boss is always the first to know. Even if it seems like pointless trivia, let the Machiavellian tell you she doesn't want to see or hear it. If she senses that you are withholding information she'll conclude you are competing with her, and things will get ugly in a hurry. This is about detoxing your environment, remember? To ensure safety, make sure the reports you share with the Machiavellian always intimate that the good work others are doing is casting favorable light on *her*. No need to be sinister or cryptic about your reports. A Machiavellian can take perfectly innocuous news and find hidden threats within it.

☐ Accept her invitations. If a Machiavellian has extended an invitation to you, that in itself is evidence that you are perceived as an enhancement to her career. Don't blow the opportunity. You may feel your peers breathing down your neck disapprovingly when your boss begins to include you. In fact, I guarantee that will happen. Just remind everyone that you are who you are. Access to the Machiavellian's institutional authority can only mean good things for the team if everybody can keep things in perspective.

☐ Frame your contributions in terms of whom your Machiavellian Boss can impress: "What you did ought to make Mr. Big a happy camper." Pinning your Machiavellian Boss's achievements onto the overarching strategic agenda of the organization builds your strategic savvy. Both are good skills to develop. Meanwhile, you're proving to the Machiavellian once again that you are furthering her career aspirations by connecting the dots between things she can take credit for and the things that will build precious equity in the eyes of those she must please to keep moving up.

The difference between a successful career and a stagnant career could depend on whether you perceive these tactics as sacrifices or opportunities. Just be aware of how your attitudes and behaviors appear in your boss's eyes. Although you and your boss might march to different drummers, your boss sets the rhythm and tempo around the office. Learning a new cadence will serve you better than forming your own drum line. Otherwise you'll probably just frustrate yourself and your boss, who in turn will drum you out.

SADISTIC BOSSES

Hello, Cruella. Telling Sadistic Bosses what they want to hear, like "Ouch," will only get them charged up to layer on more punishment—sometimes subtle and sometimes overt. Take, for example, the practical joker Sadistic Boss who puts up signs reading "When I want your opinion, I'll give it to you." Ha-ha. Sadistic Bosses apparently don't realize that people see through the pseudo-humor for what it is: a reminder of who has the power. I'll never understand why people think making light of the power disparity in the workplace is supposed to make it okay.

Like a cat toying with but never quite killing a mouse, a Sadistic Boss won't let you get away. He will keep you alive just to torture you. If you try to transfer out of his department, he will show up at your door wearing a huge grin, holding up your transfer request with D-E-N-I-E-D written across it in big red letters. You'll pinch yourself to wake from the nightmare, only to find that you're just pinching yourself and he is still standing there—wearing that evil grin. He might even post the notice on the refrigerator door in the break room for you to discover after everyone else has seen it. If you try to go around him or above his head, he will go to the Pope if necessary to get your transfer request rejected. Once you allow a Sadistic Boss to know you're wounded you'll never get away. Pain is like catnip for a Sadist.

Some people call these bosses Bully Bosses. Sadists do bully people as a rule. The more you demonstrate that the abuse is hurting you, the more abuse you'll get from a Sadist and a Bully. Showing imperviousness to the abuse or giving pushback might dissuade a Bully (who is probably just trying to make you feel the depth of pain he feels). It's more complicated to explain what's behind the Sadist's punishment. When the Sadist has institutional authority to wield, the core motivation almost becomes immaterial. Sadistic Bosses get off on pain...your pain.

If you work for a Sadistic Boss, make sure the signs of your suffering are clearly evident. As described here, it is imperative to let your groaning, gnashing of teeth, and rending of garments be heard over cubicle walls, around corners, and from across the room. Satisfied that you are suffering adequately, your Sadistic Boss might overlook you for the moment and search for victims who seem to be only marginally miserable.

A few things to keep in mind when dealing with a Sadistic Boss:

☐ Give every appearance of being busy and overworked. Don't overtly challenge a Sadistic Boss regarding your workload, but try groaning a lot: "This Avery report has me backed up two weeks—I don't know if I can make deadline. On top of that, I just found out I have to retrace all the overages for the past six years." Make your workload appear excessively burdensome. The Sadistic Boss might smile approvingly and presume that you have enough on your plate to keep you suffering—even if the suffering didn't come directly from him. The overages thing might be a stretch, but as long as you know you're working hard and adding value, what's a little hyperbole now and then?

☐ Always be ready to respond quickly, though not merrily, to a Sadistic Boss. Take on the additional work he gives but don't look happy about it. Make sure to mention that you'll get to it right after the other 12 things he has asked you to do since you came in this morning. Understand that to a Sadist, pain is power. Your pain—his power. Fighting his power only plays into his game. To preserve your sanity, you must find a way to discern between what is truly important and what is not. This discernment must be accomplished in the context of who wields the most institutional authority around you. You don't want to bury a hatchet in your own head.

☐ Sadistic Bosses want to believe that you are bent to the point of breaking, but they don't want you actually broken. That would mean you'd be on medical leave where the Sadist couldn't get at you. (A truly gifted and creative sadist can demand that you work from your hospital bed instead of watching reruns of *Jeopardy.* But he can't force you to work from your casket.)

Sadistic Bosses are truly on their game when they can keep you and the others reporting to them *almost dead*.

- ☐ Don't organize activities in a Sadistic Boss's department. Keep them underground and ad hoc. Don't dress up in your softball uniform before leaving the office. If your Sadistic Boss sees you on your way out to have fun, you'll wind up working late and missing the game. Perhaps you can preprogram groaning sounds to play on your PC speakers, a la Ferris Beuller, after you've slipped away. On second thought, scratch that: Even a satirical business book on bad bosses can go too far. If a Sadist discovered such a ruse, it would be open season on you. Your cubicle, however, should look like a war zone, with reports piled to the ceiling and wastebasket overflowing.

- ☐ Don't ever let him catch you doing nothing. Idleness invites punishment in the form of crushing workloads. I'm not saying you should fake working—you've got plenty to do to keep yourself occupied in productive activities without being deceitful. To create a better working environment for yourself, you want to work on important and personally rewarding activities. If you've ever tried to kick back and lighten things up around a Sadistic Boss, I don't need to remind you what happens.

- ☐ Watch his eyes. Whatever pain he dishes out, he has felt it before from someone more powerful. This is most assuredly true of the Bully, as well. For whatever reason, pain has become a way of life for both. Sometimes making eye contact will open up an unspoken corridor between you and he'll back off a little, as long as your gaze is empathetic and fearless. Any sign or scent of fear and you'll be history. If making eye contact only makes him rage at you, disengage.

You are best served in a Sadistic Boss's department by appearing busy and focused and entirely without good cheer, not that a serious attitude will be hard to come by. This doesn't mean you can't be upbeat and positive when you're outside of the Sadist's orbit; on the contrary, this will enhance the possibility that someone might recruit you away from your Sadistic Boss.

The fact that your boss is a Sadist is probably not news to anyone, inside or outside of your department. People higher on the organizational food chain know more than you might think, despite the fact they don't acknowledge it when you're around. If you are sour and dour, everywhere and with everyone, they won't know if the problem is you or your boss.

Finally, never talk down about your Sadistic Boss in front of his superiors. In fact, never talk down about any boss anywhere. If others see you being positive when you're away from your boss, they'll feel sorry for your situation and might even admire your tenacity for keeping a stiff upper lip in the face of such negativity. With a Sadistic Boss, play it smart but play it nonetheless.

Masochistic Bosses

Saying what a Masochistic Boss wants to hear—"You're a piece of slime"—is not exactly appropriate, and it could come back to haunt you if it's overheard by someone who's unaware of what you're dealing with. Unfortunately, complimenting Masochists only annoys them, and they usually respond by doing something particularly despicable to set the record straight.

As the moniker implies, Masochists believe that they should be punished, *must* be punished, and will suck everyone within their sphere of influence into their black hole of worthlessness. Their need to be punished is so intense, they will punish themselves if nobody else will. In extreme cases, a Masochistic Boss won't believe that anyone can criticize her well enough to be trusted. Masochistic Bosses are not Idiots in the classic sense. But they're about as uplifting as a paperweight. Masochistic Bosses attract codependents like flies to a Sunday picnic. The codependents try like crazy to fill up that black hole in the Masochist's soul, which of course is impossible. Yet the Herculean effort continues day-in and day-out. The codependents shovel affirmations down the Masochist's throat for all they're worth, and the Masochist vomits them all back up. If you want to play exorcist, that's up to you.

Departments run by Masochistic Bosses are easy to spot. For starters, very little ever gets done except for the occasional 911 call to talk the Masochistic Boss down off the ledge. Getting something accomplished might move the department an inch or two closer to meeting its goals. That might start to look a bit too much like success, and as we all know, success is the opposite of colossal failure. So that's out. Masochistic Bosses make sure their departments fail so that upper management will mete out punishment, which of course the Masochist cherishes.

The best way to deal with a Masochistic Boss is to get out of her department. There is no way these people will ever feel good about themselves, nor will they ever allow you to accomplish anything that might make them look or feel good. Doing something that makes you look or feel good might result in your Masochistic Boss saying "Oh, great. Good for yo-o-o-ou. I suppose you're going to get promoted now and knock me off the management ladder. Well, go ahead. Do whatever makes you happy." It's enough to make you take your accomplishment, wad it up, and throw it in the trash. Except that your Masochistic Boss will probably have already put the trashcan over her head and beaten it against the wall.

Things to keep in mind when dealing with a Masochistic Boss:

☐ A win/win for some Masochistic Bosses means that somebody else's win can be interpreted as their loss. Convoluted, I know, but I don't know any simpler way to explain it. A Masochistic Boss sees her life as a colossal failure and wants to enroll you in said failure. Your Masochistic Boss may very well believe that any success you enjoy will make her look like a loser in comparison. That's good—for her and for you—if you can survive the whiplash. Good for you is good for her because it makes her look bad.

☐ Most bosses expect to be included in e-mail distributions and announcements of special events because they want to be able to decide if they are attending or not, depending on what's in it for them. The Masochistic Boss, however, will simply want to confirm that anybody and everybody is wherever she is not. But even that may not be enough. The Masochistic Boss will also want to make sure that anybody and everybody is having a good time—nay, a better time—without her.

☐ Don't engage in your Masochistic Boss's negative conversation. You never want to encourage her, either. Whereas other boss types typically want to receive credit for your accomplishments as that will serve their various agendas, the Masochistic Boss will want no part of your success except when it makes her look bad. If you have something brilliant and helpful to contribute, especially something that might garner praise or recognition, leave her name out of it. Shining the spotlight on a Masochistic Boss will just annoy her.

☐ Acknowledge the bad things that can happen. The bizarre twist unique to the Masochistic Boss comes into play again, here. Whereas most people do a SWOT (strength, weakness, opportunity, and threat) analysis to predict and prepare for possible problems and exploit advantages, the Masochistic Boss is afraid that everything will go successfully as planned. She wants risk analysis to tell her the likelihood of success so that she can be prepared to tank the project at the last moment if necessary. If there are any team wins in a Masochistic Boss's department, they mostly happen when she is on vacation or sick leave.

☐ Don't invite her to the party. Your Masochistic Boss would rather have the painful pleasure of sitting home alone knowing everybody else is having a good time. Under more normal circumstances (if you can call working for a Machiavellian and/ or a Sadistic Boss a "normal circumstance"), the boss will usually come if there is something to be gained. The Masochist is happiest alone because she is most miserable alone.

☐ Use body language counterintuitively. Do the opposite of what you would normally do for most other bosses—that is, ignore your Masochistic Boss. Find a way to essentially say, "I know you're under an immense amount of pressure. But you deserve it after all, and your ultimate failure is a foregone conclusion. Furthermore, if it were in my power to terminate you and put you out of your misery—I mean, fulfill your self-fulfilling prophesy—I would. But, the best I can do is help tarnish your reputation. I hope that helps."

I rarely advise quitting, but as W.C. Fields once said, "If at first you don't succeed, try again. Then give up. There's no use being a damn fool about it." Or words to that effect. The best way to deal with a Masochistic Boss is to get out. But be careful how quickly you move out of her department. Regardless of what kind of boss you'll be transitioning to, everything—recognition, inclusion, attribution for success—will be reversed. Between having to learn to drive on the opposite side of the road and getting whiplash from instant agenda reversal, it could be dangerous. My advice: Get out before you injure yourself in the trap she has set for herself. That is, unless you're a sadist. In that case, you can play with the Masochist the way a cat plays with a defenseless mouse, and the both of you will live happily ever after. Now *that's* a win/win.

PARANOID BOSSES

A Paranoid Boss is another piece of work. To a Paranoid Boss, everything and everybody are out to get him, including you. Working for a Paranoid Boss can be a real treat, as he perceives everything as a threat. Everything you do is an attempt to subvert him—or so he thinks. What can you do? Again, very little. Paranoia is a sticky wicket. It exists largely in the Paranoid's imagination, which is not accessible to you or anyone else.

The God Boss uses his imagination in a very different way. You could say the God Boss is over-the-top optimistic about his place in the universe, while the Paranoid Boss is overly pessimistic. The Paranoid Boss believes everybody is out to get him. The God Boss believes that he is un-gettable. The Paranoid Boss spends his energy searching out and exposing the many conspiracies against him. Sometimes he actually finds one. But most of the time he has to invent one. Either way, the focus and leadership that should have been committed to departmental objectives is wasted, and the whole operation goes in the tank—thus confirming his suspicion that someone was conspiring to sabotage his operation all along.

Escaping a Paranoid Boss is not hard. If you can make her believe you're part of the conspiracy, he will do everything he can to have you punished, which in most organizations will result in your transfer. Although it's ethically suspect, you might want to try coughing at meetings. Your Paranoid Boss will immediately stop whatever he's doing and say, "What? What's going on?" Look around the room and say, "Nothing." Approximately 90 seconds later, signal one of your coconspirators to cough. Tap out Morse code on the top of the conference table and have one of your coconspirators tap back. When your Paranoid Boss demands to know what's going on, shrug your shoulders. The more you deny his accusations, the more he will suspect you and work to have you removed from his department.

Tips to keep in mind when managing a Paranoid Boss:

☐ Keep your activities in plain sight. If you're having a conversation in the break area and spot your Paranoid Boss looking your way, wave at him to come and join you. If he won't, smile and continue your conversation as openly as possible so as not to appear to be reacting to his rejection of your invitation. On your way back to your office, stop by your Paranoid Boss's office and say, "Phyllis and I were just talking about...." He might not believe that you were actually talking about what you claim you were talking about, but at least you didn't turn your back on him to continue your conversation.

☐ As you would with the Machiavellian Boss, copy your Paranoid Boss on everything. This is not to say he won't scour your e-mails for evidence of conspiracy. There is nothing you can do about that. You can, however, script language that will help keep him tuned into clear channels of communication. "As we discussed in our last meeting..." indicates that whatever you're about to discuss has already been opened up to public consumption. "You might want to double check with Ralph or Phyllis..." indicates that you're open to being checked up on by others.

☐ There comes a point when it seems there is nothing else you can do, short of moving into your Paranoid Boss's office so he can overhear every phone call you make and look over your shoulder as you write e-mails. The break room example extends to meetings that your Paranoid Boss would typically not attend. Invite him to everything, and send him updates on what transpires when he isn't there.

☐ Leverage someone he trusts, if there is such a person, to help him feel less threatened. Socializing is probably the last thing you want to do with your Paranoid Boss, but it might be the best way to earn his trust. Plus, if he relaxes a little, he might reveal to you why he's so paranoid. That information will be most helpful in managing him from that point forward.

☐ Sharing everything with your Paranoid Boss is a good way to dilute his fear of secrecy. However, demonstrating that you are sharing this information far and wide might have the effect of making him want to be part of the larger conversation. That's where you want your Paranoid Boss to be at the end of the day, in the larger conversations. This is actually a sneaky way of deliberately placing the Paranoid Boss in a paradoxical bind. You want his inner dialogue to begin questioning itself: *If everybody is talking about this stuff openly, right in front of me, where are the secrets being hidden?*

☐ Put on the uniform. Instead of following the herd out of the office for the company softball game (which your Paranoid Boss will interpret as a sure sign you're all on your way to an underground meeting), encourage your coworkers to put on their softball uniforms before they leave. Not that you can't conspire against your boss while dressed in softball uniforms, but at least you will give the appearance of doing something legitimate. And of course invite him to come to the game. If he doesn't, bring pictures and a post-game report to the office the following morning. Text photos to him during the game. This is a distinct departure from the "sneak out of the office at any cost" approach you should take with the Sadistic Boss.

There is a limit to what a Paranoid Boss will believe, even in his own imagination. If everybody is wearing softball uniforms at the end of the day, and you send him text messages or e-mails featuring shots from the game, it makes it awfully hard for even a skilled Paranoid to suspect that you're actually in a dark cellar somewhere, conspiring against him. If you walk past his office on your way to lunch with the gang and pause in his doorway long enough to ask, "I'm going out to lunch with the gang—do you want to come?" I'd say to you, "Job well done." If you bring him back a slice of pie from the restaurant or offer him the leftover pizza upon your return, I'd say, "Brilliant move."

Paranoid Bosses are not completely hopeless. Start conversations with a disarming preamble such as "May I share something with you that has been on my mind?" Naturally, your Paranoid Boss will anxiously expect a confession that you've been out to get him. Other openers, such as "My inner voice tells me that I should..." or "Do you ever wonder if..." will help keep his bow pointed into the wind. I call this *loading your conversation.* In the same way a film director decides what belongs in the frame and what doesn't, you can direct your conversation to a place where your Paranoid Boss will feel simpatico with you.

As you can see, you can do a great deal to influence your environment in a positive way. Conversely, deciding *not* to intentionally shape your environment the way you want it will only help bring about the environment you *don't* want. Inaction around the office is not innocuous. Passivity has its consequences.

RELUCTANT BOSSES

Some people just don't want to be the boss but they need the money. The masterminds that make organizational decisions, especially decisions regarding talent management, succession, and human and organization development in general, are notorious for defying all of the evidence that screams "Don't promote me!" As an executive coach, I've lost count of how many brilliant subject-matter experts I've had to talk off the ledge because they long ago gave up what they loved doing, were naturally inclined toward and gifted at doing, and accepted a new job that essentially wiped everything they loved and lived to do off their calendar. This disconnect is at the heart of countless sad stories in which people "choose out" of their organizations yet stay on the payroll until they retire or someone forces them out. When the economic woes of 2008 and beyond took retirement off the near-term table for many who couldn't wait to get out, many bosses who didn't want to be bosses—who *never* wanted to be bosses—settled in to endure several more long years of being just that.

The fiscal implosion notwithstanding, at the bottom of all this is simple economics. The brilliant organizational minds of the 21st century continue to ignore what has been rubbed in their faces for far too long: People will move away from what they do best to get paid more money. As long as the greatest compensation and benefit packages are awarded to those who manage other people, the most critical retainers in an organization will be herded into positions where they will no longer do what the organization is trying to retain them to do. Organizations continually ignore people with Good Boss potential and instead promote stellar technicians and top salespeople into entropy.

This is all part of a phenomenon I call *Idiot aggregation*, which I explain more fully in Chapter 4. For now, suffice it to say that moving people away from what they love doing and extorting them (remember that money thing) to do something they hate does not create enthusiastic or skilled bosses. As younger generations find themselves invited into the ranks of management with increasing regularity, many of them are finding management equally distasteful. The biggest difference between a middle-aged person swallowing hard and accepting a job he or she hates for the money and a Millennial taking a job he or she hates for the money is the degree to which the latter will verbalize his or her displeasure. Give a Millennial a job he or she despises and you're going to hear about it. God bless them. It's time somebody stood up and said, "This job stinks."

Tips to deal with a Reluctant Boss:

☐ If you wind up working for a Reluctant Boss, by all means empathize. Don't say, "Gee, I'm *so* glad you're the boss." He might think you're mocking him. If your Reluctant Boss is in his 30s or older, he will likely be fairly resigned to it and, true to his age, won't say much, unless you go to a bar with him after work.

☐ If the Millennial lexicon is too jarring for you, learn to say, "Bummer. This job must really stink," in your own special and appropriate way. While acknowledging the unpleasantness of the untenable situation your Reluctant Boss finds himself in, push ahead and offer to pitch in and help lighten the load. Saying "No problem, let me take care of that," might put you on your way to doing something the Reluctant Boss should be doing, but isn't. You might score points for that.

☐ Giving yourself a performance review because your Reluctant Boss can't be bothered is not as much of a stretch as you might think. Reluctant Bosses actually appreciate it when you fill out all the paperwork for this sort of thing. Ask your Reluctant Boss to forward you the files that HR sent three weeks ago and have been buried in his in-box ever since. Rate yourself. There's probably no appreciable money in the till to give your-self a raise anyway, so save your Reluctant Boss the trouble and take what you can get.

☐ Let the Reluctant Boss do what he loves to do. If he was a happy code warrior before he became an IT manager, let him write code. If he was a happy salesperson, let him go out on calls. If he was a happy analyst, let him analyze. You know the one thing he doesn't want to do is hang around the office and watch you do what he is no longer officially allowed to do any-more. So set your schedule in such a way that you can operate at the highest level of success possible without reminding your Reluctant Boss that you are there. If he notices that you're there, act as though you don't need or want anything.

I wouldn't be a good executive coach unless I believed in the eternal possibility of redemption, even in the most dire of circumstances. So pay attention to the mixed signals your Reluctant Boss may be sending out. He may actually be taking a fancy to managing others after all. He won't say that in so many words, but if he starts saying things like "I really want to know if this position is working out for you," he might be growing into management without realizing it. If there is even a spark of interest in what is going on around him, get some dry leaves, twigs, and kindling. Blow on the spark, fan the flame, and see if you can't help generate some heat. If a Reluctant Boss becomes more willing to actually *be* the boss when you're around, it could just be that you helped make the experience somewhat more pleasant.

The difference between a more-or-less invisible or absentee Reluctant Boss, and a hard-boiled, "Get the heck away from me" Reluctant Boss is usually revealed in how the Reluctant Boss's direct reports handle themselves. If the direct reports confirm the Reluctant Boss's suspicion that employees are a huge pain, the employees are likely to experience pain. If the direct reports can act like mature adults and be relatively self-managing, the Reluctant Boss might actually try to get into the management thing a little. You can play a decent-sized role in that by helping your peers understand that your Reluctant Boss is really a talented person capable of handling the job. "He just needs enough space and oxygen to get comfortable with the concept," you explain. If you look at the gap in management performance as an opportunity that the Reluctant Boss created, you could come out a hero.

Reluctant Bosses can go one of two ways: They can just burrow in deeper and deeper, avoiding all contact with their direct reports, or they can slowly acquire a taste for leading others. If your Reluctant Boss is totally absorbed with the computer and cannot be interrupted for seven hours a day, he is burrowing and, quite possibly, headed for a mineshaft disaster. On the other hand, your skill at managing up might make all the difference. If your Reluctant Boss is wired-in to his computer only three hours per day, it's time to study the surroundings, read the artifacts, and piece together what's going right—and order up some more of it.

Unprepared Bosses

Better you should have a Reluctant Boss. At least Reluctant Bosses keep whatever they know or don't know about management to themselves and out of your face (usually because they don't want to see your face). Unprepared Bosses, on the other hand, *want* to be the boss even though they simply do not possess the basic skills to manage others. In a bizarre twist, however, they can sometimes generate a decent followership based on their personal charisma. Personal charisma might be what got them promoted in the first place, in spite of their complete lack of leadership credentials.

I anticipate some squawking from Bennisian and Druckertonian leadership purists who are probably saying "Leadership and management are not the same thing!" Yeah, yeah. I have two Master's degrees, a HOD PhD, and student loans that will outlive me. I understand the concept. But every person paid for managing the performance of individual people and teams must be able to inspire some measure of followership. Even managers. Or perhaps I should say, *especially* managers.

However, when the ability to inspire followership is the only thing a new boss has going for her, trouble is bound to follow. It will only be a matter of time before whatever glaring personality deficiencies she has erupt, only to be amplified by the elevated visual platform and increased volume that come with a management position. In the earliest stages of an Unprepared Boss's first term, it's difficult to tell if there are any noticeable gaps in her management skill set, much less if she is certifiably insane. The fact is that nobody realizes that most bosses are wacko until they are firmly ensconced in their positions. Or, as is usually the case, the wacko boss functions fairly normally through a number of promotions until he or she crosses that invisible-but-lethal threshold that triggers the meltdown. That's usually when the e-mail arrives or the telephone rings in the executive coach's office.

Unprepared Bosses don't know that they don't know what they don't know. Fair enough. In the absence of such enlightenment, they assume that everyone should react to situations the way they do. Unprepared Bosses have a lot to learn—scratch that, everything to learn. The question is, can they learn it fast enough to avoid the inevitable train wreck that management ignorance can lead to? If you work for an Unprepared Boss you must make a decision: Do you jump in and help the Unprepared Boss learn what she needs to learn quickly to keep her afloat? And if so, why? You need to determine early on if you believe that she has the potential to become an effective boss (and is thereby valuable to you), or perhaps even a Good Boss, if she is given the opportunity to acquire essential leadership skills. If you guess wrong, you might birth a monster that will eat you alive. If you decide to oppose your Unprepared Boss, either actively or passively, someone else might get your goodies. Worse yet, the first thing your Unprepared Boss might learn is to weed out opposing influences—such as you.

A few things to keep in mind when you have an Unprepared Boss on your hands:

☐   Who is ever truly prepared for parenthood? This is the third time I've used the monkey-see/monkey-do analogy, but first-born children in families are either going to get the same parenting their parents received, in a classic trans-generational hand-me-down, or the intentional and complete opposite of that. Either approach can be flawed if approached arbitrarily.

☐ Likewise, if a new boss has no management or leadership training, she is likely to fall back on imitation, *n'est-ce pas*? It's been the same since the beginning of humankind. If Adam and Eve had been better parents, son number one might not have whacked son number two.

☐ Everyone raises his or her parents in a certain sense, so now is a good time to put that experience to good use. Your parents were going to be your parents no matter what, even if you wished against all wishes that you could trade them in. Who hasn't had the same feelings about their boss? It makes sense to manage up.

☐ Keep your mind clear and believe in your heart that the good you do for others has a direct correlation to and is cosmically aligned with the good things that are happening to you. The others I am referring to include your Reluctant Boss as well as your peers and subordinates who function under the Reluctant Boss's institutional authority.

☐ Resist gaining popular authority at your boss's expense. Like the proverbial I-Boss you will read about shortly, an Unprepared Boss is often someone people like to make fun of. Some people take great offense to an Unprepared Boss's inability to give them everything they want; to this mocking or angry employee, the boss is really a surrogate parent. And apparently not a very good one. If I've said it once, I've said it a thousand times: *No one ever enhanced his or her career by making the boss look stupid.*

☐ Pitch in and help the Unprepared Boss learn on the job. Learn what? How to manage by walking around, both literally and virtually, to find people (read: you) doing what they're supposed to be doing. How to recognize people (you) for the positive things they do so they'll do them more often. How to reward people (you) for the value they add to the organization. How to create an atmosphere of collaboration and 360-degree support in which everybody can cross-pollinate everyone else's efforts.

☐ Despite my reminders that managing up is a form of enlightened self-interest, it's not all about you or me. In a team
environment, it is truly about everybody. That's the environment
I want to work in, and that's the environment you can help an
Unprepared Boss build and sustain. If your Unprepared Boss
twists in the wind, so will you. It's a great temptation for many
to watch their Unprepared Boss fail in a role for which she simply lacked adequate preparation. But someone higher on the
organizational food chain than you gave your Unprepared Boss
the institutional authority to be your boss. To the smart person,
one who can control his or her Inner Idiot (you know, the one
that loves to watch bosses suffer), this is a great time to resist
such temptation and realize that your Unprepared Boss is your
entrée to position and power, and the opportunity to influence
the organization in ways that you feel align with truth, justice,
and the good old global perspective. If the Unprepared Boss
lacks the skill to manage down, in all likelihood she will lack
the knowledge of how to manage up. Helping your Unprepared
Boss prepare for presentations, big meetings, and important reports, and generally manage up effectively can be your opportunity to move up. How cool is that?

BUDDY BOSSES

I don't need any more friends, do you? When I originally wrote that in
2003, I was being a bit too glib. Fact is, people are the joy and the purpose
of my life and work. There is no way I can live out my faith without people
to help and serve. I would be a sorry executive coach if it were all about
me and my ego. A wealthier executive coach, perhaps. But one who is
true to my certification? No. Nevertheless, I'm a much better servant than
entertainer and, ergo, more fulfilled and stimulated when I can enjoy the
support, encouragement, and accountability that can only come from fel-
lowship with like-minded folks. The trouble is that a Buddy Boss assumes
he is like-minded when he is anything but. Not that we shouldn't respect
diverse points of view and seek to be inclusive and receptive to multiple
points of view. But Buddy Bosses want to crawl inside your head and take
up permanent residence.

Buddy Bosses are so determined to occupy the same space in the universe with you that you'll welcome any excuse to elude them. This includes

working. "Sorry, boss," you rehearse saying in the mirror, putting on the most pitiful face you can conjure. "The CEO just gave me a deadline directly. Didn't she copy you?" Logic like this places a Buddy Boss in a paradoxical bind. If you are fired, he loses a buddy and has to break in someone new to replace you. So distressed is he by your potential unavailability, he won't question why the CEO might be giving you orders directly.

Tips to keep in mind when handling a Buddy Boss:

☐ As a matter of self-preservation, invite your Buddy Boss to everything. He is going to come anyway. Your Buddy Boss will be hurt if he finds out you didn't include him, and you'll be saddled with a sulking boss, which would only appeal to a sadist. A wounded Buddy Boss is a pitiful thing, indeed. After days of enduring his slumped posture, tears, and sniffles, you'll wish you had just included him in the first place.

☐ Share information openly with your Buddy Boss. This will make him feel included. Sharing information openly is a sound organizational practice anyway, so make it a habit. Remain mindful, though, that most of the boss types—with the exception of the Good Boss—are not concerned first and foremost with best practices. You can immobilize a Buddy Boss to a degree by flooding him with information, which in turn keeps him out of your way temporarily while you try to get some work done.

☐ Request meetings with your Buddy Boss. A Buddy Boss might, like a mother hen, enthusiastically gather his chicks around him, but if it's always at his suggestion, he might eventually become annoyed, saddened, and even resentful. Cue the tears and sniffles. If you request a staff meeting at least once a week, the time can be put to productive organizational use, and your Buddy Boss will be pleased that you took the initiative. To him, it means you care. He'll gladly let you plan and conduct the meeting, which puts the ball in your court (read: the power in your hands) to shape the environment and move your agenda forward. Provided you are one of the good guys (as most readers of this book are), that's a good thing.

☐ Post pictures everywhere with your Buddy Boss in them. Visual demonstrations and reminders of his inclusion in all things will be emotionally reassuring to him. When he starts to get weepy about never being included in anything, ignore the comment and say with a sigh, "Gee, Boss. Remember that Punt, Pass, and Kick competition we sponsored?" Point to the picture on his desk. "You had that 8-year-old beat until the last kick. And personally I think she cheated." Each year on his birthday, give your Buddy Boss another annual scrapbook that shows how loved he is. In this day and age of electronic publishing across platforms, make sure to include a DVD and send photos and videos to his iPhone and iPad just as you would with a Paranoid Boss. Load his Facebook page with the same inclusive images, tag him in photos, and set your program to automatically poke him once an hour all weekend.

☐ Regularly send him missives to remind him that he's not alone. It doesn't take very many words to say "Hi"; the "How are you doing?" part is implied. Sending pictures and funny stories to his e-mail address also promotes his sense of inclusion. Include his home e-mail address that on the CC line and make sure he is snared in your net of friendliness wherever he is, especially on vacation. That is, if you can get him to take a vacation without you and your family.

☐ Beware the confessional. Your Buddy Boss will devote endless hours to hearing your confessions and making his confessions to you. This can distract you from getting any appreciable work done. When his confession begins, ask politely if you can hear it later because there are too many pressing issues at that moment to give him your complete and undivided attention. This is a true statement and allows you more control over when you can be distracted. Make a big deal out of when you schedule the conversation and send your Buddy Boss constant reminders from your Outlook calendar. He will be pleased, and his separation anxiety contained, in anticipation of your upcoming conversation.

Perhaps the biggest challenge with a Buddy Boss is time management. Set time limits. When your Buddy Boss asks, "Do you have a minute?" Tell him you have three, and they're all his. Then put aside any distractions that might pull your focus away from your Buddy Boss. Sit him down, sit opposite him, make eye contact, and don't blink for three minutes. Then stand up and walk away, thanking him for sharing. This behavior modification technique is usually quite effective if applied consistently. If every time he asks for your time, you set a limit, he will tend not to ask when his intention is to engage you in an open-ended conversation. This technique works on needy people amazingly well, be they bosses or subordinates. For decades now, I have taught these techniques for giving a few uninterrupted minutes a day and thereby saving hours of unstructured, unending interruptions. The techniques work.

Time and again I've seen bosses and employees preempt their neediest employees or bosses by going to them and asking for three minutes of *their* time each morning. More often than not, that eliminates the knock on your door later. You need to be on your game to avoid having a Buddy Boss surgically removed from your hip. With any luck, you might get transferred to an Idiot Boss.

IDIOT BOSSES

Be thankful for small blessings. Unlike the God, Machiavellian, Sadistic, Masochistic, Paranoid, Reluctant, Unprepared, and Buddy Bosses, the I-Boss is simply a chronically clueless mutant from the evolutionary journey of the species. The wagon of human development hit a bump somewhere, and the I-Boss was left sitting in the middle of the road in a cloud of dust, rubbing the bump on his head. From there, he wandered into a nearby office to use the toilet and, before long, was running it—the office, that is. This is the real world.

If you thought cluelessness was the only obstacle you were going to deal with in the workplace, I hope this chapter has been helpful in disabusing you of that notion. The balance of this book will make reference to the top-10 boss types, although I default more often than not to understanding I-Bosses, for there are so many of them (remember, I was one). So I won't completely exhaust the subject of the I-Boss here. In the spirit of true recovery, however, I must confess that despite my best efforts to the contrary, I am still an Idiot with an ambitious and over-eager Inner Idiot, ready at all times to pop out and make me look like a colossal moron—all driven by my intention to look impressively erudite and wise. That, or to make people feel sorry for poor, pitiful me. The good news is that your I-Boss probably won't:

☐ Think he's God, as a God Boss does.

☐ Be shrewd enough to surgically slice her way to the top, as a Machiavellian Boss is.

- [ ] Gleefully cause lacerations, leaving you bleeding all over his desk, as the Sadistic Boss would.
- [ ] Mutilate herself, or ask you to mutilate her, and bleed all over your desk, as a Masochistic Boss would.
- [ ] Suspect that Ninjas are going to sneak in and attack when he is not looking, as a Paranoid Boss would.
- [ ] Hide under his desk to avoid having to do any boss stuff, as a Reluctant Boss would.
- [ ] Struggle to stay afloat regardless of her desire to be a boss, as an Unprepared Boss would.
- [ ] Plug his umbilical cord into your fuel cell and start living off of your Chi, as a Buddy Boss would.

Be kind to your I-Boss. Do it for me. If it all seems too overwhelming, don't be discouraged. That's what a Higher Power is there for. That's why there are 12 steps, to help each of us dial into our Higher Power and tune out the noise of confusion that dealing with wacko bosses can create. Once again, the second step in our 12-step program for Recovering Idiots helps us put things in perspective so we can get a grip on what we need to do to deal with bad bosses and/or avoid becoming one ourselves.

THE SECOND STEP: "I REALIZE THAT THE CHALLENGE OF AN I-BOSS IS TOO BIG FOR ME TO HANDLE BY MYSELF AND I NEED A POWER BIGGER THAN ALL THE JARGON-SPEWING BOSSES IN THE UNIVERSE—GOOD, BAD, OR OTHERWISE—TO KEEP ME FROM GOING *COMPLETELY* CRAZY."

Santa Claus might be a myth, but I-Bosses are real, and I believe that God loves I-Bosses just as much as the rest of us. If not, why did he make so many of them? They are here to test our faith, secure our sanity, and teach survival skills. You see, all things *do* work together for good. The boss who doesn't kill us will make us stronger. If it weren't for I-Bosses, we might start thinking we really can control the world around us. With a delusion like that, you and I are just an I-Boss waiting for a corner office in which to set up shop. Our real sanity depends on confessing powerlessness and sincerely and completely turning our I-Bosses over to the omniscient, omnipresent, and omnipotent care of our Higher Power.

Idiot Bosses keep us honest. If we didn't have them around, how could they enrich our lives? As the country song asks, "How can I tell you how much I miss you if you won't go away?" Be thankful for your I-Boss. He might be the easiest to work with and the least threatening to your health of all the other boss types, save the Good Boss. I remind you yet again: Make sure your boss is an I-Boss before you start applying I-Boss intervention methods and techniques. Attempting to use I-Boss solutions on other boss types is like running a cross-platform application with incompatible software. At best, you will crash the system; at worst, you might set off an intermolecular reaction causing the planet to implode, creating a black hole sucking all known matter in our galaxy into nonexistence, and leaving only Idiot Bosses in charge until the next Big Bang. I-Bosses are apparently immune to things that would kill mere mortals.

Remember, not every boss is an Idiot, and not every Idiot is a boss. The best you can do is be prepared to deal with whatever comes your way. Let go and let God. Instead of thinking of yourself as a victim of an I-Boss or any other boss type, think of yourself as a vessel, created to bring love and redemption to the most loathed character on this planet and beyond. The Step Two exercise that follows will help you determine if you are a victim of a bad boss or a volunteer for the distasteful treatment bad bosses can subject you to.

STEP TWO EXERCISE

Keep your radar on high alert, scanning your surroundings at all times for every boss type. Now that you are becoming a skilled diagnostician of various boss types, you will be better prepared to quickly distinguish between the variety of boss blips you encounter, and immediately begin applying the methods and techniques contained in these pages. You are probably ahead of me in realizing that these diagnostic skills and palette of possible interventions apply to anyone with these disorders, not just bosses who have been imbued with institutional authority to impose their ignorance and/or character defects on the less powerful. The scope of this book, however, deals with the latter.

Call them bogies or bad guys all you want; we all share the same family history, so take out your legal pad, draw a vertical line down the center, and do your Franklin balance sheet comparison. Make your left column a list of how a victim would respond to boss behaviors from the boss type in question. The right column should list the parallel responses that you would expect from a person empowered by knowledge and empathy. As much as you might hope and pray for it, your boss is not going to be sent to the Island of Misfit Toys with all the other bad bosses. So study and compare your lists, giving your boss the same benefit of the doubt that you might accord to a friend or close relative. Can you see how the two lists, one made from a victim's perspective and the other made by an empowered and empathic person, portray radically different points of view? One column will reek of unending strife, while the other will have the scent of springtime. One column will portray gloom and doom, whereas the other is hope in bloom. The more you and I struggle to control the things over which we have no control, the deeper we sink into the vat of victimization.

If there is anything empowered and enlightened boss whisperers can share with us (paean to author Laura Crawshaw), it's the difference between trying to swim up Niagara Falls, which is roughly the equivalent of thinking we can fight back and change something we had nothing to do with creating and cannot cure nor control, versus floating with the current on an inner tube of acceptance. "Wait a minute!" workshop participants often blurt out at this point. "If I didn't cause my boss's disorder and can't cure or control it, I can't be anything *but* a victim."

"Slow down," I say calmly, maintaining a safe distance. "It's never that black and white."

In other words, scratch the all-or-nothing, black-or-white thinking. There will always be some things you and I alone are powerless to change. Those we leave to our Higher Power. However, there will be places and things where you and I can have an impact. Ergo the Niebuhr prayer for the "wisdom to know the difference." If we master and demonstrate the necessary serenity, courage, and wisdom, we can bring out the best in any boss, even the Idiots. The key to our peace and tranquility is establishing reasonable and attainable expectations. This exercise can go a long way to accomplishing that.

As at-will employees, you and I can always vote with our feet. Each one of us functions and has choices that fall along a continuum, from resigning and walking out singing "Take this job and shove it," to "I'll do anything for you boss, anything, 'cause I owe everything to you." Somewhere in between those extremes is your personal homeostatic sweet spot, a place where you can accept what you can't change and exert genuine influence on the things you can change, beginning with your own attitude, over which you have total control. If you're truly smarter than your boss, this is how you can demonstrate it, at least to your own satisfaction and for your own sense of inner peace. The more deeply you examine the divergent perspectives on your balance sheet, the more you will begin to see victimhood as volunteerism. You and I choose which side of the page to occupy. In that, there is tremendous power and control. When the real Idiot stands up, make sure it's not you volunteering for the job.

3

Characteristics and Competencies for Boss Types

In 2003 I pondered whether Idiot Bosses were the product of nature or nurture. Were they a fly in the ointment of evolution or a product of God's sense of humor? (Yes, God has a sense of humor. Have you ever seen a duck run?) As an executive coach, I can't tell you how often I'm told, "Stuff happens. Nothing caused it. Nobody's fault. Next question." Well, I say again, *stuff never just happens.* Tracking on Paul Watzlawick's notion that "one can never not communicate," I also believe that there is *always* a reason for human behavior. Either consciously or unconsciously people will do things or not do things, but never without reason.

When things explode and fall apart, it is because somebody created something explosive and lit the fuse. Either intentionally, by mistake, or perhaps merely through sheer negligence, often with the best intentions, somebody created the conditions that made the explosion possible. As an executive coach who always coaches in the context of the organization— that is, *constantly seeking to align what people do best with what the organization needs most*—I'm trying to identify, isolate, and unpack the behavior that led to the explosion and to redirect that energy into more productive and less-incendiary activities. By contrast, coaching motivated High Potentials who merely need to grow into their potential and expand their leadership skills sets is the icing on the cake of coaching.

Often I position the recovery step and associated exercise at the end of a chapter. But Step Three and the Step Three exercise *is* the chapter. There just happens to be a mountain of information to address on the front end. That is if you want to read about the characteristics and competencies of all boss types. You might prefer just to focus on your boss's type, which will shorten your time spent in Chapter Three.

THE THIRD STEP

Understanding how your natural characteristics and learned behaviors have set you on a course of tolerance or intolerance for stupidity is essential if you are to become more adept at dealing with your boss, assuming you're the smarter one. Without self-awareness, framed in the context of your Higher Power, how will you ever know if the discomfort and frustration you attribute to your boss is real or a product of your imagination? How will you ever know if your boss's dysfunctional behavior is truly dysfunctional or only appears so as a result of lens distortion when viewed through your particular lens? Most likely, for you and your boss, it is a combination of both.

Surrendering your will and your life to your Higher Power is important because he created you *and* your boss. You and your boss are both swimming in the same water, so to speak. You are different creatures within the same system. But how different are you, really? You might fit together in some providential way you just haven't figured out yet.

To me, Higher Power is synonymous in part with higher *intelligence.* We all need the perspective of a Higher Power to guide us through this study. When you and I surrender to a Higher Authority, we begin trying to succeed in the context of a system or higher order in which we and our bosses (and subordinates) are hopefully complementing one another through our natural conditions and learned competencies. What the boss lacks, we fill in. Hopefully, it works in reverse as well. Even if it doesn't work in reverse, we keep filling in anyway.

Step Three Exercise: "We decided to turn over our will and our lives to our Higher Power—as we understand him."

The Third Step exercise involves combining who your boss is and what he or she has learned with who you are and what you have learned to create a Good Boss scenario. The Third Step exercise is to (1) identify the boss type you're having the most difficulty with and (2) determine which characteristics and competencies you can supplement in your relationship with that boss type that might transform the combination of *you and your boss* into something that resembles a Good Boss relationship. You heard that right. If you want the experience of a Good Boss, it might be that you will need to make up the difference. Are you willing to be that much a part of the solution as to supplement what your boss might be lacking or will you slip back into merely complaining about your boss's shortcomings? It's your choice.

Background for the Exercise

As the first decade of the 21st century gave way to the second, many private sector and public sector corporations, public agencies, for-profits, and against-profits were drafting leadership competencies. Some organizations rolled out competencies that were actually natural, born in characteristics as well as learned attitudes and behaviors that became defining human characteristics. I refer to the latter as competencies because treating deeply ingrained characteristics and learned competencies in the same way diminishes the important difference between the two.

At the risk of becoming entangled in semantics, a human characteristic is essentially a person's default setting. A person will do something because "it's the way she is." Or, a behavior "defines his character." It's an individual's umbra, so to speak. Only with deliberate and intentional learning does one build a competency that is contrary to or absent from a person's natural (or very early developed) character. Our Higher Power understands all this. We could stumble around trying to figure it out for ourselves, or accept that we're part of a larger system and allow our Higher Power to reveal to us what we need to know if we're open to receive the knowledge.

The Matrix that follows contains published competencies I've studied from various organizations across the country and around the world. Some of these characteristics/competencies in my clients' corporations form an organizational framework for my coaching. The identified characteristics/ competencies of an organization's culture form the *context* in which coaching engagements take place.

When you think of the various definitions of "competent," including "adequate," "sufficient," and "the ability to do what is required," it doesn't sound to me as though the organizational designers, learning and development experts, and organizational behaviorists who launched the competency craze sought to set the bar very high for leadership. It sounds as if all leaders need to be is "adequate" and "sufficient" with "the ability to do what is required." I might have suggested the rubric of "leadership excellencies" instead of competencies. But nobody asked me, and who am I to push back against the tidal wave of Human Resources and Learning and Development opinion? So, behold Dr. Hoover's Excellent Character/Competence 10 × 10 Matrix for All Boss Types:

Note: The first vertical line in each category is *Characteristic*. The second vertical line is *Competency*.

Boss Type	1. A Curious & Studious Person	Skilled in Research & Inquiry	2. An Empathic & Realistic Person	A Skilled Negotiator	3. A Fair & Appreciative Person	Skilled at Dispute Resolution	4. A Confident & Responsible Person	Skilled at Constructive Confrontation	5. A Caring & Attentive Person	Skilled at Listening & Assessing Needs	6. An Open & Transparent Person	A Skilled Communicator	7. A Clear Thinker & Future-Focused Person	A Sound, Strategic Planner	8. Natural Technical Inclinations	Skilled at Application and Execution	9. Other-Focused & Organizationally Astute	A Skilled Coach	10. Intelligent & Hungry to Help Others	A Skilled Teacher & People Builder
God Boss	✓	✓									✓									
Machiavellian Boss	✓	✓		✓								✓	✓			✓	✓			
Sadistic Boss	✓	✓											✓			✓				
Masochistic Boss									✓	✓	✓					✓	✓			
Paranoid Boss	✓	✓														✓	✓			
Reluctant Boss				✓									✓			✓	✓			
Unprepared Boss	✓		✓	✓	✓		✓				✓					✓				
Buddy Boss	✓			✓					✓	✓	✓					✓			✓	
Idiot Boss	✓			✓							✓									
Good Boss	✓	✓	✓	✓	✓	✓	✓	✓	✓	✓	✓	✓	✓	✓		✓	✓	✓	✓	✓

NATURAL HUMAN CHARACTERISTICS AND THE COMPETENCIES LEARNED IN ADULTHOOD

The first vertical line in each category is what I consider a characteristic. The second vertical line is a competency. Though nearly every characteristic or competency exist in some organization's competency list somewhere, I've reshuffled and mixed and matched them a bit to create alignments that I find most functional and helpful in leadership behavior.

So as not to put executive coaches and learning and development professionals out of business, virtually everyone is capable of learning and applying almost any knowledge to some degree. This Matrix, however, reflects what you can expect from a boss type *before* he or she engages in coaching or another learning solution. Once people are coached or embark on a successful learning journey, which they might or might not be willing to do, they can potentially get credit for the competency if it is demonstrated consistently over time. The Matrix demonstrates how coaching, learning, and development can completely reshape the picture.

Characteristic 1: A Curious and Studious Person

Corresponding Competency 1: Skilled in Research and Inquiry

More than just mere curiosity, the first characteristic is upgraded to an inquisitiveness sufficient to warrant study, even if it is merely watching a television documentary on the subject. Surfing the Internet or reading a book on the subject are better yet, as is studying Idiot Bosses through a literary lens, as you're doing now. Enrolling in a master's program on dealing with Idiot Bosses (if there were such a thing) would be considered approaching really serious. Skilled research and inquiry refers to a structured approach to gathering data, analyzing it, and documenting what has been learned, thus adding to the body of knowledge so that more learning can take place.

The God Boss

God Bosses are checked off in the curiosity and skilled research columns because they can demonstrate tremendous curiosity—mostly about themselves and the formal documentation of their reigns. God Bosses could even be considered competent in that they have been known to study theology to promote self-awareness. They will often employ scribes to assist in this process.

The Machiavellian Boss

Machiavellian Bosses get check marks in the curiosity and skilled research columns because they want to know the blueprint and architecture of the organization they intend to run one day. This curiosity can lead to staying up all night poring over and analyzing organization charts (lists of enemies) and succession plans. A Machiavellian politician (redundant, I know) is the epitome of someone skilled and highly competent at researching pathways to power.

The Sadistic Boss

Like God Bosses and Machiavellian Bosses, Sadistic Bosses get checks in the curious and studious characteristic and competency column, but not for healthy reasons. Sadistic Bosses are always in search of what causes the greatest discomfort to their direct reports and assorted enemies. So curious are they, that researching their direct reports' pain thresholds to identify their breaking points is a common practice.

The Masochistic Boss

Masochistic Bosses really don't care how their lives came to be colossal catastrophes; they just assume they are and will continue to be. Thus, they feel no need to become skilled at research and inquiry. No check marks.

The Paranoid Boss

Unlike Masochistic Bosses, Paranoid Bosses are obsessed with what's going on around them. This insatiable curiosity, like the curiosity of the God Boss and Machiavellian Boss, is not necessarily good for the individual or the organization, but it is powerful. Paranoid Bosses will go to great lengths and invest much time in researching the plots and conspiracies against them, which usually means observing, tracking, and analyzing activities with a high degree of lens distortion.

The Reluctant Boss

Reluctant Bosses don't become reluctant through any sense of curiosity or formalized research. Therefore, no checks for them in the curiosity or skilled research column. If a Reluctant Boss did, in fact, go to boss school and research the art and science of management, he or she might not be so reluctant. A caveat here: The Reluctant Boss *might be* very curious and astute in research, but not in an untreated state when it comes to successful bosshood. Coaching and refocus of these characteristics and competencies could produce check marks quickly.

The Unprepared Boss

The Unprepared Boss is the first boss type to split the curiosity character/competency column. They are curious about what it feels like to be the boss and have people report to them. They are not, unfortunately, curious enough to study how to be a Good Boss. Unprepared Bosses tend to remain unprepared because they mostly just enjoy the experience of bosshood.

The Buddy Boss

Buddy Bosses carry their umbilical cords around in their hands in search of someone to attach them to. That seems to be the extent of their curiosity—whose life can they plug into and begin siphoning into their own tanks? Buddy Bosses have no check mark on the competency side of curiosity and studiousness because they leave all the learning about life to you. They'll just stitch themselves to your hip and where you go, they go.

The Idiot Boss

Idiot Bosses are curious in a childlike way. They are checked off as curious characters as a courtesy. In truth, their curiosity is very limited and not driven by a desire to learn, but to just be fascinated with simple things. Idiot Bosses' curious natures can usually be thoroughly engaged by simply giving them a rubber band to play with at meetings. That can keep them occupied for hours.

The Good Boss

As you can imagine, Good Bosses are constantly curious about how things can be made better; in the tactical, transactional, operational moment and in the crafting of future-focused strategic plans. They study the latest research and conduct their own literature reviews to remain current and inspire new thinking. Seminars and workshops, either in the classroom or on-line, are often filled with bosses who are curious and invest time, energy, and other resources in researching how to be a better boss who builds better organizations. Check, check.

Characteristic 2: An Empathic and Realistic Person

Corresponding Competency 2: A Skilled Negotiator

An overactive empathic gland can be a bad thing. Flaming codependents (such as myself) can give away the farm in the cause of making others happy. To be an effective coach, I need to keep my empathy between the navigational beacons of practicality. It will help you to do the same as you deal with your boss. Being realistic with the ability to negotiate effectively for yourself and in the best interests of others and your organization as a whole is critical to being a Good Boss and a good employee.

The God Boss

No check for God Bosses on empathy. If they were truly a Higher Power, that would be different. But God Bosses, being faux, small "g" gods (and even then, only in their own fertile imaginations), don't score well on empathy or realism. No check mark for God Bosses under the negotiation competency either. God Bosses tend to decree more than they negotiate.

The Machiavellian Boss

Machiavellian Bosses are not known for their empathy or realism beyond the reality they can impose on less-powerful people. Negotiation, however, can be a competency for Machiavellian Bosses in that they will recognize the organizational power others have in as much as it will get them closer to the coveted top of the pyramid—hence, the checkmark.

The Sadistic Boss

The last thing Sadistic Bosses can tolerate is the experience of what they are doing to others. Even if their sadism is the result of their own pain, Sadistic Bosses desire reverse empathy, if anything. But, they don't seem to have any conscious desire for it. Realism has little place in a Sadistic Boss's life except to keep abused direct reports just alive enough to keep feeling the pain. Like the God Boss, negotiation skills don't appear to have much useful purpose in the Sadistic Boss's life.

The Masochistic Boss

Masochistic Bosses can't seem to get past their own feelings of failure to identify with anyone else's feelings about anything. Masochistic Bosses are anything but realistic, and they lose every negotiation, be it for themselves or for the organization that employs them. Masochists don't make for good negotiators as they snatch defeat from the jaws of victory.

The Paranoid Boss

Paranoid Bosses are all about their own fears and could care less about how others are experiencing them or the universe as a whole. They are, of course, not realistic—unless everybody truly *is* out to get them—which might be the case with the Masochist Boss who cries "Woe is me" once too often. Because every negotiation will be based on paranoia, I'd hardly call Paranoid Bosses competent negotiators.

The Reluctant Boss

Theoretically, Reluctant Bosses can be empathic by nature and even realistic to some degree. But I hesitate to give them that because they are so anxious to withdraw and disengage. No checkmark in the empathy or realistic side of the column, and none in the negotiation side, either. If Reluctant Bosses were better negotiators, they wouldn't be walking around in shoes they never wanted to fill. Again, I believe if the reluctance issue were successfully addressed, two check marks could appear here. But not in current state.

The Unprepared Boss

Unprepared Bosses are capable of walking around senior leadership meetings and other gatherings of peers (other bosses) and identifying with how great it must feel for all of them to be bosses. A sentiment the other bosses might or might not share, thereby making it a shaky foundation for awarding a check in the empathy side of things, but a check goes there nonetheless. They can be realistic in as much as they accept they are the boss. Unprepared Bosses do, however, have enough purpose-driven negotiating skills to get offered the corner office.

The Buddy Boss

Buddy Bosses can be so excruciatingly annoying that I can't in good conscience issue a check mark suggesting they possess sufficient character to empathize or be dependably realistic. Nor can Buddy Bosses be depended upon to negotiate well because they are likely to weight their negotiations on you and your desires to ensure that you remain their friend. Although having a Buddy Boss negotiate with your needs and desires at heart might appeal on first blush, it is the wrong foundation upon which to conduct business negotiations.

The Idiot Boss

Idiot Bosses are by nature and definition clueless creatures who are unaware of how their thoughts, words, and deeds affect others. No check. However, I place a check under competence as a negotiator, mostly as an amusement. Idiot Bosses, like all Idiots, can be so oblivious to the consequences of a negotiation gone bad that they can appear to be bold and fearless to the other side of the negotiation and can therefore extract some remarkable concessions completely unawares.

The Good Boss

Good Bosses are not all that interesting to write or read about because they *get it* and they *do it.* Getting it rarely results in theatrical and entertaining disasters. It is in their characters to empathize, and they are eminently realistic because they fully appreciate the experience of others. Check. They are often competent and circumspect negotiators, appreciative of how the other side perceives things. They will typically negotiate boldly yet appreciatively for all parties when they are representing the interests of their employees, their customers, and the organization that employs them. Check again.

Characteristic 3: A Fair and Appreciative Person

Corresponding Competency 3: Skilled at Dispute Resolution

By "appreciative" I'm describing someone who goes beyond gratefulness. To me "appreciative," as in Appreciative Inquiry, is about valuing, esteeming, and honoring what brings life to individuals, relationships, and entire organizations—actually looking for the positive and productive in self and others. At its simplest, it's a "glass half-full" attitude. If it is in someone's nature to be fair and appreciative, competency in negotiation is sure to follow. Good negotiations can preclude and preempt conflicts and disputes. However, competency in resolving conflicts is an even more powerful part of a leader's skill set than the general issue of negotiation. When things have reached a point of conflict, a natural inclination toward fairness and the ability to not just recognize but truly appreciate alternative points of view are essential if you hope to work successfully with the disputing parties.

The God Boss

God Bosses are so not the real thing. The Higher Power we seek in our Idiot Boss recovery process is all about fairness and appreciativeness. No check for God Bosses on fairness and appreciativeness, as they are most commonly "fair" only to themselves at the expense of others, and certainly they only appreciate themselves. God Bosses love to render judgments, however. They could receive a checkmark under dispute resolution, as for Idiot Bosses under negotiating, mostly for humorous effect. Playing Solomon and threatening to cut the baby in half is the God Boss's style. But their brand of dispute resolution ("Off with their heads!) is not the least bit skilled, and usually not funny. No check.

The Machiavellian Boss

Machiavellian Bosses, like God Bosses, frame fairness in what it means to them. They appreciate only things that accelerate their climb to the top of the pyramid. No check for fairness and appreciativeness.

I could have placed a check under conflict resolution for many of the same reasons cited under the God Boss—swiftness and decisiveness of judgment and execution—but there is a more hideous agenda at work with the Machiavellian. No check. (Author's note: God Bosses and Machiavellian Bosses are often promoted to positions of tremendous institutional authority because they can nip conflicts in the bud and compel people to move ahead. When it comes to God and Machiavellian Bosses, the "bulldozer technique" would be more appropriate than "dispute resolution." Of course, the bulldozer technique, while tolerated and even rewarded for a while, will frequently result in an e-mail and/or phone call to the executive coach.)

The Sadistic Boss

Fairness and appreciativeness are not even blips on the radar of a Sadistic Boss. No check. If anything, Sadistic Bosses want people to experience unfairness because it intensifies the pain they are meting out. Conflict and dispute resolution are anathema to Sadistic Bosses who love conflict with anyone less powerful than they so that the Sadistic Boss can "resolve" the issue as painfully as possible. No check.

The Masochistic Boss

Masochistic Bosses steer clear of fairness and appreciative behavior because someone might be fair and appreciative with them, thereby ruining the architecture of failure they have so painstakingly constructed around themselves. No check. Masochistic Bosses are particularly fond of disputes and conflicts because they prove the hopelessness of the Masochist's existence. Masochists lose any dispute or conflict they find themselves engaged in. No second check, either.

The Paranoid Boss

Paranoid Bosses believe the only fair resolution to any conflict is for those conspiring against them to be brought to justice. That, the Paranoid Boss would appreciate. Trusting no one, Paranoid Bosses can't receive a check that would indicate that fairness and appreciation are part of their essential characters. Nor can they receive a check for competency in resolving conflicts and disputes—at least in any realistic way—because they never trust the other party. This is a character defect, or, as we say in our Idiot Recovery meetings, a *character defense*, and it precludes the ability to resolve conflict and/or live by agreed-upon resolutions.

The Reluctant Boss

Reluctant Bosses have feelings, too, so it seems reasonable to say that they could have a strong sense of fairness. Perhaps it is their sense of fairness—coupled with how unfair things can be around the office—that frustrates them. They are also capable of appreciating people for who they are and their contributions. Give them checks for fairness and appreciativeness, although they might mask them well. Reluctant Bosses tend to shy away from confrontation because that's boss stuff. No second check.

The Unprepared Boss

Unprepared Bosses are not the mercenary and maniacal personalities that Machiavellian Bosses are, despite the desire for power that they both share. Unprepared Bosses are more likely to just want a position that puts them in charge of a limited area with a limited number of direct reports, and might have it in them to be fair to and appreciative of people to the best of their unprepared ability. Give them a tentative check. Unprepared Bosses are not competent at any of the finer points of being bosses. They can't receive a check that would indicate there is a developed skill where there is none.

The Buddy Boss

Fair is merely another place the Buddy Boss wants to go with you and your family when it comes to town in August. However, I give him a check under appreciativeness in deference to his over-the-top admiration of you. A Buddy Boss will resolve conflicts and disputes in your favor to *gain* your favor, whether the resolution is fair or not, so no check there.

The Idiot Boss

Cluelessness *uber alles*. Idiot Bosses may think they are being fair, but it's not in their core character to know for sure. They can also be appreciative, but who knows what they think they're being appreciative of? It may seem as if I'm being hard on Idiot Bosses, and perhaps I am, because I am a recovering I-Boss. I've been obsessed with my interpretation of and obsession with fairness throughout my life, which has often resulted in my overdoing it and treating myself and others *un*fairly. Despite being a recovering I-Boss—or should I say, as part of my recovery—I've become certified in alternative dispute resolution. However, we're operating in a pre-recovery, current state mode. No check yet.

The Good Boss

As you have come to expect, it is in a Good Boss's essential nature to understand fairness and apply it in all things. The same is true of appreciativeness. Good Bosses are *good finders*, as motivational speaker Zig Ziglar first referred to them. A solid check belongs under fairness and appreciativeness for the Good Boss. Competency in conflict resolution is a foregone conclusion for Good Bosses. They will take their natural inclinations and balanced understanding of fairness, develop them, and put them to practical use. Give the Good Boss a check for competency in dispute resolution.

Characteristic 4: A Confident and Responsible Person

Corresponding Competency 4: Skilled at Constructive Confrontation

In the nature versus nurture debate I edge toward nurture in the issue of confidence. Confidence comes from knowing that what you expect to happen will, in all likelihood, happen, and is based more on experience than hope, desire, wild fantasy, or luck. Confidence can be in a person's character, even if the outcomes they are confident of are not the ones they necessarily want.

As for competence in the art of constructive confrontation, the ability to skillfully confront problems (we don't confront people) and keep principles above personalities is a learned competence. Constructive confrontation is, among other things, nipping problems in the bud—not abruptly and clumsily as a God Boss or Machiavellian Boss would—but skillfully, with an eye to the best outcomes for the most people. Confront important issues *before* they become expensive problems. Confrontation is not synonymous with conflict. In fact, constructive confrontation is the best way to avoid conflict. Confrontation simply means to deal with something or someone directly and face-to-face. Confrontation is inevitable. You can choose to confront a problem while it is small enough to manage and is affordable to fix or wait until you have no choice but to do damage control. Waiting too long to confront important issues and behaviors allows them to become infected and abscess until the after-the-fact confrontation deteriorates into accusations, defensiveness, blaming, and the ever-popular corporate pastime, search-for-the-scapegoat. Being an effective CEO means confronting early and often. If your boss won't do it, you do it—or, just sit back and wait for the conflict.

The God Boss

God Bosses would probably appreciate being so titled because, let's face it, when they bellow, things happen. That's confidence based on experience. No check there, however, because that is not a *responsible* way to lead. Much too old school. Confident and responsible go hand-in-hand because a person who accepts responsibility and is willing to be accountable for his or her actions is less likely to fall victim to or cause others to be victimized by false confidence. Nor is there a check under competency in constructive confrontation because God Bosses confront unilaterally. It is part and parcel of constructive confrontation to ensure that all relevant and reasonable voices are heard and acknowledged when addressing problems.

The Machiavellian Boss

Don't mistake bravado for confidence. Machiavellian Bosses get a check under confidence, but lose it when the responsibility factor is applied. Make no mistake, Machiavellian Bosses, like God Bosses, can be enormously effective at getting things done. They can also be very confident in knowing that when they push buttons, things will happen. But this is a book about helping you survive while working for them. Thus, the responsible part applies. A confident and responsible person will develop and refine the methods and techniques to confront difficult issues in ways that build people up rather than dismember them as sacrificial lambs. Machiavellian Bosses lose the check mark under constructive confrontation because their confidence in winning is based on their ability to make people lose.

The Sadistic Boss

Sadistic Bosses can appear decidedly confident in themselves and their abilities. By definition and experience, they should have confidence that they possess the institutional authority to make people suffer. But, like

God Bosses and Machiavellian Bosses, Sadistic Bosses lose their check-marks for confidence and responsibility on principle. It is simply not responsible to build confidence on abusive behavior. Sadistic Bosses do not confront constructively. That needs no further explanation, so no check mark there.

The Masochistic Boss

Masochistic Bosses are the very antithesis of confident, although they can be genuinely confident that anything they sabotage as far as their own career goes is likely to fail. The trip-wire is, again, responsibility. It is irresponsible for any leader to sabotage anything as a way to fulfill a self-defeating prophecy. Masochistic Bosses are too much into self-abuse to be credited as confident and responsible by nature or competent to confront difficult issues constructively. Can the principles and techniques of con-structive confrontation be learned and successfully applied by a Masochistic Boss? Yes, but they haven't been learned yet. No check.

The Paranoid Boss

Paranoid Bosses are confident in their belief that someone and/or everyone is out to get them. That is not only unrealistic, but irresponsible, in a fashion similar to the Masochistic Boss. Can a Paranoid Boss learn and successfully apply the principles and techniques of constructive confronta-tion? Again, it's possible, but without the trust that Paranoid Bosses are so unwilling to extend to anyone beyond their cat or dog—and even that "trust" is guarded—it is impossible.

The Reluctant Boss

Reluctant Bosses are usually unable to develop their latent potential because of their, well, reluctance. However, because this reluctance is of-ten based on an experience with a bad boss, along with their desire not to be one, there is hope. In this case, better experiences with their own boss, in which they experience good results from good boss behavior, will lead to greater confidence and greater willingness to confront constructively. That said, if a Reluctant Boss is reluctant simply because she doesn't want the responsibility of being the boss—oops. In current state, no check for confidence, nor for skill at constructive confrontation.

The Unprepared Boss

Unprepared Bosses are often confident in their ability to get promoted, which may be based in part on their responsibility. Check mark. Similarly, Unprepared Bosses are often sufficiently motivated to develop greater accountability through applying the art of constructive confrontation, but only when they understand how such competency development prepares them for bigger and better boss assignments. But Unprepared Bosses typically aren't skilled in the art of constructive confrontation; if they were, they would be extremely well prepared to be the boss.

The Buddy Boss

Unfortunately for Buddy Bosses, there just isn't much in the way of confidence to build on, unless you want to lend them some of yours. Buddy Bosses are confident only when they are plugged into your own energy and enthusiasm. They are responsible as long as it doesn't interfere with the intimate friendship they imagine they are enjoying with you. No check. A dyed-in-the-wool Buddy Boss would never engage in constructive confrontation. To confront any issue that might require a difficult conversation, no matter how constructive and positive the techniques, principles, or outcomes, is just too much for a Buddy Boss to risk. No checks at all.

The Idiot Boss

If neither the God Boss nor the Machiavellian Boss is allowed a check mark under confidence, how could anyone in good conscience give one to an Idiot Boss, no matter how much he or she swaggers? Any confidence an Idiot Boss demonstrates is likely fake. Constructive confrontation is a far more comprehensive and sophisticated process than monkey-see/monkey-do. Idiot Bosses may be dim bulbs, but they are bulbs just the same, and it is possible for them to burn more brightly under the right circumstances. In current state, however, they receive no check for constructive confrontation.

The Good Boss

It is always refreshing to reach this part of the Matrix. A Good Boss's confidence regarding his responsibilities comes from thoughtful reflection on experience, which results in reasonable assurance that what he expects

to happen is likely to happen again. Good Bosses are inherently responsible enough to do their due diligence through study, reflection, experimentation, and documentation of their experiences. Therefore they are fully accountable for their choices. As icing on the Good Boss cake, they go beyond personal accountability and share responsibility when things go wrong, no matter who messed up. Accountability and responsibility are part and parcel of constructive confrontation. Check and double check for real confidence based on real experience, and for competencies honed during the study and application of constructive confrontation.

Characteristic 5: A Caring and Attentive Person

Corresponding Competency 5: Skilled at Listening and Assessing Needs

As Norman Vincent Peale, minister, *Guideposts* magazine founder, and author of *The Power of Positive Thinking* and dozens of other books, once said, "Nobody cares how much you know until they know how much you care." Caring and attentiveness can't be taught in the classroom or online if they aren't already present in a person's natural character. However, skill at listening and assessing needs can be learned through technique if the student is sufficiently motivated. I encounter managers and executives who seek help in these areas once they realize that these deficiencies can be a career breakers.

The God Boss

Some God Bosses consider the fact that they don't bellow "You're fired!" every five minutes to be evidence of their caring nature. God Bosses who continue to bellow "You're fired!" every five minutes have abandoned any pretence that there is any correlation whatsoever between them and a truly caring Higher Power. The only time you'll find a God Boss being attentive is when she is looking for someone to zap off the face of the planet. No check mark for caring and attentiveness. Listening is not a strong suit among God Bosses either, because they think their own voices are the only ones worth listening to. Being omniscient in their own minds, God Bosses don't want to hear anyone else's original thinking. All in all, their listening skills have atrophied over time and gone the way of our vestigial tails. The only needs God Bosses assess are their own. No check marks in Column 5.

The Machiavellian Boss

Like the God Boss, the Machiavellian Boss is a self-absorbed creature who cares plenty about her own agenda, but little else. The only things she pays attention to are perceived impediments to her career ambitions or the chasm between her and the top spot on the proverbial pyramid. No checkmark. Interestingly, Machiavellian Bosses are skilled listeners. They are acutely dialed into any verbal and nonverbal signals and messages that have a direct impact on their ascent to the summit. The lack of regard for the needs of others disqualifies the Machiavellian's highly developed listening skills. No check mark.

The Sadistic Boss

A Sadistic Boss can't easily be mistaken for a caring person, no matter how loosely you might define "caring." Sadistic Bosses are cats who love to bat mice around for their personal amusement. It is doubtful that a cat toying with a mouse would ever be accused of caring for the rodent. A Sadist's attentiveness is equally maniacal in that it only serves in the boss's efforts to torture the bossed. No check. Sadistic Bosses listen for the type of groaning and wailing that indicates suffering is taking place. What Sadistic Bosses *don't* hear, however, are the cries from the hearts of people who are truly in pain. Likewise, assessment skills among Sadistic Bosses are usually only used for the purpose of pain planning. No check mark.

The Masochistic Boss

Just because Masochistic Bosses feel most comfortable predicting and even taking an active role in their own failure doesn't necessarily mean that they aren't caring and attentive people. Although they are obsessed with their own failure, Masochistic Bosses usually don't begrudge turning a caring and attentive ear to others. For this reason they can be good listeners and mentors to those who report to them. *Just because my career is a complete and utter disaster*, reasons the Masochistic Boss, *doesn't mean that yours has to be.* As I mentioned in Chapter 2, the Masochistic Boss often has a strong desire for her peers and/or direct reports to succeed so that her career will be an embarrassment by comparison. Check marks for the Masochistic Boss's capacity to care, listen, assess, and attend to needs effectively.

The Paranoid Boss

Like God, Machiavellian, and Sadistic Bosses, the Paranoid Boss is hopelessly absorbed with his own problems (or what he imagines are problems). No check marks for caring and attentiveness for the Paranoid Bosses. Is a Paranoid Boss a skilled listener? Yes, among the best. But the listening is purely for defensive purposes. The same applies to assessment. Paranoid Bosses are great at assessing the dangers they face—or so they think. Because the conspiracies they are so afraid of exist only in their imagination, their capacity for accurate assessment is diminished. No checks for the Paranoid Boss. (Sometimes a Paranoid Boss will wear on his employees to such a degree that said employees will take up a collection to pay a band of Ninjas to sneak in and assassinate him, just to get it over with.)

The Reluctant Boss

Reluctant Bosses can care about and be attentive to the needs of others as well as their own needs. That might be why they're reluctant to become bosses in the first place. The main challenge with a Reluctant Boss is her reluctance to exercise these gifts for fear it will encourage her superiors to award her additional boss responsibilities. Although a Reluctant Boss might care, she is not apt to be attentive. If she were, she would *want* to be the boss. Likewise, if the Reluctant Boss were a skilled listener and proficient in needs assessment, she would likely want to occupy the boss's chair where such things are not only appropriate, but productive. No checks.

The Unprepared Boss

I've already suggested that the intense desire of Unprepared Bosses to *be* bosses can be leveraged to motivate them to learn and apply Good Boss behaviors in the interest of remaining bosses and becoming even bigger bosses. As such, they are coachable. In current state, however, Unprepared Bosses usually don't get promoted based on how caring and attentive they are; it's usually based on the fact that they produce results—a good thing, but not necessarily an indication of a caring or attentive M.O. Unprepared Bosses have the potential to listen effectively and to assess individual and institutional needs if doing so will build a platform under

them for expanded boss responsibilities. In current state, these are not necessarily what got them promoted as much as a sheer desire to have the corner office. No checks.

The Buddy Boss

It's not all that much of a stretch to award a check mark to Buddy Bosses for their characteristic caring and attentiveness. If anything, caring and attentiveness are overused natural characteristics for Buddy Bosses. Buddy Bosses have veered slightly off the navigational beacon in their attempt to not merely study you, but to become you. They get a check mark for caring and attentiveness, but it's a qualified check mark for the aforementioned reasons. Buddy Bosses can be skilled listeners as well. But what are they listening for? Probably your needs so they can fulfill them and, by doing so, purchase your friendship. A shaky foundation for listening and assessing needs, but the behavior is there and can be refined though coaching and learning. A provisional check.

The Idiot Boss

The eternal cluelessness of I-Bosses precludes them from being relied upon to care for or attend to the needs of others. Nothing vicious, malfeasant, or premeditated here—on the I-Boss's part or mine. I-Bosses just don't get it, and if they ever do get it, they'll forget it by this time tomorrow. As for the competencies of active listening and needs assessment, no check marks for I-Bosses here, either. I-Bosses can learn active listening skills and the intricacies of needs assessment, even as they pertain to talent acquisition and learning and development throughout the employee lifecycle. Current state, however, is Idiotville. No checks.

The Good Boss

Good Bosses are naturally endowed with a caring nature. Good Bosses will eagerly grow and develop in the competencies of effective and affective listening. That translates to skilled techniques in how to hear all of what others are trying to say as well as hearing the emotions behind the remarks. This requires being attentive, which Good Bosses are. Attentive and wise. Good Bosses listen well and assess who has natural inclinations toward organization-enhancing behaviors as well as who does not, and

work hard to move everyone possible from merely competent communities of practice to genuine mastery. Check both boxes for Good Bosses.

Characteristic 6: An Open and Transparent Person

Corresponding Competency 6: A Skilled Communicator

Wouldn't you like to do business with an open and transparent real estate agent? Auto mechanic? Wouldn't you like to be married to an open and transparent person? Wouldn't you like to work for one? Rhetorical questions. The implication here is honesty. When it comes to characteristics impossible to acquire in the Corporate University, honesty is near the top of the list. Like the "H" word, the "M" word (morality), and even the "E" word (ethics), isn't something to introduce to an employee for the first time during an onboarding or assimilation process. If someone's moral or ethical construct is shaky upon entering the organization, it will, in all likelihood, continue to be unstable or even deteriorate over time, and no amount of book learning is going to help that. Threats of imprisonment, physical torture, confiscation of digital gaming devices, or other aversion behavior modification might help. But again, a human being's character is established long before he or she shows up on your doorstep as a boss, employee, peer, vendor, or customer. Beware, dishonest, immoral, and unethical people can be surgically skilled communicators.

The God Boss

God Bosses like to share information, alright. "You're fired!" "I am unhappy" is another piece of information that God Bosses are often heard saying. *I am unhappy* are three words loaded with multiple meanings and subtext. "I am unhappy," when uttered by a God Boss, roughly translated, means "You and everyone on this continent are about to experience a teachable moment courtesy of the wrath of god." God Bosses tend to be open and transparent because they don't think they have any natural enemies. Check it off. God Bosses love to hear their own voices echoing in the mountains, valleys, and canyons of industry. However, there is a listening component and a sensitivity factor to consider, not to mention using communication to strategically advance the cause of the organization. Not there with a God Boss. No second check mark.

The Machiavellian Boss

Machiavellian Bosses love to withhold information and operate covertly. Skilled communicators convey messages in a compelling and memorable manner. Lessons taught by Machiavellian Bosses are not soon forgotten. You'll be in a meeting, minding your own business, when you suddenly look down and see your Rolex on the wrist of a severed arm lying on the conference table in front of you. *That looks like my watch*, you think. *Come to think of it, that looks like my wrist and arm.* You obviously said or did something the Machiavellian Boss found detrimental to her agenda. Bottom line: You'll never do or say that again for so long as you have a limb yet to sever. There is more to effective communications than clarity of message. If it were not so, the God Boss would have earned a check for skilled communications.

The Sadistic Boss

Sadistic Bosses (sometimes Bully Bosses, as described in Chapter 2) are not awarded a check mark for openness and transparency even though their intentions are pretty transparent. Withholding critical data from their subordinates often results in their subordinates walking off cliffs and into spinning airplane propellers...much to the amusement of the Sadistic Boss. Sadistic Bosses treat information as a commodity to be used in their economies of suffering. No check mark. Sadistic Bosses can be counted on to communicate clearly when they have a mind to. It would be a huge disappointment to Sadistic Bosses if their victims weren't aware of the disparity of power they are trading on: their superior power versus your inferior weakness. Again, clarity of message alone doesn't earn a check mark for skilled communication.

The Masochistic Boss

Masochistic Bosses share as much of their twisted perspective as possible and thereby earn a check mark for openness and transparency. Not only do Masochistic Bosses naturally share information about their catastrophic circumstances, they share *ad nauseum*. Masochistic Bosses are anything but skilled communicators, however. They can be downright clumsy communicators. Because most carbon-based life forms don't naturally default to personal failure or self-inflicted suffering, the Masochistic Boss's rants about being a failure and deserving to be punished cause people to blanch, scrunch their foreheads, shake their heads, and mumble, "What?" No check mark for skilled communications for Masochistic Bosses.

The Paranoid Boss

In stark contrast to Masochistic Bosses, Paranoid Bosses are not naturally inclined to be open or honest because of all the ways information in the wrong hands could come back to haunt them. To the Paranoid Boss, any hands other than their own are guilty until proven innocent, which is impossible. No check mark for a natural characteristic of openness and honesty. No check mark for being a skilled communicator, either. Perhaps it is because the Paranoid Boss's worldview and perspective are so warped that nobody seems to care if he communicates effectively. Most people would prefer that a Paranoid Boss be mute.

The Reluctant Boss

Reluctant Bosses are capable of being open and transparent, but rarely are. If you ask them about something they are interested in, they will share information with you all day. It is the role of being a boss, of dealing with people problems and managing in general, that they don't want to talk about. "Leave me alone," doesn't sound terribly open and transparent. Reluctant Bosses get no checkmark here, nor do they receive one for being skilled communicators. Inasmuch as Reluctant Bosses are not naturally calibrated to share information about the things bosses need to share information about, skilled communication in the current state—not so much.

The Unprepared Boss

Unprepared Bosses are generally open and transparent. They get a check mark for that. They don't see any reason to veil their ambition and will often speak openly about their qualifications for lofty positions of institutional authority. Unfortunately, it is often the case that the information they are sharing is inaccurate—at least, when it comes to boss business. Unprepared Bosses share information, pontificate, even, about things they would be better off not sharing. Not skilled communication. No check. A wise person once said, "I choose not to speak unless what I have to say is an improvement on silence." Excellent advice for Reluctant, Idiot, and Buddy Bosses in particular.

The Buddy Boss

Buddy Bosses are verbally incontinent. As such they get a check mark for being open and transparent. They do tend to talk only about social stuff, but that is all they think about. It is difficult to determine if Buddy Bosses are skilled communicators. It can be argued that they make every attempt to lock others into conversations that never cease, listen well, and give feedback. If competence in communication were based solely on intent, a check mark for the Buddy Boss would be a no-brainer. But, a skilled communicator pays attention to the agenda and affect of others in the conversation. The neediness that Buddy Bosses are (in)famous for can blind them to anything that matters to their "best friend." No check mark for the Buddy Boss for skilled communications.

The Idiot Boss

Idiot Bosses can be nearly as chatty as Buddy Bosses. However, if you give an I-Boss that rubber band to play with he can't stretch rubber and talk at the same time, and will be silent until he gets bored and starts talking again. Never forget that I-Bosses are capable of Groupthink solitaire. Give them a check for openness and transparency. Skilled communicators they are not. Among the many things they share on their way to earning their previous check mark, they are sometimes absolutely correct. It's the broken clock is right twice-a-day thing. Whether by sheer coincidence or through a fleeting burst of brilliance, these moments can be dangerous because most people assume that anything coming out of the mouth of an Idiot is unreliable—even if it is. The I-Boss receives no check mark for being a skilled communicator.

The Good Boss

Good Bosses tend to be good across the board. They understand how important it is to be open and transparent and have no reason not to be. They are acutely aware of how valuable trust building is and methodically do things that build credibility. Not keeping secrets nor talking behind closed doors or people's backs is a big part of a Good Boss's credibility. Good Bosses keep people informed. They sense the relative value of informed people over uninformed people. This character issue of openness and transparency may stem from a Good Boss's inherent integrity and sense of empathy. Just as they like to be kept informed, they naturally extend that courtesy to others as a matter of maintaining credible alignment between their beliefs and their actions. Give a check mark to Good Bosses for their willingness to be open and transparent as well as skillfully communicate.

Characteristic 7: A Clear Thinker and Future-Focused Person

Corresponding Competency 7: A Sound, Strategic Planner

Organizational leadership competencies often deal with strategy, as well they should. Bosses with questionable skills and/or credentials are often dysfunctional when it comes to thinking clearly, exercising good judgment, and creating a vision for the future. It's no wonder that their direct reports and others get frustrated with them. Clear thinking suggests awareness of the moment in the context of past experience and future possibilities. Of the things managers and executives are paid to do, thinking clearly and thinking ahead are near the top of the list. Future focus is clearly an expectation for the executive. Constantly being in a reactive mode is often the result of not creating a strategy and executing on it. When that happens, it is usually the employees who pay for the sins of their leaders. Managing up should include helping your boss plan for the future because, if he or she doesn't, you'll wind up working late to make up the difference.

The God Boss

God Bosses are always thinking in the moment, and even then they are thinking only about their personal and immediate gratification. No check mark for God Bosses when it comes to clear thinking (they are delusional, after all) and certainly not in considering the future implications of their actions. Neither can this delusional boss receive a checkmark for being a sound strategic thinker; well-versed in the craft of creative and innovative processes and strategic applications. God Bosses are too myopic to render an accurate description of what is, much less contemplate "what if?" They actually believe that if something is needed in the future, there is no use in planning for it now. The God Boss will simply will it so into existence when the time comes.

The Machiavellian Boss

Machiavellian Bosses have very clear vision of the future state of their career and of the organization. Machiavellian at the top, the organization below. Though this might not be the vision of the future anyone else in the organization subscribes to, the Machiavellian Boss is certainly thinking clearly and focusing on the future. Check. Although Machiavellians are among the most skilled strategic thinkers and planners imaginable, their strategies are self-absorbed and can't be thought of as "sound" in an organizational context. To Machiavellian Bosses, their personal success (not the organization's) is not the best thing, it is the *only* thing. No check.

The Sadistic Boss

Sadistic Bosses are clear thinkers. The fact that they can assess the present state clearly and construct a reasonable facsimile of the future is evidence that they have clarity in their vision, albeit through a demented lens. Sadistic Bosses tend to demonstrate their strategic planning chops by inventing and applying new and improved torture techniques. Again, not what I would call "sound" strategy. Despite the sometimes incredible creativity and innovation in their visions of the future and overall strategic planning, Sadistic Bosses receive no check mark in the strategic planning column.

The Masochistic Boss

Unlike her Sadistic counterpart, the Masochistic Boss's twisted perception of what and who is threatening her makes it hard to check her off in the column of clear thinking and future focus. No check mark for clarity. I suppose we could give the Masochistic Boss a check mark for her ability to both plan for and bring to pass her own personal career disaster scenario. However she loses the check mark because the entire premise is a fantasy. Even though the failure the Masochistic Boss anticipates often comes to fruition, it is not the result of strategic planning as much as a defeatist attitude on the part of the Masochist.

The Paranoid Boss

Paranoid Bosses aren't naturally clear thinkers, capable of realistic discernment in the moment, when reflecting on the past, or contemplating the future. Paranoid Bosses believe that everyone is out to get them—not necessarily because they *deserve* to be gotten, as the Masochistic Boss believes, but because, well, because everyone is *out to get them*. The Paranoid Boss's paranoia can become a self-fulfilling prophesy, as everyone eventually gets tired of the paranoia and contributes to a collection to finance the aforementioned Ninja "hit." No checkmark can be awarded to the Paranoid Boss for clear thinking despite his future focus. Being a survivalist of sorts, Paranoid Bosses are always on the defensive and really don't need to ascribe motivations to others for wanting to attack them. They simply believe that attacking them is what everyone else has on his or her mind. That's not being strategic. No check.

The Reluctant Boss

It can be argued that Reluctant Bosses have a very clear view of the present state, understand (and long for) their past, and show some flexibility when it comes to contemplating the future. Reluctant Bosses don't want to accept the promotion because they could wind up being a horrible boss, something they may have been subjected to in the past. I award a check for the Reluctant Boss's natural ability to think clearly in the moment and out into the future, even if it's not a pleasant thought. Avoidant behavior is always strategic in nature because of what *could happen.* Their strategy to avoid leadership responsibility is not necessarily what the organization wants from them, and is therefore not sound. It's the lack of soundness or ultimate benefit to the organization that costs the Reluctant Boss a checkmark for strategic planning.

The Unprepared Boss

Whereas the Reluctant Boss has some potentially sound reasons to be leery of bosshood, the Unprepared Boss tends to overlook and/or turn a blind eye to the potential pitfalls of unskilled bosses. Reluctant Bosses know that people sometimes have justifiable causes for boss-i-cide and, in extreme cases, not a jury in the land will convict them. Unprepared Bosses assume they will be accepted as bosses based solely on their newly bestowed institutional authority and their pure desire to be the boss. That's not clear thinking. No check. If Unprepared Bosses were strategic, they would have considered the need for leadership skills and acquired some. No check.

The Buddy Boss

Buddy Bosses are out of luck on the clear thinking and future focus front for much the same reason that God, Masochistic, Paranoid, and Unprepared Bosses are. The super-high social neediness coefficient at play in the Buddy Boss makes the relational dynamic an overused strength. Overused as in *off the charts.* Buddy Bosses can't pass the natural clarity of thinking and appropriateness of future focus test in the context of being a boss. No check. Unfortunately, the creativity and innovation a Buddy Boss will invest in planning the upcoming holidays at your house won't meet the current state threshold required to receive a check mark for strategic planning.

The Idiot Boss

I-Bosses can see people and situations clearly only if you rub their noses in the situation the way one might housebreak a puppy. Unfortunately, for most employees, rubbing their boss's nose in anything is a disagreeable waste of time and energy, especially if the I-Boss doesn't connect the dots between the undesirable experience and the desired new behavior. No check mark for your I-Boss when it comes to clear or future focused thinking. Even if he is well trained to go through the motions of strategic planning, it is pretty unlikely that an I-Boss will understand why he's doing what he's doing. Put another way, expecting an I-Boss to make a serious and valuable contribution to strategic planning is like asking the village Idiot to perform gall bladder surgery using only plastic tableware from your local fast-food establishment. Neither the knowledge nor the tools will be adequate to the task. No check mark.

The Good Boss

Good Bosses have the knowhow and the tools that I-Bosses don't. If for any reason Good Bosses don't have the knowledge and tools handy, they find them. Good Bosses are naturally capable of and drawn to clear thinking that considers the future implications and historical precedent of the ideas being considered in the moment. They want their thinking to be clear, realistic, and useful. Check the box. Good Bosses naturally consider "what is?" as well as "what if?" and are the people most organizational policy makers should specify as the architects of the strategic plan. Put down another checkmark for the Good Boss for strategic thinking and planning.

Characteristic 8: Someone with Technical Inclinations

Corresponding Competency 8: Skilled at Application and Execution

I chose the term *technical inclinations* to level the playing field a bit. *Technical abilities* seemed to disproportionately favor technical types. Technical abilities can be a generational thing. My 14-year-old nephew, Charlie, has forgotten more about writing code, digital processing, and platform migration than the CEO of Intel has learned since the turn of the century. Maybe that's a stretch. But not much of one. The kid retrofits his hardware to operate unpublished enhanced gaming software that he and his friends write and no hardware has yet been developed to play. My nephew is also versed in application and execution at a level I'm not qualified to write about. What needs to be done, they do. Let's see how this plays out with various boss types.

The God Boss

In most any job there are baseline technical abilities required. By the term *technical*, I'm referring to anything that is in the domain of the left brain: digital communications and processing, physics, math, game theory, that sort of thing. Geek Squad stuff. God Bosses are God Bosses because they can out-bellow everyone else. Perhaps God Bosses developed their skill at bellowing to compensate for the fact that they're not naturally drawn to or naturally skilled with all things technical. Although some people with enormous technical expertise can become bellowers, God Bosses get no check mark here. Generally speaking, God Bosses don't have the competence for the skilled application and execution they demand from others. The fact that they're incompetent with application and execution is part of what makes them so irascible. The sound of bellowing is a fairly reliable indicator that whatever the God Boss is demanding is something he is not comfortable or competent in producing himself. No check mark for competency.

The Machiavellian Boss

Machiavellian Bosses tend not to be technically inclined, either. If they were, they would probably just hack into the corporate database and re-classify themselves as CEO. Why bother to fight their way up the ladder? If Machiavellian Bosses have been driven to learn anything, it is how to apply knowledge and execute, both figuratively and literally. Application and execution are the twin edges of the Machiavellian's Stiletto (heels). Machiavellians can produce results, even if it's not in the cause of quality leadership, the killer instinct of the Machiavellian is something to behold. If you have a stealth mission that needs to be "executed" with extreme prejudice, hire a Machiavellian and give her a check.

The Sadistic Boss

Sadistic Bosses can have natural technical abilities. It's hard to say that technical inclinations are the rule with Sadistic Bosses. In my experience, no. Like their Machiavellian counterparts, Sadistic Bosses are highly skilled at application and execution, but for slightly different reasons. For the Machiavellian, the pain is nothing personal and lasts no longer than necessary to get the point across. Sadistic Bosses will strike repeatedly to cause continuous endless pain and suffering. Although this book is ultimately about quality leadership and higher quality followership, it's also satire and sacrilege. I'm tempted to give Sadistic Bosses points (and a check mark) for their competence in application and execution. It's a shame the results they get are not more altruistically motivated.

The Masochistic Boss

It is not unusual for Masochistic Bosses to be naturally gifted in tech-nology and therefore get a check mark for technical inclinations based on their superior intelligence. There are low-intelligence Masochists, of course, but they seldom get tapped for bosshood. I award a check here because Masochistic Bosses are so frequently technical contributors to their organizations. Masochistic Bosses also rank high on application and execution. The problem with Masochistic Bosses is their tendency to sabotage their own accomplishments. Masochistic Bosses have been known to bring brilliant work into a meeting, listen to someone else pres-ent comparable work, and then tear up their own work under the table rather than present it. The check mark here assumes that not all of the superior work is sabotaged or destroyed and gets through to be applied and executed.

The Paranoid Boss

Paranoid Bosses are frequently technically gifted people. But they usually use their technical inclinations to set up surveillance and entrap the conspirators. Because there are no conspirators, Paranoid Bosses tend to waste a lot of time and technical expertise tilting at windmills (technologically speaking). They deserve a check mark nonetheless for their natural inclinations toward technology and the way they embrace it. Paranoid Bosses also deserve a check mark for their competency with application and execution. If they are working on a project for corporate security, they will likely produce the most stellar intelligence imaginable. If you ever want a really comprehensive report on your competition, just tell the Paranoid Boss that the competition is on a secret mission to get him fired. Paranoid Bosses will throw every resource at their disposal at the problem.

The Reluctant Boss

Tremendous technical inclination and intelligence are often the reasons why the Reluctant Boss is asked to be the boss. This boss type is often supersmart when it comes to technology. Unlike Unprepared Bosses, Reluctant Bosses are smart enough to realize that this natural gifting in technology does not qualify them to manage people. A check mark, however, for Reluctant Bosses based on their technical predispositions. Reluctant Bosses in their current state are also typically adept at application and execution, which is often the reason they are under pressure to accept the boss spot. Just as Marshall Goldsmith likes to remind us that what got us here won't necessarily get us any further (or words to that effect), it's important to realize that it is often Reluctant Bosses who put the brakes on their own upward mobility. Reluctant Bosses get the check mark for their competency—one could even say mastery—in application and execution.

The Unprepared Boss

Unprepared Bosses can be and often are technically gifted. This technological savvy is frequently the foundation for an Unprepared Boss's belief that she is ready for management, even though technical expertise in itself is unrelated to the ability to manage others. Even worse is when organizational policy-makers, most often senior level tech heads who have reached the same conclusion about themselves, promote technically-gifted-but-unprepared bosses in order to have someone nearby with simpatico. Give the Unprepared Boss a check mark for technical gifting even though it might be used as sole criteria for promotion, which is shortsighted. The Unprepared Boss could almost receive a check for competency in application and execution—as a sole contributor. Just because they can apply and execute alone, doesn't prepare them for bosshood. No check.

The Buddy Boss

Buddy Bosses can actually earn a check mark under technical inclinations. Buddy Bosses are bright enough and are usually excellent video gamers and social networkers. That's one of the reasons they bond so well with your pre-adolescent children, which, of course, makes you want to hurl. Put a check under technical inclinations for Buddy Bosses even though they will sometimes feign difficulty with applications in an effort to lure you into helping them. I considered awarding a check mark for application and execution because of how well a Buddy Boss can pull of a social event at your house. But, that hardly helps the organization, at least in a palpable and profitable way.

The Idiot Boss

Idiot Bosses lack sufficient intelligence to be technical. They're clueless, after all. The check mark for technical inclination is withheld even though savants appear now and again as I-Bosses. In the early 1980s Idiot Bosses were the ones who tried to use White Out on their monitors. Clueless creatures such as Idiot Bosses simply don't have enough bricks to build a house, much less apply or execute on a strategic plan. An outhouse, maybe, but not a house one can occupy. Even when Idiot Bosses are blessed with enough bricks to build a mansion, they will forget to use mortar. At the end of this or any other day, save the check mark you were thinking about giving the Idiot Boss for application and execution out of sheer sympathy.

The Good Boss

In Dr. Hoover's Excellent Character/Competence 10 X 10 Matrix for All Boss Types, Good Bosses seem to be good at everything. Surprise. Going way out on a limb here, I'm going to make an executive decision and pull the check mark from the Good Boss's natural technical inclination column. Good Bosses are good at recognizing, rewarding, and investing in the growth and development of others. Isn't it more refreshing to have a boss who admits lacking technical ability and seeks help, as opposed to some Idiot who lacks technical ability but tries to fake it? It's more valuable for a boss without natural technical inclinations to have the institutional authority and natural impulse to seek help from, recognize, and reward those who do. Good Bosses don't take credit that is due others and rarely ever take credit that is due them, deferring instead to the work of their team members. This creates an optimal atmosphere for application of knowledge and execution on strategy in a collaborative environment. Put a check mark under the application and execution column for Good Bosses.

Characteristic 9: Other-Focused and Organizationally Astute

Corresponding Competency 9: A Skilled Coach

Some competency lists speak of focusing externally. Many consider this to be a focus outside the company to maintain the competitive edge and advantage. In my book (since this *is* my book), an external focus begins where my skin ends. If we have an extrinsic perspective that enables and encourages us to pay attention to customers *inside* of the organization, it will be a natural extension for us to also focus on customers *outside* the organization. Know who the players are and how they all contribute to organizational success. Being organizationally astute means more than knowing that your company makes money—but how exactly. We can become great coaches, either internal or external, to organizations if we honor that external focus, ask people powerful questions, and listen as they share powerful answers. If we keep our egos out of the conversation, great epiphanies will occur to benefit the individual and the organization.

The God Boss

You must be joking. God Bosses are not focused on other people for any other reason except submission. They see other people as a faceless mass to be bellowed at, not as individuals with individual characteristics, talents, and abilities. Except in the case where someone has a skill or competency that the God Boss finds particularly useful, such as peeling grapes or playing the lute, there is typically no individual recognition at all. As for being organizationally astute, God Bosses know where the throne room is. That's about all. No check. God Bosses do not make good coaches. After all, why would someone so delusional and self-absorbed bother to listen to others (which is the core component of good coaching) long enough to hear anything they say? God Bosses make no pretense about where their subjects are in relationship to them, and that relationship is not one of trust and mutual respect. No check mark for God Boss as coach.

The Machiavellian Boss

Machiavellian Bosses are intensely other-focused in that they tend to see individuals who are either helping them achieve their goal of attaining the summit of the pyramid or hindering them. As such, Machiavellian Bosses typically inventory everyone in the organization who has direct or indirect influence on the Machiavellian's agenda. Are Machiavellian Bosses organizationally astute? A Machiavellian Boss knows every nook and cranny in the organization and can spot a vulnerable executive who can be stepped over or easily removed from a mile away. Check. Do you believe that anything about a Machiavellian Boss adds up to good coaching material? Neither do I. As a coach who is dedicated to the healthy growth and development of coaching clients and the organizations that sponsor their coaching, I can't in good conscience bestow a check mark for coaching skills where the Machiavellian is concerned.

The Sadistic Boss

Sadistic Bosses knows their prey very well, studying their victims closely to determine each person's weakness and breaking point. Sadistic Bosses are organizationally astute only so far as to determine how much they can get away with before HR calls in an executive coach. Sadistic Bosses receive no check mark for their focus on others because (1) it is intended for evil (which alone would not disqualify it) and (2) it is not tied into any organizational awareness or appreciation. As for coaching, would you bare your soul to someone who has sworn an oath to cause you maximum suffering, using any device available? Would you hand a Sadist a hammer to hit you with? (Masochists are not allowed to answer.) No check mark for coaching, either.

The Masochistic Boss

Failure is a highly personal thing to the Masochistic Boss. Most of the focus that she expends on others is related to her desire to pale in comparison. The Masochistic Boss isn't focusing on others as much as she is projecting her agenda of failure onto others. Organizationally astute? The Masochistic Boss only observes the organization as a bunch of people who are better at everything than she is. No check mark. Masochistic Bosses could potentially make good coaches in that they are often highly encouraging of others, but that "encouragement" gets old fast. Masochistic Bosses battle everyone to be the biggest loser, and I'm not talking about the scale. Masochistic Bosses just can't string together enough good other-focused coaching qualities without sabotaging them along the way to earn a check mark.

The Paranoid Boss

Paranoid Bosses are extremely other focused in that they are acutely interested in who has it out for them, which they presume is everyone. Paranoid Bosses count conspirators to fall asleep the way that the rest of us count sheep. As for being organizationally astute, I don't see any practical value in the Paranoid Boss's perception of the organization as a dangerous environment. No check mark. Despite their laser-like focus on others, Paranoid Bosses are not good coaches because they will invariably assume that their coaching clients are part of a vast, underground conspiracy against them. So much for trust and transparency. What should be powerful questions asked by the coach, intended to inspire deep self-reflection on the part of the client, will become targeted interrogation techniques intended to expose the conspiracy. No check mark in the skilled coaching column for the Paranoid Boss.

The Reluctant Boss

If Reluctant Bosses were other-focused, they would not be so reluctant to lead others. This doesn't mean that Reluctant Bosses are completely self-absorbed in the way that God Bosses or Machiavellian Bosses are. But they are *other-avoidant* when it comes to leading. Reluctant Bosses might be more organizationally astute than we give them credit for. They understand how things really get done in a politically charged atmosphere and want no part of it. No check mark. As for being good coach material, being other-focused as a positive leadership characteristic means there is a desire to be a skilled helper. The inclination to help others is baseline for coaches and mentors of any kind. A Reluctant Boss could go through the motions of being a coach, but the reluctance to step up and truly engage keeps the box below "a skilled coach" blank.

The Unprepared Boss

Unprepared Bosses receive no check marks below "other-centeredness and organizational astuteness" either, because they are more eager to enjoy the power and prestige of rank than they are to pay attention to others. If Unprepared Bosses were experienced and fairly proficient at the other-focused servanthood dimension of leadership before they become bosses, they would be prepared to lead. Learning about finance and P&L responsibilities is a function of training. Sadly, Unprepared Bosses are often promoted based on strong P&L skills, while demonstrating zero people skills. As far as coaching their direct reports or others in the organization, I suppose an Unprepared Boss could advise on ambitiousness. But, giving advice is not what coaching is about. Coaching is about providing a safe environment where people can engage in the type of self-discovery that will make them more effective and successful at what they do. No checks in column nine for Unprepared Bosses.

The Buddy Boss

Buddy Bosses pay a great deal of attention to others in that they are constantly scanning the horizon for new friends. Buddy Bosses are famished for friendship because, like vampires, they get their strength from others, not from inside. Organizational astuteness requires that a certain ironic distance be maintained between the individual and the corporation so as to allow perspective and objectivity. Buddy Bosses can't be more than an arm's length from anyone. I can't check the others off for their inappropriate focus or for being unable to see the organizational forest for the trees. Buddy Bosses certainly put in enough time with others to be considered for coaching. However, that time will never be quality time spent focusing intensely on coaching clients and their challenges. That knocks the Buddy Boss's check mark out of the box under skilled coaching.

The Idiot Boss

Unfortunately for I-Bosses, they won't pick up any more check marks here. I-Bosses who can be immobilized for 30 minutes while studying the complexity of a rubber band are oblivious to the universe of interesting and fascinating people around them. Neither is organizational astuteness a strong suit of the I-Boss. Organizations are complex, living organisms. Rubber bands are not. Imagining an I-Boss coaching a coworker or subordinate makes me want to simultaneously laugh and cry. The damage an I-Boss can do when attempting to coach is directly proportionate to the needs of the coaching client. The more desperately a coaching client needs the help of a coach, the more the I-Boss's cluelessness is likely to compound the problem. Skilled coaches, be they certified executive coaches or managers who coach, need to be other-focused, empathic, organizationally astute, and knowledgeable about business processes as well as individual and corporate human behavior—things that the I-Boss will never be.

The Good Boss

Good Bosses' most valuable contributions come outside of any technical box. Otherwise, keep the person an individual contributor. A boss who is highly proficient in technical stuff *and* who truly rates as a Good Boss is a natural wonder. Truly exceptional. Other-centeredness is what Good Bosses are all about. Good Bosses automatically consider the needs of others as equal to if not greater than their own—and all within the context of the organization. Another check mark. Good Bosses are naturally inclined toward and seek expert development in the craft of coaching. With their intense desire to help others grow and develop and reach their full potential, Good Bosses tend to make great coaches when introduced to the craft. Good Bosses study and practice coaching technique in order to build the strongest possible competencies in their missions to align what people do best with what organizations need most. Check mark again.

Characteristic 10: Intelligent Person Who Is Hungry to Help Others

Corresponding Competency 10: A Skilled Teacher and People Builder

As you're about to see, the complementary characteristics of intelligence and hunger to help others, along with competence in teaching and building people up, are goals too lofty for anyone who hasn't seriously considered the awesome responsibilities and obligations of leadership. Organizational policy-makers typically resolve this dilemma by unbundling the combined characteristics. In a high-tech or high-content firm (like an advertising agency) organizational policy-makers often contend that superior intelligence is a sufficient criterion to grant a promotion into leadership. The same organizational policy-makers also say that a hunger to help people, taken alone, is an insufficient criterion for promotion. Unfortunately, the biggest genius in the world is not very valuable as a leader without a desire to help others. A great inventor, perhaps. A great leader, probably not. Intelligence alone doesn't suggest a bias for action, but helping others does. We can't help others grow and develop if we're idle. We must put things and keep things in motion for growth and improvement to occur. Whereas some lists of leadership competencies speak of having a "talent mindset," I refer to the same notion as "people building." No huge difference, except that I firmly believe in what Spencer Hayes, the architect of Southwest Publishing, said about building people. Leaders in Spencer's organizations have told me that he often teaches leaders who work for him that their primary responsibility is to *build the people who build their businesses.* It is hard to align essential leadership behaviors any better than that. To me a "talent mindset" means a commitment to building people throughout the entire employment lifecycle, from recruitment to retirement, and even beyond. As I've already mentioned, teaching something is the best way to learn it. So becoming skilled teachers makes all of us skilled learners.

The God Boss

God Bosses don't appear as a rule to be as intelligent as they are noisy. The trick with moderate intelligence is to make the most of it, as many self-made millionaires have proven. People with superior intelligence often find themselves employed by someone with significantly inferior intelligence. Lesser intelligence or not, bellowing God Bosses don't appear to be invested in helping others. If they were, they might pipe down and listen for a change. No check mark for the God Boss under the intelligence and helping others column. Bellowers don't teach. Nor do they build people. Bellowing God Bosses, intelligent or not, are not hungry to help anyone but themselves. With no additional check marks in column 10, God Bosses receive only three out of a possible 20 check marks overall. One must wonder why they are on the payroll at all.

The Machiavellian Boss

Machiavellian Bosses have superior intelligence. They are strategic, cunning, and ruthless, and do their best work below the radar, dismembering rivals and other impediments—leaving a signed business card behind to let others know "who did this." The Machiavellian Boss is only concerned with helping the Machiavellian Boss and thereby loses the column 10 check mark she could have earned were it for intelligence alone.

The Machiavellian is a gifted teacher in that you only need one lesson to change your behavior forever. However, the Machiavellian's victory is based on everyone else's loss and you don't want people in your organization to practice what the Machiavellian teaches. No check marks in the final column for Machiavellian Bosses, bringing their total positive leadership characteristics and competencies to seven out of a possible 20.

The Sadistic Boss

It is doubtful that the most skilled attorney in the land could convince a jury, even a rigged jury, that Sadistic Bosses, no matter how intelligent they might be, have any interest in helping others. No check mark for Sadistic Bosses under the intelligence and helping others column. As for teaching and building people, the only thing a Sadistic Boss is interested in teaching his subordinates is that there is no hope for relief from the pain and suffering he is causing. Some people make the mistake of thinking a Sadistic Boss can be bought. They believe that the pain and suffering are just intended to drive up the price for freedom. Unfortunately for the subordinates of Sadistic Bosses, the boss simply enjoys the suffering of others, and no amount of money will change that. Besides, the company is already paying the Sadist well to abuse you. With no check for teaching and people-building, Sadistic Bosses tally four out of a possible 20 check marks for positive leadership characteristics and competencies, placing them between the God Boss and the Machiavellian Boss. Not particularly good company to keep in my book.

The Masochistic Boss

Masochistic Bosses are funnier than their God, Machiavellian, or Sadistic counterparts. Unless you work for one. Masochistic Bosses, like Machiavellians, have at the very least a reasonably high IQ, but remain horribly dysfunctional in the area of Emotional Intelligence. Intellectually rich and emotionally poor, Masochistic Bosses are only hungry to help others when it makes them look bad by comparison. But in most organizations helping others makes one look good, not bad. So the Masochistic Boss finds herself in a paradoxical bind. Accordingly, Masochists are rarely found helping others. Their time is mostly invested in hurting themselves. No check mark for Masochistic Bosses in the intelligence and hunger for helping others category. The likelihood that a Masochist will make a good teacher is practically nil, as her focus remains too solidly locked into failure as a self-fulfilling prophesy. The "You're so much smarter and talented than me" attitude can make any achievement on the part of her direct reports or students feel yucky. Masochistic Bosses score five out of a possible 20 check marks. The Stiletto-wielding/wearing Machiavellian beats her by two, which probably makes the Masochist happy.

The Paranoid Boss

The Paranoid Boss can be super-intelligent. But whereas Machiavellian Bosses use their intelligence to gain something tangible, Paranoid Bosses, like Masochists, use their intelligence to imagine something that doesn't exist and then set about to prove it. Paranoid Bosses might be much smarter than the average bear, but can't claim a check mark under the intelligence column because they have no desire to help others—rendering their intelligence useless for leadership. No check. Paranoid Bosses make terrible teachers for many of the same reasons they make crappy coaches. They are just not other-focused except to unearth evidence of conspiracy. Not only do Paranoid Bosses have no interest in building up other people, they apparently don't have much interest in building themselves up, either. The Paranoid Boss only earns four check marks out of a possible 20.

The Reluctant Boss

What a bummer that the rule is to promote people based on technical ability, raw intelligence, and/or sales performance rather than on leadership ability and Emotional Intelligence that will increase everyone's performance. Then again, executive coaches earn much of their income after an organization promotes a scary-smart person with gargantuan technical skills into a leadership position. Why? Because the organization soon realizes the error in its ways, turns around, and hires said coach to help the mega-smart, upwardly mobile tech-a-zoid behave as if he or she has the Emotional Intelligence, human relations skills, and/or empathy he or she should have demonstrated prior to the promotion. No check marks for Reluctant Bosses on intelligent hunger to help, teach, and/or build people. The Reluctant Boss just wants everybody to leave him alone. Four out of a possible 20 check marks could be interpreted as lots of headroom for growth on the part of the Reluctant Boss.

The Unprepared Boss

Unprepared Bosses can also be IQ proficient and EQ deficient. Unprepared Bosses can be awarded promotions based on their intellect, if not for shoving their way to the head of the line. But IQ as a natural human characteristic is not a good predictor of EQ, as Howard Gardner, Daniel Goleman, and others have described it. Just because someone is book smart doesn't mean he or she is heart smart. The same can be claimed in reverse. Too much heart smarts can potentially make head smarts look awfully dumb. Unprepared Boss receive no check mark under the intelligence and hunger to help people column. In current state the unprepared Boss's focus is not on teaching and people building as much as it is on career building and learning where the next promotion will come from. No check marks for the Unprepared Boss in column 10 leave him or her with seven out of 20. That's a tie with the Unprepared Boss's closest cousin, the Machiavellian.

The Buddy Boss

Buddy Bosses can be intelligent and more than willing to help others, but their insatiable neediness sometimes overshadows everything else. Buddy Bosses are motivated to help others inasmuch as helping others guarantees relationship. They can sometimes even accomplish these relationship-building goals in intelligent and creative ways that also help the business. Give them a check for strong hunger. Buddy Bosses can learn to teach well and build people up. But in their current state they don't typically take time to teach or build beyond just getting and staying connected. No check mark for the Buddy Boss on teaching and building, which brings the Buddy Boss's tally to seven check marks out of a possible 20 across the Matrix. Wow. A three-way tie with the Machiavellian and the Unprepared Boss. What an unlikely bedfellow the Buddy Boss makes with the other two.

The Idiot Boss

Things were looking up only until we turn the page to the Idiot Boss and free fall down the God Boss's level. As a recovering I-Boss, this shows how far your humble author sank before attempting to learn a better way to lead. More realistically, it indicates how far below sea level I was before I ever realized there was such a thing as the art and science of management and leadership—management being mostly science, and leadership mostly art. As for intelligence as a natural characteristic, there is little for me or other recovering or untreated I-Bosses to brag about. I do have a hunger for helping others, from colleagues, friends, and family members to coaching clients and the residents at the homeless shelter on 15th Street. But, as previously mentioned, organizational Kahunas more frequently promote technicians over altruists. As an untreated I-Boss, trying only to appear intelligent, I was much more promotable, but much less helpful. Untreated I-Bosses are still too entangled in the underbrush of their cluelessness to become skilled at teaching or people building until someone does those things to them first. Idiot Bosses (in their natural and untreated state) receive only three check marks out of a possible 20. Definitely low tide. God Bosses, also scoring three out of a possible 20, are not the kind of company I care to keep. Time for me to change the things I can.

The Good Boss

My bias for leadership excellence is squarely in the camp of the one I call the Good Boss. Out of 10 boss types on the Character/Competence 10 X 10 Matrix for all Boss Types, there is one complete set of check marks in the 10th column. Good Bosses are rarely if ever the most intelligent or most technically gifted people in the organization. They receive a check for intelligence on the Matrix as a sort of consolation prize for losing one in technical ability. More than that, the Good Boss's pronounced hunger to help others props up the intelligence factor. Teaching and building the people who build the business is just plain smart. Good Bosses score 19 checkmarks out of a possible 20—95 percent—clearly making them the boss of choice for fun and profit. That doesn't mean all natural characteristics are bestowed in equal measure, but they're virtually all there to some degree—and used positively. What Good Bosses don't come by naturally, they appreciate the need to supplement with learned and applied competencies.

THE MILLION-DOLLAR QUESTION

How many times have you heard the expression "Don't stand there like an Idiot"? Some readers might think the million-dollar question is "How does an Idiot stand?" That would be a $2 question. Here's the big money inquiry: To avoid hiring an executive coach to help selected managers and executives develop the qualities the organization wants them to demonstrate as leaders, why not hire and/or promote people into management and executive positions who already demonstrate those desirable qualities? You know what the qualities of Good Bosses are. Your organization has probably spent *beaucoup* time developing a list of competencies and leadership expectations that resembles mine in some fashion. Why not load the ranks of management and leadership with individuals who have a proven track record in those characteristics and competencies?

As you continue through this book, think about why such a simple solution is so universally ignored in organizational life. Ponder how it is that a horrible boss can nonetheless have good characteristics. It's not the strength; it's how it's used. It's not only the weakness, but how it hinders relationships and personal productivity. The difference between being a Good Boss—one who builds the people who build the business—and any other boss can be found more in the margins and subtext than in the headlines. In the headlines, every boss that gets promoted is written up as the Second Coming. Below is what you can do to help yourself and your organization to only bring coaches like me into the building to expand and develop unrealized leadership potential—not to talk people off of the ledge.

STEP THREE EXERCISE REVIEW

Regardless of whom you give the credit to, each of us was created uniquely and wonderfully—with character and potential. It's a beautiful thing when we become aligned with our original characteristics and purposes. Combine who your boss is and what he or she has learned with who you are and what you have learned in order to create a Good Boss scenario. To review, the Third Step exercise is to (1) identify the boss type you're having the most difficulty with, and (2) determine which characteristics and competencies you can supplement in your relationship with that boss type that might transform the combination of *you and your boss* into something that resembles a Good Boss. What can the two of you accomplish together in terms of leadership style?

CURRENT STATE VERSUS FUTURE STATE OF THE BOSS TYPES

The Matrix on page 81 indicates how the boss types rate in their current state. The checks represent where their potential could possibly be tapped (with reasonable certainty), re-purposed, and expanded, or they could essentially just learn something new and turn it into a competence. Despite some extremely dysfunctional natural characteristics, many of those characteristics can often be leveraged to serve a productive purpose. To Machiavellians and Unprepared Bosses who are obsessed with power and position, for example, teaching and building up teams of competent people can be a way to gain and sustain power. It won't happen in the natural current state. It takes deliberate effort. But it can be accomplished with extremely favorable results.

An Opportunity to Grow

Regardless of the open, unchecked boxes on the Matrix, hope and optimism spring eternal (and nearly everywhere). People can learn to do things that are against type, that oppose their natural characteristics, and can learn and apply that learning brilliantly. It can be extremely hard. The ancient Eastern philosophy teaches us "When the student is ready, the student's inner Idiot will do something incredibly stupid to screw things up," or words to that effect. But those moments of situational stupidity are teachable moments. If we are never challenged, we won't grow very much. The same is true for our challenged bosses. Maybe that's not important to you, but you might never have been an Idiot. It's the seminal lesson. Making peace with your Inner Idiot is the first step on a long road to recovery, bringing you personal peace and a peaceful coexistence with other Idiots. Making peace with your Inner Idiot is an early step in developing simpatico with and compassion for the Idiot or other boss type you work for.

If you are the boss, remember that business is about people. People make the stuff other people buy and use. People provide services other people need, want, and pay for. Good Bosses never forget that. Everybody has a situation suitable to his or her unique talents and abilities. Find yours. Find the optimal opportunity for your team members to be actualized. There is no more effective way to pump up the bottom line. All of this, if you haven't noticed, demonstrates a tremendous bias for action.

Teaming up with our Higher Power is the best way to tap into the best you have to offer and the best everyone around you has to offer. It begins when we decide to turn over our will and our lives to our Higher Power—as we understand Him.

Idiot's Epilogue

Much time could be spent here comparing the Idiot Boss to the Good Boss because, as improbable as it might sound, Idiot Bosses can and often do make the transition to Good Bosses. Amazing, isn't it? I mentioned earlier that I'm harder on I-Bosses than any other boss type because I am one—although recovering. So satire and sarcasm have somewhat obscured any positive potential in I-Bosses as I have described them. In truth, for the I-Boss, or any other boss type, to make it to Good Boss is only possible with the miracle of divine intervention, through which all things are possible. Thank you, Higher Power.

When I surrendered my will and my life to a Higher Intelligence, floodgates of awareness opened. I let the flood wash over me and cleanse me of prideful, controlling impulses. I didn't need to know everything. I just needed to seek and be open to the answers. A caring Higher Power, whatever or whoever you believe that Higher Power is, wants all of us to live peacefully with difficult bosses and, more than that, to become edifying bosses to others. We just need to exchange our stubbornness and willfulness for the serenity that comes from surrender. We'll be okay. He'll see to that. To have a boss of choice, we must be employees of choice.

4

Idiot Procreation

The term *Idiot procreation* doesn't refer to male and female I-Bosses gathering at trade shows and hooking up. It refers to the strange yet universal phenomenon that occurs as naturally and frequently in organizations as cancelled bonuses. A glimpse into the average I-Boss's day will help you understand how their population grows.

As I travel around the country attempting to save organizations from themselves, I sometimes arrive too late. Between the time I receive the panicked telephone call, book my flight, and pull my rental car into the parking garage, the entire organization is likely to have crossed over into the I-zone—a state caused by the fusion of neurological synapses, usually following an attempt to apply logic and reason to an Idiot Boss's thinking and behavior. Those who are suddenly and unexpectedly adrift in the I-zone have not become Idiots; their mental faculties have merely been disconnected from their power sources. The experience is similar to typing away at your computer late at night when the power goes out. Everything is instantly dark and silent. In the I-zone, your brain goes dark and silent along with everything else. You become one with the power failure. It's an internal virus from which few recover. Imagine being in good health and of sound and body as you arrive for work. You present your I-Boss with the brilliant middle-range plan you stayed up for three days and nights rewriting. He looks at it with a blank expression and asks, "What's this?"

A voice inside your head screams, *It's the mid-range report you asked me to do over again for the third time, you idiot!*

"Why are you wasting time on this instead of doing important work?" your I-Boss continues, clearly oblivious to the voice inside your head. Your inner voice tries to scream again, but nothing comes out this time. A pop-up window on your mental desktop reads: "This program has encountered a fatal error and will be shut down." It's too late to do anything but watch your sanity disappear. Your internal monitor screen winks out and everything goes quiet.

I often arrive at the organization only to find people in the I-zone: weary workers with shoulders slumped and bags under hollow eyes that have peered once too often into the corporate abyss. Standing among these zombies as they wander aimlessly through sterile corridors, I wonder how much sooner I would have needed to arrive in order to prevent the wholesale destruction of gray matter, broken souls, and irreversible nerve damage. There is no sound to accompany the macabre scene except a low moaning that doesn't seem to come from anyone in particular. It's like the poorly looped soundtrack from a B horror movie.

As I stand in the hallowed halls of American enterprise, a mob of moaning, shambling corpses parts around me like the Red Sea. I can't imagine how they manage to avoid running into me as I stand there. *They must have some kind of sonar*, I think to myself as I slowly shake my head and ruminate on what might have been. The lifeless expression worn by the zombies is the opposite of the perpetual smile so many I-Bosses wear. I've never been able to figure out how perpetual smilers manage to bite and chew their food, much less talk, without moving their jaws.

Just then, I feel a slight tug on my sleeve. I turn and there is a ghost-ly looking young woman, once vibrant, now gaunt and sallow. "Why do they make Idiots into bosses?" she asks, staring off into space. Her voice is monotone and scratchy, as if someone pulled the ring attached to the string in her back a hundred times too many. Her sunken eyes search the angles where the walls meet the ceiling, as if the answer to her question might be written near the junction of horizontal and vertical surfaces.

I've been here and done this too many times to hazard a quick response. I just wait. As I suspected, she doesn't wait for an answer to her first question before asking a second. "Why do Idiot Bosses multiply like rabbits?" Her voice is still raspy. This time she looks at me, but I realize she is sensing my presence more than actually seeing me. I step slightly to the side. Her eyes don't follow. Suddenly, the door swings open to the men's room. Her Idiot Boss strolls out in a carefree, almost cavalier manner that flies in the face of the beleaguered moaning masses around him. "Hey, Dr. Hoover," he calls out to me, zipping his pants at the same time. The ghostly woman releases my sleeve and is absorbed once again into the river of walking dead. *How can he be so glib?* I think to myself. *He must see these people. Why doesn't he acknowledge them?* But by then he's glommed onto me, extending his hand for me to shake. Yech.

"We haven't seen you in a long time," says he, referring to a brief consulting appearance I made five years prior to help develop a corporate communications strategy. Before the strategy could be implemented, the company's earnings hit a bump in the road, the top brass panicked, and all extravagances were cancelled, especially those they needed most. The plan was scrapped in an effort to drive costs out of the business. Instead, the last vestiges of intelligence, enthusiasm, and motivation were driven out.

"Too long," I say flatly, scanning the morbid scene around me.

"What do you mean?" he asks innocently.

Instead of amusing me, his sheer stupidity evokes anger. I feel as if he is taunting me, intentionally trying to bust my chops. *Nobody can be that stupid,* my inner voice snarls. "Didn't you call *me*?" I ask aloud, trying to sound genuinely curious. I am curious. If you're going to receive payment for your consulting, it helps to know who hired you.

"Oh, yeah," he recalls. "I did call you. People were really starting to go bonkers around here after I decided we needed to quit wasting time on meaningless activities. But, you can see they've quieted down." He holds his arm out in the direction of his office and we start walking.

"Define meaningless," I query, ever the Socratic coach, even on consulting visits. I think I know where he's going with this, but I want him to say it in his own words.

"I ask people to do certain things and they act like I want them to kill their mothers." I can see he is close to connecting the dots. That's what good coaches/consultants/counselors do: We help our clients put two and two together so they not only understand they have four, but fully appreciate what four means and where it came from. The hardest part in helping Idiots connect the dots is getting them to realize they need at least two dots before they can connect anything. But Idiots have no problem connecting one dot. They'll draw single dots all day long, if left without adult supervision. It makes them feel busy and useful. More importantly, they never have to deal with the complexity of contemplating how two dots relate to one another. God forbid if you ever asked them to consider triangulation. Their heads would explode.

I had to help this I-Boss, fresh from the restroom, find at least one more dot if I was to do him any good or help restore cognitive functioning to at least some of his staff. Despite how cynical we coaches and consultants can be in moments of unwinding, we really do want to help our clients. We come in the door with a genuine desire to leave things better for having been there, regardless of the money. The money is nice and it helps make the Volvo payments, but I can honestly tell you the desire to make things better than they were before I arrived has nothing to do with money. It's an overactive affirmation gene that every good coach and consultant is born with—a good characteristic if it doesn't turn into sympathy. A good competency if it is used for recognition and encouragement of positive boss behavior.

By helping bosses get better I make life easier and more fruitful for their team members. Yet despite my optimism on the way in the door, I often leave feeling utterly defeated. Some coaches and consultants will say they're never discouraged, which makes me question their veracity across the board. I tend to like and trust people on the front end until proven otherwise. After initial coaching sessions with most of the boss types listed on the Matrix in Chapter 3, I leave wanting to hire a hit man. In truth, the hit man fantasy comes and goes quickly, sometimes in an instant. Once I'm past it, my optimism kicks in, and I seize on the upside potential that my client has stored away inside and get genuinely excited about the prospects of succeeding together.

As I conversed with this I-Boss amidst the sea of zombies, my inner voice said, *Call Guido*. Inner voices can bring good or bad news. When I was practicing mental health intervention as an intern registered with the California Board of Behavioral Sciences, my supervisor modeled true cynicism. Supervision sessions for mental health professionals can be the most politically incorrect rant sessions imaginable. Who'd have thought it? No psychologist will ever admit to this, and I never taped a supervision session, so you'll just have to take my word for it. I remember my clinical supervisor, in describing a schizophrenic she was treating, asking rhetorically, "Why do the voices always tell them to kill, to hurt themselves, or to live under an overpass? Why don't they say, Take a bath, get a job, and pay your therapist?" She got out of the business shortly after that and joined Alcoholics Anonymous.

While walking and talking with this particular I-Boss the voices inside my head were saying *Find the nearest janitorial closet and lock yourself in before you kill him or jump out the window.* Then a second inner voice joined the conversation. You know you're in trouble when multiple inner voices start weighing in. *Which is it?* my rational inner voice demanded. *Do I kill him, kill myself, or crawl under one of these desks? If I jump out the window first, I won't kill him, and I won't have that on my conscience for the final three seconds of my life. But, would I really regret killing him as I fall to my own death? Or would the final, homicidal act of a desperate coach be a gift to the world he leaves behind?* Many business executives would need to change their underwear if they ever knew what their consultants were thinking about them at any given moment.

"What exactly did you ask them to do?" I asked aloud as we walked.

"I asked them to rework the mid-range plan," he said nonchalantly.

"Rework?"

"Yeah, do it over again."

"How many times had they done it before?" We reached his office, a glass-walled cell featuring a panoramic view of the entire floor, from the coffee nook to the copy room.

"I dunno—two, maybe three times."

"How do you think they felt about doing the same report two or three times?" I asked, settling into an armchair facing his desk. The question was typical Socratic consulting/coaching, leading the horse ever so gently to the water. My question was much too leading for non-directive coaching purists. But even so, I could tell this horse stood a good chance of dehydration.

"No idea," he answered honestly as he closed the door and sat down behind his desk. I had to give him half a point for that. Sitting down without incident, that is. "You said they are going bonkers." He motioned toward the sea of zombies moving methodically in all directions outside the glass walls of his office. In there, with the door shut, we couldn't hear the low-pitched moaning that gave the zombie parade its eerie edge. The lack of a soundtrack made the sight even weirder than before. More than glass partitions insulated this I-Boss from his team members, and indeed from reality itself. At least he saw them out there. That was a start. That was a seed. I decided to go with it.

"What makes you think they have a problem repeating the same task over and over again?" I asked, tilting my head toward the zombies.

"Look at them," he said. "You would think I asked them to carry loads of bricks up 30 flights of stairs." This guy was a few bricks short of a load himself and he was starting to make me feel really uncomfortable. Being a professional, I breathed deeply and rotated my shoulders backward to loosen up the muscles that had been steadily tightening in my chest since he emerged from the men's room. I knew it was going to take a while for his elevator to rise 30 floors, so I resigned myself to be patient and tried to remember that I was being paid for this.

"Why do you think they look that way?" I continued, trying to point him toward the second dot that he needed in order to make the connection.

"I guess they would rather just be goofing off," said he.

No dot.

"Goofing off?"

"You know."

"I do?"

"Wasting time."

"Oh," said I. "If left to their own devices, your team members would just waste time?"

"Yeah," he sighed. "What can you do?"

You can stop thinking like an imbecile. I didn't actually say that. I just thought it. I can't speak for other coaches, counselors, and consultants, but I have terrifying dreams that my microphone switch will one day malfunction and I'll say aloud what I'm actually thinking. These dreams feel eerily similar to naked dreams, which, in a way, they are.

"What were they doing when you asked them to stop and rework the mid-range plan for the third or fourth time?"

"I dunno," he said, getting a bit irritated. "Why the third degree?" Clients can get snippy when pushed too far. They're aware of who works for whom. I decided to press on anyway. I owed it to those formerly hard-working, formerly dedicated, former human beings on the other side of the glass. And I owed it to my client and the corporation that was paying all of us.

"This is important," I said. Instead of raising his eyebrows at the directive comment, he actually leaned forward and listened more intently. Cluelessness can have a silver lining. "Were they doing something you assigned to them when you asked them to drop what they were doing and rework the mid-range plan?" I was highlighting dots left and right. Still he couldn't seem to draw a line between any of them.

"Probably," he said, leaning back in his chair. "What does that have to do with anything?" My horse had not only reached the water, he was standing in it, and yet he still refused to drink. I abandoned Socrates and took out my invisible magic marker.

"It works like this," I began. (My nondirective better angels began to weep as I became increasingly directive. It's like the Chinese proverb: Teach a person how to connect the dots and there is hope. Connect the dots for a person and he's still an Idiot.) "When you ask your team members to do something, that thing becomes a priority. They will jump into the task with the intention of doing a good job." I was referring to early career people before a long line of I-Bosses snuffed out their passions and turned them into hopeless cynics. "When you interrupt their work to shift their efforts to a new task, that diminishes the importance of what they're already doing."

"So...?"

"So, every time you ask them to do something and then ask them to abandon that task, they become increasingly cynical about the real importance of either task."

"Cynical...?"

"It's like the boy who cried wolf," I explained, in hopes that a child's tale would resonate with him.

"Why did the boy cry wolf?"

"It's not *why* he cried wolf," I said without moving my jaw. "The point is that the boy cried wolf when there wasn't a wolf."

"That was stupid," he scoffed.

"Yes," I blurted out, barely containing my enthusiasm at the hint of a breakthrough. "It was stupid to cry wolf when there was no wolf. Do you know why?"

"It was stupid because there was no wolf."

"True," I said. "Can you drill down deeper and think of a bigger problem his actions might cause?"

He hesitated for a long moment and pinched the bridge of his nose as he tried hard to conjure an answer. I waited. "I don't know," he sighed amidst a gush of air from his lungs as if a balloon had been untied. Slapping his open palms on his desk to signify his growing frustration, he added, "This is stupid."

I could see that his meter had expired. Giving someone an answer as opposed to helping him discover the answer violates centuries of Chinese wisdom, but I needed to catch a plane. "When the boy first cried wolf, everybody took him seriously and ran or hid. But, there never was a wolf. Finally, they became cynical. Then, when a real wolf appeared and the boy cried wolf, they didn't heed his warning."

"Are you saying that I cry wolf?"

I touched the end of my nose with one finger and pointing at him with the other.

"Are you saying when I give my people something to do, I should let them finish it?" I repeated the gesture. Just when I was starting to think his elevator was out of order, it was moving again. "But, what will I do?"

"Do?" I asked.

"If I give them assignments or let them choose their own assignments—won't that get boring?"

"Boring for whom?"

"For me."

Just when I thought I was leading him, he led me right into the heart of the matter. Although I credited him with opening an understanding previously hidden from me, I didn't offer to reduce my fee. But, now at least he had two dots to work with.

"Wow," I said. "What an epiphany!"

"Epipha...?" he said blankly.

"Never mind," I continued. "Boredom has you switching gears on everyone and frying their brains."

"Do you think so?"

"There's your answer."

"Where's my answer?"

"If you were engaged in the ongoing mission of the department, you wouldn't be bored and keep interrupting what people are trying to finish."

"Engaged in the ongoing mission?" he asked. "Wouldn't that be micromanaging? I went to a seminar once and they told us not to micromanage people."

"It's a little late for that," I said aloud. Admittedly that was pushing the envelope, but I sped ahead before he could react. "Who reads the mid-range plan?"

"The executive committee, I guess."

"Has anybody ever come back to you and asked for an explanation of variances from the mid-range plan?"

"No," he said thoughtfully, stroking his chin. "Once they're finished and presented, they go up on the shelf and never get opened again."

"Except when you get bored?"

"Yeah, I figure it couldn't hurt to do a little tweaking."

"Okay, let's connect the dots," I came right out and said. "You know the mid-range plan is an exercise in futility. Your team members know the mid-range plan is an exercise in futility. Yet, you ask them to keep revisiting it."

"Not a smart thing, now that you put it that way."

"Right," I affirm. "That is micromanaging in the worst sense of the term. You're looking at your department as if it were a beehive that exists to amuse you."

"I wouldn't say that," he protested.

"You don't have to say it; I just did." I had long since abandoned coaching principles and was emboldened by the rush that consultants get when they're on a roll. "What if I were to say you can *macro*-manage by becoming a strategic trailblazer and clearing a path through the bureaucratic jungle so your people can be more productive?"

"Really?"

"Really. You will be entertained, even challenged. And your people will come back to life and do amazing things."

"When can I start blazing trails?"

"You already have," I said, raising my hand for a high five. My client returned the high five and added a fist bump and a smile for good measure.

The story I just told you is a fantasy. I don't conduct myself in coaching sessions that way, and real I-Bosses don't "get it" that quickly. Plus, I always miss my flights. But I-Bosses *can* get it, given sufficient time, gentle guidance, and encouragement. I've seen some radical turnarounds in my time. I've even been the catalyst for many of them. More commonly, however, I-Bosses go without intervention, coaching or otherwise, and are mostly influenced by other I-Bosses, in which case bad behavior only gets worse, and the body count in their departments grows to staggering proportions. And that's where Idiot procreation comes in.

STEP FOUR: "WE MUST INVENTORY OUR OWN IDIOTIC BEHAVIOR."

This kind of thing keeps me humble and pumps up my empathetic muscle group to Mr. Universe proportions. When I'm drawing on every ounce of creativity and influence I possess to teach some sorry son-of-a-goat I-Boss how to connect dots, I need to be mindful of where I came from and how difficult the journey was for me. As I said at the beginning of the chapter, sometimes flying into a righteously indignant rage just feels right, even when it's wrong. To paraphrase Sigmund Freud, sometimes an Idiot is just an Idiot.

Apart from the question of where Idiots came from, if you are serious about trying to successfully work for one, it's important to understand how Idiots wind up in leadership positions. Just as Idiots don't intentionally set out to become Idiots, neither do most Idiot Bosses intentionally set out to become bosses. In this sense, it's important not to confuse I-Bosses with God, Machiavellian, Masochistic, Sadistic, Paranoid, Reluctant, Unprepared, Buddy, or even Good Bosses.

That Loud Sucking Sound

To reduce the cockamamie thing to its lowest common denominator, Idiot Bosses leave a black hole–like vacuum where intelligence, vision, and wisdom ought to be. The natural universe abhors the vacuum and begins sucking hard to fill it. If intelligence, vision, and wisdom are wandering by at that moment, the story will have a happy ending. But when's the last time that happened? Usually some random, meaningless, irrelevant idea gets sucked into the vacuum and becomes company policy.

An Idiot might initially become the boss for any number of reasons. He might be the only available candidate because everyone else in the department has jumped out of windows or is cowering in a janitorial closet. Or perhaps the Idiot found a proposal on the floor, picked it up, and was standing looking at it when someone higher on the food chain walked by. The Kahuna thought it was the Idiot's creation and promoted him. Sometimes Idiots apply for a promotion because it looks like fun, and accidentally appear competent long enough to get the job. But by the time their true character emerges, it's too late.

Don't you wish you could vote for your next boss? Of course you can always vote with your feet, but wouldn't it be nice if somebody asked before promoting the clueless? Fat chance. I'm suspicious of the democratic process anyway. A democratically elected office is supposed be self-cleansing and purge itself of incompetence, complacency, and corruption. In practice, the first order of business for elected officials is to short-circuit the democratic process and make their jobs as secure and lucrative as those of the bureaucrats who run federal, state, and local government. Cue the incompetence, complacency, and corruption.

What "sucking up" really means

When an I-Boss is promoted, especially near the top, the sucking can be felt throughout the organization. When an I-Boss moves up a notch, she leaves a vacuum (and more suction) in her wake. The vacuum that Idiots in high places create is then replicated at every level. It's a type of automated, systemic inbreeding, and the bloodline becomes more anemic with every reorg. Here's a story that may help illustrate my point: The grand matriarch of a wealthy family on Lookout Mountain, Tennessee, once welcomed a new bride into the family who came from outside the ancestry. Instead of turning up a haughty nostril toward the commoner, the matriarch welcomed her by saying "We need some new blood in this family. There are enough babbling idiots on this mountain already."

Unfortunately, Idiots are only Idiots by comparison. Only non-Idiots can point out that they are, in fact, Idiots. Therefore, the people who make Idiots feel the least like Idiots are other Idiots. Guess who those Idiots choose to surround themselves with? The higher and more powerful the I-Boss, the greater his ability to pad his staff with additional Idiots. The Peter Principle is correct in that people are often promoted beyond their level of competence. What Larry Peter assumed happened next, however, is oftentimes wrong—not because Larry lacked the intelligence to call it correctly, mind you: He just passed away too soon to conduct the longitudinal research. Idiots don't stop rising in the organization once they are promoted beyond their level of competency. Since when has competence been a prerequisite for executive office? I've been a Fortune-100 executive and I can personally attest that my position was based more on how comfortable I made my boss feel than how intelligent or competent I was. Incompetence, especially in the area of human motivation and understanding, can be a first-class ticket to the executive suite.

The only thing keeping some I-Bosses out of higher office is a God, Machiavellian, or Sadistic Boss who can outsmart, outmuscle, and outsteal the I-Boss while he is in the restroom. Just when you thought it couldn't get any worse, organizational designers get rid of the Idiots by plugging their spots with God, Machiavellian, Sadistic, Masochistic, Paranoid, Unprepared, Reluctant, and Sadistic Bosses.

ONCE IGNITED, THE FIRE SPREADS

Even if an I-Boss is created by accident or through a misunderstanding, it is no accident that Idiots are promoted. It's one of the more unpleasant aspects of human nature rearing its ugly head. The principle bearing the name of the late Larry Peter only explains a portion of this phenomenon. Even though increasing one's cognitive capacity is a tall order, it is possible for people promoted beyond their level of competency to nonetheless recognize their dilemma and work to increase their competencies, or at least seek assistance from more competent people. In the case of Idiot Bosses, there is sparse evidence they were ever competent to begin with; certainly, they lack the human characteristics of curiosity or reflection that might give them a clue that they would ever need such competence.

Indeed, many Idiots get into positions of leadership for the wrong reasons, by accident, or from the luck of the draw. Or perhaps they were just walking nearby when the sucking started. The point is that, just as I did, they might eventually discover there is much more to leadership than meets the unenlightened eye. But once they're there, the thought of doing the honorable thing and resigning doesn't enter their mind. Instead, Idiot Bosses, like their counterparts in professional politics, start to tap dance as fast as they can, and things just deteriorate from there.

INSTITUTIONALIZING INCOMPETENCE

If you think there are more I-Bosses than any other kind of boss, you're right, especially in large organizations where Idiot procreation is most common. For those for whom competency has never been a factor, is it any wonder they are least threatened by (and, most of the time, downright comfortable around) other Idiots?

There are both micro– and macro–mushroom effects. When Idiots discover they are not capable of doing what their job requires, they look for someone else to do it. They don't want to give up the perks and prestige of their position. Such is the inherent flaw in classical, bureaucratic, hierarchical organizations. The only way to get more is to move higher. Enlightened organizational designers don't attach the concept of "more" to the concept of "higher." They find innovative ways to reward productivity and contribution without institutionalizing incompetence.

The mushroom effect

The micro–mushroom effect is usually a departmental issue. A lower-level I-Boss, possibly an Unprepared Boss, does not have the budget or the authority to create and fill unjustified positions, and hence he becomes an insufferable aggravation to his team members the way the zombie king was to his. A Peter Principle candidate who has been promoted beyond his competency might not be aware he is unqualified to lead other human beings in activities he managed to muddle through before as a peon.

But what about the truly competent person who is promoted into management based on her skills and abilities? This is another example of inherent flaws in bureaucratic, hierarchical organizations. (Can you tell I don't like them?) For a skilled and competent person, moving into management is her only way to earn more money and acquire more power. The reason for the promotion, however, has nothing to do with perks for the promoted. To the managers and executives higher up the food chain, promoting the person with superior skills and abilities is a way to generalize her performance. If she is extremely good at something, she can make everyone else good at it, too. Or so the logic goes. Such logic is, in a word, illogical. Leading other people, which involves guiding their professional growth and development as well as motivating them, calls for a highly specialized skill set and a servant's mentality, neither one of which the new manager probably has nor ever wanted to have.

Making widgets, writing code, cold calling, and building financial models are all important functions. You wouldn't ask a wizard at widget-making to stop making widgets and start cold calling, unless you were an Idiot. Only an Idiot would ask a code warrior to take customer service calls. That's one factor that contributed to the demise of dot-coms. You wouldn't ask an accountant to head up the engineering department or an engineer to head up accounting—despite the fact both are linear thinkers who live to calculate and extrapolate. Anyone with half a brain realizes that someone who has demonstrated tremendous competence in a specialized skill and who has, in all likelihood, spent most of her adult life mastering it, thrives when doing whatever it is she's so good at.

All common sense notwithstanding, the most common promotional practice in hierarchical organizations is, unfortunately, to separate people from the tasks they love and put them in charge of less talented people doing those things. Crudely stated, traditional promotions in hierarchical organizations require new bosses to teach pigs to sing. The newly promoted boss, being a rare species of singing pig, only annoys the common porkers in the department, who have no desire or intention to sing. The net result of the whole caper is a herd of annoyed pigs and a resentful former singing pig with no opportunity to vocalize.

Promote based on talent

Don't let my glib and flip tone fool you. Despite the unwritten and unspoken rules of organizational life that I chat about so casually, this is truly important stuff. I urge you to be part of the solution, no matter how ridiculous the problem or idiotic the people who caused it. I need to keep reminding myself, as I'm reminding you now, that it's my choice to be the victim, volunteer, or victor in this process. You and I, armed with this enlightened knowledge, can be the driver that helps put the check marks in the Character/Competency Matrix in Chapter 3. A check marks the spot where genuine effort to learn and grow can cover a multitude of sins.

Facilitating the personal and professional growth and development of others is something some people have a natural ability and desire to do. These folks are as naturally suited to leadership as number crunchers are to accounting. The trailblazer concept of clearing the way so others have the space, resources, and oxygen necessary for optimal operation comes naturally to servant leaders (aka Good Bosses). Like their specialized, competent counterparts, they have a desire to continue learning and refining the skills they are naturally suited for, and the learning never stops.

If organizational chieftains really want to dominate their respective industries, they will position their gifted leaders in positions of leadership and let them blaze trails for the super-competent widget makers, code warriors, cold callers, and number crunchers. But this rarely happens. The general rule holds that top executives place widget makers, code warriors, cold callers, and number crunchers in positions responsible for the professional growth and development of other people. Plus they usually do it without preparing the new leader. Wrong, wrong, wrong. The widget makers, code warriors, cold callers, and number crunchers no longer get to do the things they love. They are forced to deal with issues of human motivation and the basic problems of day-to-day living—in other words, other people's problems. You are left with a bunch of angry and/or confused bosses, who are by no means Idiots. Terrible leaders, yes. Idiots, no. And now they're being paid a lot of money. They're not going to step down. Maybe one in a million will. Most will exchange their happiness and vocational fulfillment for the cash and benefits. They are being held hostage in the hierarchy.

The mushroom cap swells with people who are being paid well for not contributing much of anything. The stem contains the harder-working people supporting the crowd in the cap. Eighty percent of the work is done in the stem while those in the cap receive 80 percent of the payroll and benefits. The cap of the mushroom burgeons as non-leaders in leadership positions surround themselves with people to insulate them from the problems people bring to their doorstep daily. The cap of the mushroom also spreads as Idiot Bosses surround themselves with people who make them feel comfortable in their stupidity. The next time you read in the *Wall Street Journal* that someone has received a big promotion in a large organization, lower the paper and picture the cap of the corporate mushroom expanding along with the caps of lots of little mushrooms throughout the organization.

Timber!

Of course, the laws of physics state that the stem of the mushroom can only support so much weight before it buckles and the whole thing topples over. We've all seen how organizations can be created to exploit changes in technology or government regulations. In the wrong hands these organizations are built, made prosperous, and even celebrated, all while being bled dry by the executives at the top of the hierarchy. Many top executives and public administrators have a license to steal as surely as James Bond has a license to kill. After the guts of these organizations are transferred into the top executives' bank accounts and the husks blow away in the wind, an outraged public cries out for justice. Too late. The horse is already out of the barn. The dedicated hard work of the unsung heroes in the mushroom stem keep it all going. They do their best to hold up all of that weight. But the cap of the mushroom can still grow too large for even the hardest-working people to support. How many corporate mushrooms have you seen topple in your lifetime? In the past 10 years? As the ancient Chinese proverb says, *If we do not change our direction, we are likely to end up where we are headed.*

THE RIGHT PEOPLE, THE RIGHT REASONS, THE RIGHT THINGS

Even though I-Bosses are inevitable, they don't need to be terminal. If you work for one, try to understand his shortcomings and make him feel less threatened. You might actually slow the growth of the Idiot population. We once thought that the only place the mushroom cap could grow indefinitely is in government, where the solution is to keep expanding the stem. The public sector doesn't need to make a profit, nor does it need to provide competitive goods and services. Still, we appear to have reached the limit to which even government can sustain out-of-control spending. In Washington and on Wall Street, conservative lawmakers spent the spring and summer of 2011 trying to cut up the federal government's credit cards and thus literally and figuratively depressed the markets, proving that the size of the mushroom cap and stem are finite even to the people who print money. Everybody, it seems, even private-sector bosses and public-sector lawmakers, are human in the end—and not without shortcomings. Good boss management begins with accepting the boss's shortcomings as part and parcel being human.

We can observe other nations around the world where virtually everyone is part of the mushroom stem. In that case, it's advisable to be in the political or social class that occupies the cap. When the entire private sector is sucked into the stem, which is what occurred in the former Soviet Union, the cap shrinks. Enormous stem, tiny little cap. Ultimately, the stem can't support its own weight and topples over. The Soviet experiment didn't last from one end of the 20th century to the other. When Mother Nature grows a mushroom, the stem is always in proper proportion with the cap.

If you are reading this book, chances are good that you're part of the mushroom stem and not the cap. My cap is off to you. Be strong, but also be smart. Even the strongest stem can't hold up a mushroom cap that has grown too big and heavy. Working smart helps shrink the size of the mushroom cap. If it's not possible to shrink it, you can hopefully slow its growth until you can get out from underneath it.

Fourth Step Exercise: "We must inventory our own idiotic behavior."

Work your Fourth Step. Continually update the inventory of your motivations and methods. Don't do things for the wrong reasons, the way I did. If you are, change your priorities and approach. Continuing down the same road will only waste your time and create a herd of angry pigs. Stand back and look at your organization. You'll see how and why those I-Bosses got to where they are. Look at the less-than-intelligent things you have done along the way. We're all part of the Idiot world—some just have bigger parts than others.

Get your hands on organizational charts for the last three or four (preferably five or six) major reorganizations. Pin them to the wall and take push pins and colored yarn to track the progress of certain executives of your choosing. Who is moving up, and who is stuck in place, moving down, or MIA? Who has surrounded himself with sycophants as insulation against problems the executive level can't handle? Are you noting any patterns? Where are you in the picture? How has your career trajectory tracked with some of the more disagreeable characters on the charts? Could it be that you have a blind spot when it comes to how much time your Inner Idiot spends in the driver's seat? It's best just to admit that your Inner Idiot is hard at work sabotaging your career or forming unholy alliances that you don't want to tell your children about, just so you can drive a Lexus instead of a Toyota.

Your Inner Idiot might be on a crusade to eliminate all Idiots from the face of the planet without first learning and applying a bit of tact and decorum. If your Inner Idiot frightens the Idiots above you on the organizational food chain, no matter how good your motives are, you've just fried your own bacon. When the sucking sound is heard, are you being swept up the ranks of the organization, are you slipping backward, or are you standing still while the Idiots fly past you?

Idiots will always beget more Idiots. By understanding the dynamics of Idiot aggregation and procreation, you can break the cycle when it's your turn on top. Be patient and encouraging with your I-Boss. How would you like to be sucked into a corporate vacuum cleaner, or, as they say in London, "Hoovered"? Study the map you created from year-over-year org charts and note the trends. They will reveal what (or who) makes the most senior Kahunas in your organization comfortable. Try to discern whether or not your clueless coefficient, be it large or modest, is contributing to your career growth, blocking your career growth, or sending you into a tailspin.

Take that self-inventory in the context of the organization. Begin to determine what role you consciously and unconsciously play in the scheme of things. When the real Idiot stands up, hope it's not you. Instead of being party to Idiot procreation, lead the party of Idiot prohibition.

5

Banishing Talent

The congressional resolution proposing an early warning system for Idiots among the general population was shot down in committee as politically incorrect. That makes me suspicious. The only people who object to issuing Idiot alerts are Idiots. That's because they don't see themselves as a threat to operational effectiveness in the workplace or to the health and psychological well-being of their team members. What many Idiots do sometimes see as a threat to their own health and psychological well-being, however, is competency. Idiots often perceive competent and talented people as threats—not because they have anything against accomplishment, but because their bosses might expect *them* to actually accomplish something. Machiavellians are shrewd enough to lay claim to your accomplishments and present them up the food chain to higher-ups as their own. Idiots would rather just keep talent out of it altogether.

In your I-Boss's twisted logic, if nobody's doing anything worthwhile, he won't be expected to accomplish anything worthwhile, either. If there are no talented people in the immediate vicinity, the Idiot Boss's chances of flying below senior management's radar are greatly improved. Ergo, the best way to make sure no one in the department demonstrates talent is to banish it altogether.

Remember the principles behind Idiot procreation from Chapter 4:

- ☐ Idiot is promoted beyond Idiot's competency.

- ☐ Idiot prefers not to tell spouse he is going to return the raise, stock options, extra vacation, Lexus benefits package, parking spot next to the building, and corner office.

- ☐ Idiot prefers not to publicly admit shortcomings (if Idiot is even aware of shortcomings); ergo, seeking coaching or any form of learning and development is out.

- ☐ Idiot begins hiring sycophants, thus forming a protective cocoon around Idiot Boss's new position.

- ☐ Sycophants occupy office space and payroll that would otherwise be occupied by talented contributors.

- ☐ All of the Idiot's energy and resources (the company's resources, mostly) are committed to protecting the Idiot Boss's dirty little secret.

- ☐ Protective cocoon deflects problems Idiot Boss is incapable of dealing with.

- ☐ Idiot Boss looks like a genius.

- ☐ If problem penetrates Idiot Boss's defensive perimeter (cocoon), and Idiot Boss screws up big time, costing company millions, Idiot Boss begins firing sycophants from easily accessible stable of sacrificial lambs.

- ☐ Idiot Boss looks decisive and powerful.

- ☐ Idiot Kahunas that hired and/or promoted Idiot Boss in the first place give Idiot Boss a promotion and a raise.

- ☐ Executive search firm is hired to locate new Idiot Boss to replace recently promoted Idiot Boss.

I'm beginning to see why 12-step programs have such a high success rate. They don't let you get away with anything. Denial is dead among the 12-steppers. But it seems like all I've been doing so far is confessing my stupidity to you and to my Higher Power—who already knows what I'm going to say before I say it, so why bother confessing? It's the self-admission part I struggle with. My ego doesn't want to deal with the fact that I've sat on both sides of the Idiot desk. I've been the Idiot Boss, and to this day I still sometimes play the Idiot employee. Despite all of my investment in my own recovery, my Inner Idiot is alive and well.

I'm beginning to realize that when my frustration boils to overflowing and I rail against the Idiots in the universe, I'm not accepting the full measure of my own past, present, or future cluelessness. As they say in the program, "If you can spot it, you've got it." We can most easily recognize the problems in others we have in ourselves. As an employee, I've often felt my talents and abilities were overlooked or ignored. As a pre-recovery I-Boss, I'm sure I must have overlooked or ignored far more talent than I ever had to offer. If you suspect your boss is not recognizing your talent, remember that many Idiots wouldn't know talent if it bit them on their big toe. Banishing talent is a common and vicious practice among God and Paranoid Bosses in particular.

Banishing talent is a blow to any organization. It can cost companies dearly in lost effectiveness, efficiency, productivity, and profitability. None of this is of any great concern to the Gods, Paranoids, and Idiots who feel the pain in their toes. They see talent as a threat to their control and the attainment of their objectives. Paranoids spell threat with a capital T. For some reason, these bosses haven't developed the Machiavellian's cast-iron constitution, which allows you to exert tremendous effort and exercise immense talent, only to have your boss snatch away the glory.

HEAD BASHING

As hard as it is to believe sometimes, bosses are human beings. Their oftentimes aggravating behavior might make you think there is a diabolical doctor somewhere programming Stepford Bosses and shipping them via UPS into companies across the country. To fight against or think you can change your boss's essential nature is like believing you can change human nature itself. Nevertheless, many people go to work each day thinking they can hold back the tides of idiocy without drowning.

For those brave, stubborn, and (I have to say it) self-righteous souls, I suggest you pause about 50 feet away from the front of your building, ask a coworker to hold the door open, get a running start, attain full speed, lower your head, and smash into the edge of the open door. When you regain consciousness, go inside and enjoy the rest of your day. Follow that routine every day for six months and you might damage the door enough for maintenance to replace it. I'm suggesting this because it makes as much sense as trying to change someone else, especially your boss. Even if you succeed in getting to him, they'll just haul him away and pull the shrink wrap off another Idiot Boss from the diabolical doctor. They'll always be able to manufacture another door or another Stepford Boss. But how many times will you be able to regain consciousness before you're out for good? Resenting the unfair way of the workplace hurts you more than it hurts them. I might remind you 100 times before you finish reading this book how toxic resentment is, because it took me 1,000 run-ins with the door to even begin accepting the concept.

I'm not saying you can't influence a change in your boss. Your boss might improve, but only after you do. I see this happen all the time. Coaching really does make a difference beyond the coaching client. But, that's not the reason to do it. You must be genuinely invested in improving your performance, your attitude, and your countenance. Then you will be better off—much better off—whether the boss follows suit or not. I can sense your blood boiling from here. However, you want peace. You want serenity. Waiting for your boss to give it to you by changing is an expectation that will set you up to fail. As we say in the church basement on Wednesday nights, "An expectation is just a resentment waiting to happen." Don't get hung up on whether your boss will change. Keep your expectations to yourself.

COMMUNICATE YOUR WAY TO SERENITY

You can't expect bad bosses to change, but you can change the way you approach and deal with them, which can change how you feel about yourself, them, and life in general. If you intentionally and regularly keep your I-Boss informed of what you're doing, your I-Boss will feel less threatened. This means premeditating "chance" encounters with your I-Boss in the hallway, or at the water cooler, or by following your I-Boss into the restroom. Yes, I'm suggesting strategic bio-breaks. For females working for male bosses and vice versa, your options are more limited. However, women can pass on information to female clerical assistants in the sanctity of the ladies' room. Working your propaganda through the clerical assistant is often more effective than delivering it directly to the boss anyway.

Don't make a big thing of it. Mix up your media. Give micro-reports on your activities face-to-face. Send an occasional e-mail. Hand in a report. But be surgical with your timing. Don't toss your communiqué on top of a huge pile of reading your boss is already resenting. Don't add your e-mail to an overflowing inbox. Monitor when your boss is bored and dispatch one of your entertaining-yet-informative missives at the appropriate moment. Don't dismiss this as pure satire. Keeping people comfortable is the secret of happy and healthy relationships. Consider the alternative. If you want to be a torment to your boss out of resentment and spite, remember to ask an associate to hold the door open for you tomorrow morning as you approach the building. No matter the content of your verbal, nonverbal, or written communications, the net result is to create the impression you are operating within your boss's comfort zone and even protecting him from unwelcome threats.

Use language that allows your I-Boss to take at least a portion if not all of the credit when reporting progress and achievements. I know he doesn't deserve it. But you're working this plan to bring more joy to your world, so let go of bitterness and resentment. They hurt you more than they hurt anyone else. In your correspondences, use phrases like "Per your suggestion...," "As we discussed in the meeting...," and "When studying the assignment you made, several options appeared...." Go ahead and bite the bullet with "Your idea really worked out well." If you don't gag, you'll experience an immediate improvement in the atmosphere around the office. Clouds will lift and the sun will shine. As much as you will be loath to admit it, you will actually feel better. So will your I-Boss. The principle is simple displacement theory: You can't harbor resentment when you're focused on complimenting others. It will dissipate like the noxious and toxic gas it is.

Communicate with caution

Don't be so obvious that your I-Boss and your peers perceive you as a kiss-up. If people call you one anyway, simply say, "I don't want to work in an atmosphere of continuous conflict. Life is too short. If keeping the boss involved and informed helps my serenity, I'm all over it." Or say nothing and merely offer to hold the door open for your resentful peers tomorrow morning.

Also bear in mind how keeping the boss informed and involved often puts control in your corner. In the information age, information is like money in the bank. I-Bosses drive people crazy with third and fourth versions of meaningless plans and reports because they (the bosses) are bored and figure they should be doing something. Keeping your I-Boss informed and just a little bit flattered will keep the Idiot off your back. What's that worth to you? Plus, giving your I-Boss a script with which to impress her own boss (I-Boss-plus-1) in the next big meeting is a good way for you to promote your agenda. Subtle but effective.

Communication techniques are effective with Idiot, Good, God, Buddy, Unprepared, and possibly Paranoid and Reluctant Bosses, where flattery can earn brownie points. Machiavellians are another breed altogether. And don't try communicating your way to serenity with a Sadistic, Masochistic, or Machiavellian Boss and then write me a cranky letter with your remaining hand claiming I didn't warn you.

I spend a lot of time explaining to abused and bruised team members in various organizations the need to take evasive action against the seemingly unprovoked attacks, slurs, and general abuse from some of their peers and bosses. What is unprovoked to you might seem justified in someone else's demented thinking. If you are in direct competition with someone, it's more obvious and understandable how anything good you do will threaten her chances to win. Just because you're not in competition with another person—your boss, for example—doesn't mean that she won't feel threatened.

Never forget that your competence is seen as a threat to those who are less competent or who have convinced themselves that anything positive for you is negative for them. Part of what I confess in Step Five is that I don't pay close enough attention to the threat that my competence might pose to others. It's my job to be aware of that, nobody else's. If I get blindsided by somebody who resents my competence, who's the Idiot? This is hard to grasp if competence in others doesn't threaten you. But to those who live in an inversely proportionate, mutually exclusive world, the fact that you're breathing means you're using their oxygen. The fact you're not competency-phobic means your guard might not be up where it needs to be.

You're open to a backhand when you least expect it. To take the full force of a punch when you have no idea it's coming can really knock you for a loop. Be aware that your natural desire to do things well and to contribute your unique talents and abilities to the achievement of organizational objectives is likely to leave you feeling as if you just ran head-long into the edge of an open door. To paraphrase another Chinese proverb: "If you understand—things are the way they are. If you don't understand—things are the way they are." To recovering Idiots, the proverb refers to the stuff we can't change. Why bother to lose sleep, grow gray hair, or pop your aorta over stuff you can't change anyway?

SHAMU MANAGEMENT

Machiavellian Bosses are not Idiots. They are as shrewd as they come. Machiavellians I've encountered might have felt my competence was a threat because they assumed that everyone thinks in terms of conquest and constant competition, as they do, and that everyone is trying to be king of the hill, as they are. Machiavellians distrust everyone but only have the power to exact vengeance on those below them on the food chain. Ken Blanchard has a possible explanation for this.

In Ken's speeches, he sometimes describes behavior modification in animals, such as Shamu the killer whale at Sea World. He talks about how the Sea World trainers start every session with the animal by simply jumping in and swimming with him, playing and frolicking as the whale wishes. Ken points out that people are often like animals in the sense that they need to be constantly reassured you're not going to hurt them before they will stop acting defensively and trust you. Although you can earn the trust of many people through consistent, non-threatening behavior over time, some people will never trust you. If their motives are not pure, it's likely they'll never fully believe your motives are pure, either.

Even if competence is not an overt threat, competency will cause some incompetent people to feel seasick. I-Bosses don't need to know what's causing the nausea to realize they are nauseous. The trick is to package your competency in ways that will benefit you and not threaten— or nauseate—your competency-sensitive boss. Tomorrow morning, when you see your boss, think to yourself, *Good morning, big whale. Wanna go for a swim?*

It's a Cruel World

I would like to believe competency in the workplace is routinely rewarded. But my experience and observations have shown otherwise. If you have been rewarded at work for your talent and competency, you've been blessed by enlightened leadership. Be grateful and throw your enthusiastic support behind any culture that recognizes and rewards excellence. On the other hand, there is nothing to be gained from getting frustrated and beating your head against a wall every time competency is punished. Punishment for competent behavior is not always part of a conspiracy. Sometimes bosses just don't know any better.

Competency is ignored more often than it is overtly punished. Having no competency to speak of, most Idiot Bosses can't be expected to recognize it in their employees. At the end of the day, competency gets you nowhere with Idiot Bosses, except perhaps banished from their inner circle for making them feel uncomfortable. That's the root of competency-based punishment or neglect—the fact that it makes certain people uncomfortable.

Competency, Creativity, and Change

True competency is usually accompanied by creativity. Competency and creativity are foreign concepts to most Idiots. To I-Bosses, there are fixed and rigid ways to do things based on nothing more than the way they learned to do things. When one is not sure of oneself, there can be comfort in rigidity. Likewise, change and uncertainty are like Kryptonite to Idiots.

Rigid people avoid change because they don't understand it and therefore fear it. True competency embraces change and resists rigidity. Many people seek rigidity in their lives as a substitute for competency. Just give them a framework in which to operate, a strict set of rules, and they will operate with confidence. The next time your I-Boss explains something by saying "Because that's how we do things around here," you'll know he is not being flip. He really likes to have fixed policies and procedures to fall back on, whether or not they make sense.

Security that emanates from structure is actually a developmental phase of childhood. You probably remember when your mom used to say, "Because I said so." And that was enough. You turned that around and used it on a younger brother or sister, saying "Because Mom said so," and expected it to be enough. What did it feel like the first time you saw Mom or Dad doing something completely uncharacteristic of the behavior you grew to expect from them? I'll bet it shook your world. I-Bosses are often developmentally arrested in that phase of childhood where things are done the way they are done because that's the way they are done. They find security, not in the competency they don't have, but in the rulebook. True competency and creativity can be rewards in themselves. To creative and competent people, change is a welcome and often stimulating challenge.

Building calluses

Like Shamu the whale, we intentionally do things to make ourselves feel comfortable and intentionally avoid doing things that make us feel uncomfortable. Hence, the formation of the concentric rings of the cocoon around incompetence during Idiot procreation. While this protective layering insulates incompetent bosses from potential discomfort, it also pushes competency further and further from the epicenter of decision-making in organizations. Sometimes the concentric rings of incompetence are formed intentionally, sometimes unintentionally. With each new I-Boss and the insulating personnel he gathers around himself, another ring is formed. There have been painful moments in my professional life when I discovered I was one of the people my boss was insulating himself against.

One boss who needed insulation from me was someone I'll call Big Bill, a former business partner. Big Bill was the majority stockholder and therefore the more powerful side of the dyad. Big Bill was a powerful businessperson, older than I, with *beaucoup* capital (hence the majority stockholder). I figured I could learn a thing or two from him, which I did. Bill was the best of mentors and the worst of mentors. I learned more about business from him than any other person in my life. I learned important principles for successful operation of an enterprise. I learned if something costs X to manufacture, you must charge X times 3 at a minimum to cover hidden costs and preserve any hope of making a profit.

I also learned how to torture people. Big Bill believed in management by intimidation. I call him "Big" not because he was big and tall, but because he had a large presence. It became quickly apparent how he had earned his fortune in the construction industry. When a bunch of contractors gather on a job site (in Big Bill's case, skyscrapers, major hotels, hospitals, and university buildings), decisions must be made about necessary alterations to original plans, how to proceed with the variances, and whose fault it is. The inevitable disputes and conflicts must be resolved quickly. In the construction business, negotiations on the job site aren't conducted as judicial processes or mediation sessions. They are conducted more like a brawl in an alley.

Bill could out-brawl them all. Imagine being belligerent enough to make construction contractors, those guys who drive the big gas-guzzling SUVs and monster trucks, throw up their hands and walk away saying "Have it your way." I saw it happen many times, after which he liked to go drink hard liquor and gloat. For someone like me who hates conflict, my relationship with somebody who made a fortune in an economy of conflict was conflicted from the start.

The ambient culture in the publishing industry where our partnership lived was and still is very different from the construction industry. There is a gentility about publishing that Bill never even tried to understand or honor. Thankfully, the "sissies" in the publishing business repulsed him and he stayed out of the end of our business that involved negotiating for intellectual properties and anything else that might tarnish his reputation as a two-fisted businessman. He left all of that up to me. As senior partner, he had an office in our facility, but he operated mostly out of his engineering firm offices and his Mercedes. He appeared around the publishing company several times a week to check up on us and/or to amuse himself. We never knew from one appearance to the next what kind of mood he would be in. He fluctuated between overt and covert intimidation. He might come in one day and go off on how there was a box of tissues in everybody's office and he would be damned if he was going to pay for everyone to blow their noses. On other days, he would come in happy-go-lucky and greet everyone with a big smile. "Hey, easy money," he would say to our graphic artist. "When are you going to get to work and stop stealing my money?" he chuckled at the guys sweating out in the warehouse. He had a great sense of humor.

Although they never took a vote, I'm sure our staff preferred the seagull approach. Seagull management, as Ken Blanchard describes it, occurs when a manager comes into an office, flies around, flaps his wings with great commotion, craps on everybody's head, and then flies out. Rather than feel the sting of Big Bill's back-handed humor, designed to remind you who works for whom, I know I'd prefer somebody to come at me with his foul attitude clearly visible on his sleeve.

Constantly reminding staff members who works for whom, even with a smile, is a power play. The unmistakable message is: me, big dog; you, little dog. I'm strong; you're weak. I'm superior; you are subordinate. I'm important; you're not. I'm irreplaceable; you're expendable. You could make a case that all of those statements are true, technically speaking. But they're only true in a context of hierarchical relationships. As much as people similar to Big Bill think this attitude makes them a lot of money, they fail to accept that those who practice a more equitable and appreciative approach to people in their employ can make a lot *more* money.

For all the good Big Bill did for me, for all of the doors he opened for me, for all the opportunities he made available to me, he still left me impaled on the horns of a dilemma. By the time I left Disney, I was a disciple of Danny Cox and the principle that team members get better right after the leader does. Hoping that your boss gets better right after you do is a tough road, but possibly the only one you have. My motto had become "Lead the way you like to be led." Whatever characteristics or behaviors I wanted from my team members, be it hard work, high energy, innovation, creativity, loyalty, efficiency, or high performance, it was up to me to model them all before I could credibly expect them from others. Imagine how shocked I was to learn what a poor role model I had become.

DAMAGE CONTROL

My management philosophy was the complete opposite of Big Bill's, and he felt compelled to take me under his wing and teach me how to treat employees. They were never loyal, according to him. They were efficient because the punishment for inefficiency was severe. They worked hard because you paid them to work hard. Bill was convinced that, despite their paychecks, people only worked hard when he was looking in their direction. I couldn't convince him otherwise. When I pointed out that our present staff was half the size of the staff I took charge of initially and that they were producing four times the revenues, he attributed the increased productivity to his surprise visits and autocratic management style. Our staff was generating revenues of close to $250,000 per person in 1984 dollars. To me, their superior performance was in spite of his influence, not because of it.

I spent time after each flight of the seagull encouraging various team members and refocusing their efforts. We had a molecular organizational design, and every work "pod" orbited around the management core. Each person was a leader in his or her own area. Granted, we were a small company, but the principles of autonomy worked well, and our people responded and performed just the way organization behavior specialists predict people with a sense of ownership and autonomy will perform.

I managed up and down the food chain, doing my best to keep Bill happy and our team members happy and productive. That meant dropping whatever I was doing when Big Bill showed up. After he made his rounds greeting/insulting our team members, he signaled to me it was time to have coffee at the café down the street. We could have had coffee in my office or his office, but that was against his rules. Bill believed in leaving the premises to discuss company business. According to his philosophy, employees will eavesdrop and become privy to information they have no business knowing (99 percent of which nobody cared to know anyway) if you stay in the office. Thinking back, the stuff we talked about offsite was mostly information emanating from our team members anyway.

Bill was also into psychological warfare. Another reason he left the office to have coffee was to create the illusion we were discussing our team members beyond their earshot. This was supposed to make them fear for their jobs and therefore work more diligently. Big Bill was The Man, and I reconciled myself to being a good soldier and charging up the hill when he said charge. In the publishing industry, he didn't even know which way to point the canons. We succeeded anyway. When I say succeeded, I mean that we grew quickly and developed a tremendous reputation in our field. When we sold the company 40 months after the day Bill and I bought it, his piece of the pie was more than five times his total investment—net.

Charging up the hill at his command usually involved doing little to impact our organizational objectives. Thank goodness he didn't like to bother with strategic planning. I would have been up to my tailpipe in mid-range plans. I felt all along that Big Bill should have been more appreciative of my efforts on our collective behalf. And I whined about him to friends, family, and anyone who would listen. Many people can identify with the tremendous resentment I harbored for Bill.

My role in my own misery

Here's the big part of my Step Five confession: I had the mother of all epiphanies, thanks to the unrelated efforts of Bill and a friend in the mental health field. I was getting my first master's degree, the one in marriage and family therapy, and one of my supervisors grew weary of hearing me whine about my business partner. One day, as I was launching into the vicissitudes of working with him for the 100th time, my friend said, "When are you going to stop worrying about him and start dealing with your role in this relational friction?"

"My role?"

"He knows you resent him and that makes him uncomfortable around you."

"Okay," I said. "I'll admit that I resent him. He doesn't appreciate a single thing I do even though I'm doing everything I possibly can for the business. I'm making him a lot of money."

"He's still uncomfortable," she said.

"Let him be uncomfortable," I shot back. She didn't need to say anything. She just patiently waited for me to stew in my own stupidity for a few moments. "All right," I mumbled. "And your point is...?"

"You can't hide resentment, no matter how hard you try. It seeps into everything you say and do. It has an unmistakable odor."

"He comments about my sarcasm all the time," I noted.

"Are you sarcastic?"

"All the time," I confessed.

She hit me right where it hurt the most. I couldn't deny I had enormous resentment toward Big Bill, just as I had had for other bosses in my career. No wonder none of them was comfortable around me. No wonder they took everything I did as an assault and my every comment as a veiled insult. On the same hand that held the accusing finger I pointed at Big Bill were those three fingers pointing back at me. Whether those bosses acted fairly or unfairly, competently or incompetently, appropriately or inappropriately, I was just as much to blame for the tension as they were. Whenever I was around them, it didn't matter what words came out of my mouth. I was always in an adversarial posture, and I reeked of resentment.

PUT THE BOUNDARY WHERE THE BOUNDARY BELONGS

As true as it all was, I didn't want to hear it. I've learned in the years since that it is not what my consulting clients want to hear, either. It's a difficult pill to swallow. It's a tough defense mechanism for my coaching clients to recognize in themselves, much less admit and work to overcome. What about your situation? Upon closer examination, are you being punished for your talent and competency, or are you poisoning the atmosphere around you, as I did? Most likely it's a combination of both, and you only have control over your part in it.

If others make your blood boil, your attitude might be helping increase the flame on their burner. Confess it. Don't let your Inner Idiot use it against you. I feel a little Pollyannaish asking the rhetorical question: Can't we all just get along? Yes, we can, but not always on our own terms. Truly getting along with bosses and coworkers rarely happens on our terms. Draw the line where you need to protect yourself and your best interests, but when the line is drawn to protect your ego and to prove you're right, it's time to erase the line and start over.

We can all get along if we accept that life and work are never perfect and that there are times and places to settle for less in the moment to gain more in the long term. There are also times when you shouldn't compromise. Deciding which is which is up to you. How serene you can be despite your I-Boss is your call. How much you allow situational stupidity to rob you of valuable time and energy is your decision. You might not be in control of what your I-Boss says or does, but you are in control of your attitude and how you respond.

Deciding to admit your role in the chaos and discomfort caused by your I-Boss is a start. You could even say it's half the battle. When I realized and accepted that I contributed to and exacerbated Big Bill's bad attitude, the tension between us immediately eased off. When my attitude improved, so did his. It was just like Danny Cox said it would be. And Big Bill was essentially the boss, the 800-pound guerilla, me plus one. Bill didn't change his essential character, but he stopped acting like a tyrant virtually overnight. Was he ever a tyrant, or was my lens distorted? I was shocked whenever I heard someone else who knew him comment on how kindly he treated them. There were only a few, but enough to help me recognize that I was catastrophizing the relationship. You and I have tremendous power to alter the climate in which we work, regardless of our I-Boss's incompetence or our I-Boss's fear of our competence. We can and should do good work. We can and should take pride in what we do. That causes us to focus on accomplishment rather than focusing on the burden we imagine someone else is placing on us. And we can present our good work to the I-Boss not as a threat, but as our contribution to the overall efforts of the team.

If you want to live a happier, more fulfilling life, live by the words of Aunt Eller from the musical *Oklahoma!* In the film version, she comforts her niece by saying "You must look at the good things in life and the bad things in life and say, 'Well, all right then' to both." I've never heard it said better. Look at the good things at work and the bad things at work and make peace with both. As the Chinese proverb says, life will be what it is, whether you understand it or not. That's why we recovering Idiots pray for serenity to accept what we can't change, the courage to change what we can, and the wisdom to know the difference.

You have very little control over your Idiot Boss, or any other boss type, for that matter. You have a vast amount of control over the type of relationship you have with them. Having said that, your control is limited to your own thoughts, statements, and behaviors. The good news is the way you think and what you say and do can improve the way your I-Boss treats you. As you become less threatening to your I-Boss, his respect for your talent and competency might well increase. Who needs control when a little bit of influence can cause such a major improvement in how others perceive you?

STEP FIVE EXERCISE: "ADMIT TO MY HIGHER POWER, TO MYSELF, AND TO OTHERS THE NATURE OF MY WRONGS."

Make the small change; reap the big reward. This exercise is simple, but hard to pull off if you're harboring boatloads of resentment. Resentment, which will be delved into more deeply in Chapter 8, serves no good purpose for you, the resentor, because it has no effect on resentees except to annoy them. If resentees are Idiots, they might not even pick up on the odor.

Here is one way of describing the stupidity of resenting: You're angry at someone you're talking to on your cell phone. You throw the phone in the toilet in anger. How does that hurt the person on the other end of the call? Go for the opposite approach, just once, in a small way so as not to compromise your sense of dignity (based as it might be in part on the nobleness of your resentment). Identify one situation or typical exchange between you and the person you resent. Rehearse responding in a way you know the resentee will appreciate (based on your copious study of this person) yet are loath to do because doing so will make you want to throw up. Next time the opportunity arises, give the appreciative response. Don't overdo it and disqualify your effort. Do it in stride, with no fanfare, and carry on with your day. If you don't notice an immediate and positive reaction, I'm a monkey's uncle. If you don't notice an immediate and positive reaction, your heart probably wasn't in it, and whatever you did had the odor of resentment all over it. No points for that.

If at first you don't succeed, rehearse and try again. If you can manage to get a sincere response out—*sans* resentment—you will alter the relationship and the environment virtually overnight. If you can refrain from resenting the fact that you had to do the work, you'll pave the way for being appreciated for the talent you truly are rather than being banished. Confess the nature of your wrongs, approach your I-Boss in a truly new and resentment-free manner, and be neither the banisher or nor the banishee of talent. Clean up your side of the street, de-threaten competence, and give talent a chance.

6

Success in Spite of Stupidity

My former obsession with fairness and perfection launched me on a self-defeating mission to prove I was right about everything. In my stupidity, I never stopped to consider if losing what I was ostensibly working for was worth someone telling me I was right. Doing the right thing was a secondary concern and doing things correctly mattered little in my quest simply to be *considered right*.

BEING RIGHT IS STUPID

Most people want to think they're right, which means that not everyone who thinks they are right can actually be right. Step back and reflect on your long-term plan, or jump ahead and take a look at your five desired goals in the Step Six exercise at the end of this chapter. What is your ideal big picture? Which is more important: achieving your desired long-term or short-term goals, or being right? Once you stop insisting on being right and granting the honor to someone else, barriers will start to fall, you'll feel energized, and the wind will fill your sails.

As long as you are engaged in a tug-of-war with someone else over who is right, your focus and energy can't be applied to goal achievement—unless, of course, your only goal is to be right. Try it the next time you lock horns with someone over something that won't alter the course of the universe. Simply agree with the blockhead and say, "You're right. The layoffs won't affect morale." Of course they will. But if they're inevitable and beyond your control, what good is arguing about it? Just nod politely. A much better use of your time and energy would be to make plans for how to deal with the demoralization. Save yourself and others who are spared the axe. All of you will be working twice as hard at a minimum. Maintaining a productive and (hopefully) rewarding work environment will be a bigger challenge than before. Don't waste time arguing about the obvious, especially with people who are too stupid to see the obvious. You have more important fish to fry. So don't be too stupid to see the obvious.

If it's your boss or someone even higher on the corporate food chain—Boss-plus-one, Boss-plus-two, Boss-plus-three, and so on—what do you think you're going to gain by convincing her she's wrong? If intentionally aggravating someone with influence and/or direct authority over your working conditions, job security, and future prospects is your formula for success, I don't want to read the book you plan to write during the copious leisure hours after you're canned. Making others feel good is so easy; it's ridiculous not to do it. Just say, "You're right. Hurricanes rotate clockwise in the northern hemisphere." Who cares? Allowing someone else to be right doesn't make you wrong. Abdicating the throne of "right" to someone immature enough to think it will matter 10 minutes, 10 years, or 10 centuries from now is the big thing to do. It's an especially grand gesture when you have immutable proof the other person is wrong. (You Googled hurricane rotation, didn't you?)

Since I've stopped battling over being right, I've come to enjoy letting people who are wrong about something think they're right. I quietly hold a private smug-fest. Best of all, I'm no longer tripping myself on the way to the finish line. I also sit back, watch the winner bask in the glory of rightness, and think to myself: *Did I look that imbecilic when I insisted on being right?*

How the Smart (and Lucky) Succeed

Movie mogul Samuel Goldwyn is credited with first saying "The harder I work, the luckier I get." I would update that and say, "The *smarter* I work, the luckier I get." Employing the principles and techniques in this book constitutes smart work, regardless of how easy or hard it might be. I admit that some of the greatest successes in my life have not come as the result of a well-structured or smart strategy. Think how much *luckier* I would have been if I had studied Samuel Goldwyn sooner. You and I don't have the power to align the planets, much less predict when it will happen. All we can do is have our ducks in a row when the universe decides it's our turn. We can't create luck, but we can be prepared to take advantage of it when it pays a visit. As Disney University's Mike Vance said, "Don't miss your opportunities." The last thing you want to be caught doing when the planets align is acting stupidly. One of the greatest tragedies in life is failing to be ready when your number is chosen. Self-help motivational books are good for helping prepare for that moment. But they can't force the moment to arrive any sooner than our Higher Power schedules it to arrive.

Books written by or about successful people often contain nuggets of truth. But the truths apply to the successful person's unique circumstances, which often include a run of luck. I think books promising fail-proof paths to wealth are mostly self-aggrandizing accounts of how rich people want the world to believe they succeeded. And they want the world to believe they did it all on their own.

The best we can do is keep ourselves in a state of readiness for anticipated and unanticipated opportunities. As Benjamin Franklin said, "Early to bed and early to rise, makes a [person] healthy, wealthy, and wise," or words to that effect. Dr. Hoover says that luck will get you the last three without bothering with the first two. But you can't count on luck. So lie down with the sun and rise with the rooster. That's all we have control over. When your new and improved relationship with a difficult boss yields dividends, you can revisit your Step Six exercise (at the end of this chapter) and relish the historical account of how you played a premeditated and intelligent role.

Consider your options

Be realistic when considering what you want to accomplish in your workday. Most people reading this book are doers by nature and have found themselves frustrated by bosses who impede progress and accomplishment. Before you crawl under your desk and withdraw from the rat race, answer some basic questions:

- ☐ Are you a rat?
- ☐ Who are you racing against?
- ☐ Do you want to be active or idle?
- ☐ If you want to be active, do you want to just be busy doing things or do you want to do be busy getting things done?
- ☐ Does "getting things done" mean advancing your career and earning potential, or cataloguing rare fungi?
- ☐ If you want to earn more and be more involved, are you willing to become a smart blip on the corporate radar screen?

Unprepared blips are continually frustrated and disappointed because blips on the organizational radar screen usually become targets. You might simply be a target for those who want to foist their responsibilities onto the first person who will accept them. Becoming a target can also mean serving as a scapegoat for someone else's poor performance. If you want to become a more active and visible player at work, be aware of and prepare for the potential downside of visibility.

Many people are highly skilled at internal and external planning for their organizations, yet they rarely apply those same planning skills to their own careers and working conditions. The act of surviving and thriving an Idiot Boss or any other boss type can be enhanced by planning your way into more rewarding activities. It's not hard to stay ahead of an Idiot Boss, so if you're not trying to hide in the janitorial closet until retirement, put your planning skills to work for you.

- ☐ Consider what you want to become involved in. Look ahead and listen to the company propaganda for activities and initiatives the department is likely to be gearing up for in the near future. Identify those things you want to be involved in and offer to do preliminary research and legwork.

☐ If you want face time with the CEO, volunteer for the charity event for which the CEO's spouse is honorary chair. Roughly translated, "honorary chair" means "chair's spouse's company will buy ten tables at $1,000 per plate." The problem is that they usually have to drag people off the street to fill 100 seats. The CEO will welcome you (and the prospect of having someone to talk to during the speeches) with open arms.

☐ Consider who is likely to be involved in the new initiatives and decide if these are the people you want to share a foxhole with. Look at who will likely be the team leader and consider how shiny this person's star is within the organization. Someone you personally enjoy a great deal may not be very popular up the food chain, in which case you could have a decision to make—comfort now, or keeping options open for the future.

☐ Consider the importance of the new activities and initiatives in the context of long-range organizational objectives. It might be fun to re-sod the corporate softball field, but will redesigning work processes put you in a more lucrative limelight? If the CEO is a maniacal softball player, by all means grab the wheelbarrow.

☐ Consider what you are best suited for. Don't try to take charge of an aerospace engineering project if your background is in advertising or public relations. It's always in your best interest to align your professional responsibilities with your natural strengths and competencies. One way to beat back the ravages of personal stupidity is to align what you do best with what the organization needs most.

☐ Consider how others see you. Although your unique strengths and competencies might be right for a project or corporate initiative, do others recognize you as a leader? You could maneuver your Idiot Boss into assigning you a project, which technically legitimizes your power. But if your peers don't perceive you as a competent leader, they will sabotage and subvert your efforts, leaving you wishing you had stayed under your desk.

☐ Consider how much time and effort you're willing to exert to overcome obstacles in your path, what amount of abuse you're willing to absorb from detractors, and whether the potential reward is equal to the sacrifice. The challenge isn't in coming under fire; it's in not being properly trained for combat operations.

SURVIVING YOUR PERFORMANCE REVIEW

In a perfect world, bosses would be eager to regularly examine the organizational population and review their performance in terms of who is contributing and who can be encouraged to step up. Yet, you would be amazed at how vigorously some managers avoid reviews. Or maybe you wouldn't be amazed. Good bosses are eager to give performance reviews to praise performance and encourage growth. Sadists enjoy giving performance reviews for the opposite reasons and thereby render them useless for their intended purpose.

Ostensibly, the purpose of the performance review is, at least in part, to determine eligibility for promotions and salary increases. In reality, most organizations go through the performance review process at least once a year after much pushing, prodding, confiscation of the boss's gaming device, and threatened litigation from HR, which is only trying to cover the company's derrière in the event of a grievance or wrongful termination suit. When employees tend to have their attorneys on speed dial, staying out of court is no small feat.

By design, performance reviews require a manager to sit on the throne of judgment. If a manager gives an honest appraisal, the team member might feel slighted or even attacked. If the manager inflates a review to protect the team member's fragile ego, the boss might feel guilty for subverting the system and rendering the review meaningless. With the possible exception of the Masochist, all of us like to think we're more valuable than we really are. (I have yet to work for a company that can't survive my departure.) One danger in the annual performance review: When bosses go through the performance review motions, what constitutes a good employee to them and what constitutes a good employee in the real world can be two different things.

If top executives are genuinely concerned about productivity and performance, they should have team members do performance reviews on their *bosses*. To organizations already doing so, I extend my heartfelt congratulations. To the others, I say, "Wake up." Bad bosses have 1,000 times more destructive potential than ineffective team members. If you can't find the courage to have team members review their bosses, at least use 360-degree feedback as the basis for performance reviews, as some firms do. It's more valid, reliable, and objective than the manager-generated performance review. Performance is reviewed every day in organizations where open communication is encouraged and information flows freely among all team members. Constructive confrontation practically eliminates the need for painful, annual performance reviews by engaging employee performance (and boss performance) weekly.

Performance review horror

My worst performance review came from a particularly mean-spirited manager who I will always believe had it in for me for graduating from college and using words in excess of two syllables. I remember thinking to myself as my manager yakked in the background: *Are we talking about the same person here? All this time I thought I was doing a good job. Does he think I work long hours because I have nothing better to do? If I'm this bad, why did he wait so long to tell me?* He wrote that I needed improvement in quantity of work, quality of work, work habits, and especially communication—then he demanded that I sign it. Based on that review alone, I'm surprised security didn't escort me from the building in handcuffs.

Don't allow a poor performance review to wound your ego. They are often a more reliable indicator of the boss's mood and ability to deal with people issues than they are accurate reflections of performance. If your boss discusses goals, objectives, habits, and behaviors on performance review day and no other day of the year, the review process lacks any kind of credibility as far as I'm concerned. (Read *The Art of Constructive Confrontation* by yours truly and see how continuous constructive conversations can be hugely beneficial to everyone involved if they are done sooner rather than later and with consistency.)

For those who still suffer under the oppressive yoke of their boss's performance reviews, the least I can do is offer some pointers. Performance reviews mean different things to different boss types. Depending on your boss's type, you can emerge unharmed or crawl out of your performance review bloodied and bruised. Regardless of the challenge awaiting you, it's best to go in with your eyes wide open.

You need to be prepared for them all. Reflect on what you've already learned about the various boss types—their likes and dislikes, their strengths and weaknesses, and their career paradigms. You must present yourself in the best possible light to your boss 12 months per year, not just 30 days before performance reviews. Violate the particular protocol of any boss type at your own peril. A bad performance review will shatter your serenity. Even if you manage to preserve a semblance of happiness and contentment in the workplace following a poor performance review, your confidence will be shaken.

THE GOD BOSS PERFORMANCE REVIEW

God Bosses enjoy the performance review process because it gives them the opportunity to exert "power over." To a God Boss, a good employee genuflects. As long as the team member being reviewed spends sufficient time on bended knee and presents suitable tithes and offerings, the review will be positive, regardless of whether or not anything is getting accomplished in the department.

To prepare for a performance review with a God Boss, choose your wardrobe carefully. Your clothing should reflect humility and submissiveness. Sackcloth and sandals might be appropriate. God Bosses take themselves very seriously. The more ceremony you engage in, the better. Burning incense and chanting your God Boss's name are nice touches. Be careful, though. Pay attention and determine what will be an adequate demonstration of your devotion without going over the top. God Bosses don't appreciate being mocked.

For your best shot at getting a raise from a God Boss, use epithets like "Your Greatness," "Your Majesty," and "Your Lordship" throughout the year. "Boss Almighty" isn't bad, either. It all sounds blasphemous because it is, but do you want the raise or not? No matter how literally you take your God Boss, always refer to his accomplishments, his glory, and his mighty power when talking business or golf. Go with the flow on this one—anyone who thinks he is God could be dangerous. Whatever he says or does, act eternally grateful.

Prepare all year long for a God Boss review by:

☐ Articulating how much you appreciate the opportunity to serve in his department in e-mails and other appropriate correspondences.

☐ Thanking him for his help and guidance on projects.

☐ Offering to do him favors or small services.

☐ Bringing him small gifts, even if they are humorous tokens and trinkets.

☐ Mentioning to his peers how his accomplishments have driven the department forward.

☐ Acknowledging his leadership in written reports and evaluations of projects.

Before you write these suggestions off as frivolous, consider doing these things for 12 months. If your diagnosis is correct and your boss truly thinks he's God, what kind of performance review do you think you'll receive? Don't worry about real productivity—you accomplish that for your own satisfaction and to earn the respect of your peers. A God Boss will evaluate and qualify you for promotions and raises based on how faithful a disciple he thinks you are. I guarantee, if he perceives you as a detractor or as ungrateful, no amount of real productivity, efficiency, or cost savings will bring you into his good graces at performance review time.

THE MACHIAVELLIAN BOSS PERFORMANCE REVIEW

Prepare for your performance review with a Machiavellian Boss by reviewing everything you have done for the company, and make sure you didn't receive credit for it. If you did receive credit, go into the performance review and immediately apologize for the mistake and promise it will never happen again. Act as if you're at a loss to explain how your name became attached to something the Machiavellian was obviously responsible for. If you're written up in the company newsletter for some achievement, demand a retraction in the following issue.

Men should keep several suits and ties in the office to ensure color coordination with the Machiavellian. Women must dress to complement rather than compete with the Machiavellian. If she comments about the similarity of your wardrobes, tell her she sets the fashion trends and emphasize how you watch her closely for guidance. Furthermore, tell her whatever she wears, drives, eats, or reads should be required for the entire organizational population.

Understand that everything the Machiavellian tells you regarding your performance is distorted through the lens of how it either promotes or impedes her career. Nod and agree to everything. Don't get into an "I'm right and you're wrong" thumb wrestling match with a Machiavellian if you want to go home with two thumbs. Prepare all year long for a Machiavellian Boss performance review by:

☐ Articulating how her work is deserving of much more acclaim from higher up in e-mails and other appropriate correspondences.

☐ Thanking her for allowing you to work on her behalf.

☐ Volunteering to take on special projects that promote her agenda and enhance her image.

☐ Selecting wardrobe and decorating your workspace in ways that suggest allegiance.

☐ Mentioning to her peers how her accomplishments have driven the department forward.

☐ Acknowledging the superiority of her leadership in written reports and evaluations of projects.

Consider doing these things for 12 months. If your diagnosis is correct and your boss truly is Machiavellian, you will receive the best marks possible on your performance review. Think of productivity as a way of accomplishing something you can give her credit for. You can still be productive as a means of self-satisfaction and to earn the respect of your peers. However, a Machiavellian Boss will evaluate and qualify you for promotions and raises based on how convinced she is that you support and do not compete with her. I guarantee if she perceives you as a threat or competitor, no amount of real productivity, efficiency, or cost savings will bring you into her good graces at performance review time.

THE SADISTIC BOSS PERFORMANCE REVIEW

The performance review is a Sadistic Boss's dream come true. A legal, sanctioned, and even required annual session of torture is almost too good to be true for a Sadist. The Sadistic Boss can hardly contain himself as his employees absorb the psychological torment, grimace in pain, tear their hair out by the fistful, and are forced to come back at least once a year for more. Sadistic Bosses would do punitive performance reviews weekly if they could.

If you want to get a raise from your Sadistic Boss, claim any increase in your income will cause you painful tax consequences. Emphasize the word *painful*. It's not the Sadistic Boss's money to begin with, and if it will cause you anguish, he'll find it's worth padding the budget for. More likely, though, he'll opt to starve you out.

Dress as if you slept in your clothes. If he comments, say flatly that you haven't slept since he gave you the medium-range plan to rewrite—*again*. (I-Bosses consider rewriting reports as entertainment. Sadists make you rewrite reports as torture.) Wear clothes that are too large so he'll think that you don't have time to eat. If you're a good make-up artist, make your face a bit more sallow, apply some bags under your eyes, and hollow out your cheeks. Pile your office or cubicle with stacks of papers and reports from floor to ceiling. Leave only enough room for one person to get in and out. If he thinks you're slaving in there (cue the moans and wails) he'll leave you alone and go hunt down someone who looks rested and well fed.

Prepare all year long for a Sadistic performance review by:

- ☐ Articulating at every opportunity how much you are struggling under the excessive workload. Never cross the line and act angry toward your Sadistic Boss about this; instead, act defeated and worn down.

- ☐ Using body language and expressions to support the grim descriptions you offer of your circumstances. Attribute your physical pain to a kidney stone. Knowing that you're struggling under this kind of compounded mental and physical torture will magnify a Sadistic Boss's sense of satisfaction.

- ☐ Pointing out the reasons why projects and initiatives imposed by your Sadistic Boss are tremendous encumbrances, even if they're not. If he's happy with the *appearance* that his power is sufficient to cause you discomfort, why should he the wiser?

- ☐ Never volunteering to take on special projects and extra workload—that's taking away your Sadistic Boss's power to control and abuse you. You must maintain the illusion, whether it is an illusion or not, that anything he tells you to do could be the straw that breaks your back.

☐ Being prepared to celebrate secretly with your peers. When and if your Sadistic Boss acknowledges your success, remain solemn, sigh, and say, "Yeah, boss, that project took so much time we got backed up on everything else." If your Sadistic Boss believes you, he might not immediately load you up with additional work.

☐ Making wardrobe and workspace decorating choices in ways that avoid exhibiting a lighthearted, carefree existence. Your work area should be piled high with work, whether it has anything to do with your current project or not. A wardrobe motif? Think salt mines.

Consider doing these things for 12 months. If your diagnosis is correct and your boss truly is a Sadist, you will receive the best marks possible on your performance review. Again, don't avoid productivity altogether; you and your peers still want to achieve a sense of accomplishment. Just don't expect a job well done to be welcomed with time off to catch your breath. The silver lining of the Sadist's dark cloud is the fact that he needs the illusion of power as much as he needs the actual power. If you play your role convincingly enough, a Sadistic Boss might accept your stellar performance as payment in full.

The Masochistic Boss Performance Review

Masochists use the performance review to prove what miserable failures they are, not what a bad employee you are. If they were better bosses, they reason, you would be a better employee. That is true, but not for the reasons they're citing. Masochists think everything they touch turns to ca-ca and they don't stop to think about how that might insult you. Don't take it personally. You didn't have anything to do with creating the Masochist's condition, and there is nothing she can say or do to turn you into fertilizer.

Wearing something drab might help because it will deflect attention off of your clothing. If you wear something bright and cheery, your Masochistic Boss will probably notice and go into a downward spiral about what a lousy dresser she is. She may indeed be a terrible dresser, but do you really want to sit and listen to that? I'd rather have her tell me I need improvement in quantity of work, quality of work, work habits, and communication.

You might be able to get a raise from a Masochistic Boss if you can convince her it will damage her departmental budget enough to draw a reprimand from her boss. If she doesn't figure that out on her own, it's up to you to mention it. As you rush out to visit your child in the ICU, pause at the door, turn, and say, "I suppose a raise is out of the question because it would really bring your boss down hard on you...." Then run. The raise should be approved by the time you get back to the office.

Prepare all year long for a Masochistic Boss performance review by:

☐ Articulating how your Masochistic Boss struggles under an excessive workload that no human being should be expected to manage. Use body language and expressions that slightly mimic her slumped shoulders and hopeless countenance.

☐ Pointing out the reasons why projects and initiatives imposed on her department are doomed from the start. Let your Masochistic Boss know how sorry you are that she has been put in this untenable situation.

☐ Volunteering to take on special projects and extra workload from time to time. This gives you the opportunity to produce worthwhile work. However, don't rush into her office rejoicing in the accomplishment.

☐ Being prepared to celebrate secretly with your peers. When and if your Masochistic Boss acknowledges your team's success, remain solemn, sigh, and say, "Yeah, boss, we really got lucky on that one. Don't you wish we could be so lucky all the time?"

☐ Making wardrobe and workspace decorating choices in ways that avoid exhibiting a dramatic contrast in self-image between you and your Masochistic Boss—she will feel minimized just being around you.

☐ Avoiding reassuring her. When things go terribly wrong, don't tell her that it wasn't her fault. Say instead that it was a common misunderstanding, or that anybody could have made a similar mistake or miscalculation.

Consider doing these things for 12 months. If your diagnosis is correct and your boss truly is a Masochist, you will receive the best marks possible on your performance review. Like all bosses, Masochists will evaluate you for promotions and raises based on how convinced they are that you understand and sympathize with their dilemma. At all times, keep your own interests in perspective. Despite the skilled ways you play to your Masochistic Boss, you don't want to be an individual martyr working for a martyred individual.

THE PARANOID BOSS PERFORMANCE REVIEW

A Paranoid Boss will give you an average performance review by marking all threes on the five-point Likert scales. He'll stare at you in silence as you come in and sit down. Clutching your  performance review in his hand, he'll shut the door, close the blinds, turn up the radio, and speak in a whisper in case the room is bugged. Some Paranoid Bosses might even search you for a hidden digital pen or other recording device. He'll tell you the review process is nothing but a veiled attempt to trick him. But he's too smart to fall for it. He'll say he gave you all average marks so as not to raise any suspicion with HR, but he still knows what you and your scheming team members are up to. It's best never to wear all black around a Paranoid Boss. Don't whisper in the office or talk into the cuff of your shirt sleeve. Don't even take your cell phone with you into the performance review. If it rings, he'll dive under his desk.

If you want a raise from a Paranoid Boss, take a deep breath, search the ceiling for hidden cameras, lean close to him, and tell him he's right: Everyone *is* out to get him, and you know who, when, what, and where. If he'll give you a raise to "cover expenses," promise to deliver a full report exposing the conspiracy and conspirators. For your personal safety, make him agree to transfer you out of his department one week before the report is due. Once out, you can forget the bogus report. How is he going to explain rescinding the transfer and raise?

Prepare all year long for a Paranoid Boss's performance review by:

☐ Keeping everything you do as visible as possible. Take every opportunity to keep all activities in plain sight of your Paranoid Boss. To the extent you are able, arrange your working space so that he can observe you from his office or regular routes of travel.

☐ Using body language that features broad, sweeping arm gestures that suggest openness, which will help assure him that you have nothing to hide.

☐ Describing how you and your fellow team members came up with your conclusions and what activities led to your results. The more you can paint a picture for a Paranoid Boss, the less he will rely on his fertile imagination to fill in the blanks.

☐ Taking on special projects as if you were working in the front window at Macy's—giving everyone involved, directly or peripherally, a brief account of the project's origins before you move on to a progress report. How you frame the information can lead to unsolicited comments coming back to your Paranoid Boss, thus indicating an open atmosphere. An open atmosphere is less threatening than the possibility of covert operations in dark corridors.

☐ Celebrating success openly with your peers and including your Paranoid Boss at every opportunity. Celebrate in the office as much as possible so he can't avoid seeing what you're doing and can't pretend he was excluded.

☐ Making wardrobe and workspace decorating choices in ways that provide maximum access and exposure. This means as few walls and partitions as possible. When you meet with coworkers, do it in the open where the boss can see you. Do it within earshot if you can.

Consider doing these things for 12 months. If your diagnosis is correct and your boss truly is Paranoid, you will receive the best marks possible on your performance review. If you have kept him updated on a daily basis with brief, "spontaneous" reports, even when there is little to report, he can't help but feel less threatened. If you give in to your natural urge to avoid the pain in the corner office and keep your work, office associations, and comings and goings to yourself, you're asking for trouble. As always, surviving and thriving in the workplace, especially under a Paranoid Boss, places the responsibility for proactive solutions on your shoulders.

THE RELUCTANT BOSS PERFORMANCE REVIEW

You'll need to write the review for your Reluctant Boss, as she never wanted to be the boss in the first place. Many organizations have addressed this issue without openly acknowledging that it is an issue or admitting any wrongdoing on the part of bosses who see no redeeming value in these reviews or who are too lazy or otherwise just flat out refuse to write them. As an executive coach I often hear the complaints of employees who either never get reviewed, despite HR's insistence on the legitimacy or legality of the process, or who receive reviews *after* bonuses have been distributed (or not distributed, whichever the case may be), thus making the exercise somewhat moot.

Whether or not it actually makes sense, Reluctant Bosses are thrilled with the idea of employees authoring their own performance reviews. Reluctant Bosses see this as a way to avoid engagement. Any boss responsibility you can remove from a Reluctant Boss's plate will only serve to endear yourself to her. Reluctant Bosses don't want any part of the management responsibility that is implicit in the performance review process. So don't require it of her. By composing your own review, you give your Reluctant Boss the opportunity to simply sign off and be done with it. If you can deliver your performance review to yourself in a mirror, your Reluctant Boss will be all the happier. Organizations that adopt the practice of employees writing their own reviews play straight into the hands of Reluctant Bosses.

Prepare all year long for a Reluctant Boss's performance review by:

☐ Being as self-directed as possible. Make no demands whatsoever on your Reluctant Boss to perform any of the responsibilities of management. That's the last thing you want your Reluctant Boss to think of at performance review time.

☐ Helping to keep your peers off of your Reluctant Boss's radar. Make a point to let your Reluctant Boss see you redirecting others away from her office. You might even mention occasionally that you managed to help so-and-so resolve his or her problem before it needed to darken her doorway.

☐ Becoming your Reluctant Boss's surrogate in departmental meetings. If you take responsibility for scheduling and conducting meetings that your Reluctant Boss would otherwise be responsible for, she will be grateful at performance review time.

☐ Becoming your Reluctant Boss's surrogate in interdepartmental meetings. Whenever you can engineer the opportunity, speak on behalf of your Reluctant Boss as to what your department is accomplishing, using the names and functions of team members that your Reluctant Boss has probably forgotten.

☐ Reporting only good news to your Reluctant Boss. Reluctant Bosses are keenly aware that any negative information implies that a management response might be required. Save your Reluctant Boss the trauma of acting like a boss by creating and sustaining the distinct impression that everything is copasetic.

☐ Using the Third Party Compliment to perfection in order to build up your Reluctant Boss in the eyes of her peers. There is no sweeter music to the ears of a Reluctant Boss than to hear compliments for the excellent people management that she never actually engaged in.

By doing these things for 12 months, you will be putting yourself in the bull's eye of your Reluctant Boss's comfort zone, such that it will be virtually impossible for her to not give you anything you ask for. Write not only your own performance review, but the reviews of others who might present your Reluctant Boss with incomplete work, thereby causing your Reluctant Boss to complete the work herself. Writing up your peers' performance reviews puts all kinds of power in your hands. Properly executed, these techniques will make you indispensible to your Reluctant Boss. The only danger in all of this will occur if you are a needy type who craves the parental ministrations of an attentive and responsive boss. In that case, you and your Reluctant Boss will be constant irritants to one another.

THE UNPREPARED BOSS PERFORMANCE REVIEW

The principle characteristic of the Unprepared Boss is an over-eagerness to be the boss, coupled with under-appreciation of the awesome responsibilities involved in competent bosshood. This makes it incumbent upon you to compensate for what the Unprepared Boss should be doing but is not doing—all while not appearing to usurp the Unprepared Boss's authority. Whereas the Reluctant Boss will abdicate authority all day long in the cause of evading managerial duties, the Unprepared Boss will bail on his managerial duties yet still expect—nay, verily demand—the rights and privileges of bosshood. This puts anyone reporting to an Unprepared Boss in a very delicate position when it comes to being evaluated. You must do much of what your Unprepared Boss should be doing as a manager. In this way, you're treating him as you would a Reluctant Boss. But beware that the Unprepared Boss will resent anything that creates the impression that he doesn't know what he's doing.

As a result, you will likely find yourself in the untenable position of bailing out your Unprepared Boss and giving him credit for being competent. It can be enough to make you gag. But the issue here is keeping your personal stupidity from blocking a decent performance review. Resenting your Unprepared Boss won't help your cause. It's not so much the resentment itself that's bad (despite its unmistakable odor), but the incredibly stupid things resentment causes us to think, say, and, worst of all, do.

Prepare all year long for an Unprepared Boss's performance review by:

☐ Acknowledging your Unprepared Boss's authority. Talk him up, not down. Your Unprepared Boss might not want to be the ultimate authority, as the Machiavellian Boss does, but your Unprepared Boss is the sheriff in your neck of the woods. Don't spit on his badge unless you're polishing it.

☐ Not challenging your Unprepared Boss's authority. Unless you have a 100-percent chance of success (which you don't, unless you're one of the CEO's progeny), don't challenge the legitimacy of your Unprepared Boss's title.

☐ Getting things done in spite of your Unprepared Boss's authority. Allowing things to go to seed, which is a naturally passive-aggressive response to your Unprepared Boss's unpreparedness, will ultimately reflect badly on you.

☐ Championing the causes that your Unprepared Boss has sworn allegiance to. The authority the organization has bestowed upon your Unprepared Boss makes it possible for him to play big shot when it comes to good causes. The bitter medicine of propping up your Unprepared Boss's self image as a benevolent dictator will go down a little easier when you consider that somebody is actually being helped in the process.

☐ Championing the cause of your beleaguered colleagues. You might get rewarded at performance review time for your contributions to the smooth operation of his department—again, as long as you avoid making him appear incompetent. The key is to give deference to your Unprepared Boss's institutional authority (as unsavory a task as that might be) as you build popular authority.

☐ Maintaining your composure. This might sound *über* simple, but keeping things copasetic around the department will lend credence to your Unprepared Boss's fictional preparedness to lead. Keeping your cool when everyone around you is losing theirs can help everyone around you, including your Unprepared Boss.

Demonstrating an ability to maintain your composure for 12 months around your Unprepared Boss is important to hammer home here because losing one's grip, so to speak, is the fastest way to let loose the dogs of stupidity. Don't give your Inner Idiot the opportunity to pop out and wreak havoc on your career. If you do, your Inner Idiot will rush, babbling incoherently, into a bad performance review and transform it into a disastrous performance review faster than you can say, *"Whahappened?"*

THE BUDDY BOSS PERFORMANCE REVIEW

Your Buddy Boss will treasure the one-on-one time with you that a performance review affords. When he suggests you meet once a month instead of only once a year, smile and ask if you get a raise every month. He might be so happy you want to spend time with him that she'll come up with the extra coinage. How bad could it be? Your Buddy Boss wants to interact with you constantly. There shouldn't be anything new to discuss at a performance review when you've been joined at the hip all year long, except the weather and your raise.

To drive your Buddy Boss into an elated frenzy, wear similar clothing and excitedly point out how you match. What a surprise. What a wonderful coincidence. It must mean you're meant to be friends forever. When the irony gets too thick, step outside for some oxygen. Don't use the emergency phone call about your child in ICU ploy. A Buddy Boss will beat you to the hospital. Just act delighted with everything your Buddy Boss says and does and, the moment you're out of his sight, do whatever floats your boat.

Prepare all year long for a performance review from your Buddy Boss by:

☐ Keeping everything you do as friendly as possible—take every opportunity to make all activities seem socially driven without embarrassing yourself in front of the cynics in the company. Arrange your workspace so that your Buddy Boss can observe you from his office or on his regular routes of travel. That contact will be enough for him if he just needs an acknowledgment fix.

☐ Using body language that features friendly, welcoming gestures that say, "It's so good to see you." It doesn't matter that you've been friendly, even giddy, every time he's encountered you for the past 15 years—if your Buddy Boss has received no assurance in the last 15 minutes, you might want to give him a wave.

☐ Using voice mail and e-mails to reassure him that he is in your thoughts. Like the Sadistic Boss, your Buddy Boss feeds on the perception more than the reality of your regular appearance. A stitch in time will save nine. A brief, preemptive e-mail or voice mail might keep your Buddy Boss out of your office long enough for you to get some real work done.

☐ Saying up-front that special projects sound like fun and will give you more opportunities to report in on a regular basis. As always, you are using special projects to write your own ticket as far as workload is concerned. You can also use them to create social interactions that will please your Buddy Boss. Now that's catching two birds in one net.

☐ Celebrating success openly with your peers and your Buddy Boss. He will love nothing more than a reason to party. Celebrate in the office as much as possible to reduce the possibility that he'll wind up at your place. He'll join in any festivities available. As with all other boss types, you're managing him to your advantage.

☐ Making wardrobe and workspace decorating choices in ways that indicate maximum affection for your Buddy Boss. This could include naming the softball and bowling teams after him on the jerseys. Pictures hung on the office walls, pinned on departmental bulletin boards, and stuck on the break room refrigerator should display your Buddy Boss with you and every other team member you can squeeze into the frame.

Consider doing these things for 12 months. If your diagnosis is correct and your boss is as emotionally needy as the day is long (i.e., he's a Buddy Boss), you will receive the best marks possible on your performance review. If you have included him in these ways, your Buddy Boss can't help but feel included. And why wouldn't you want your work environment to be as friendly as possible? It falls to you to get anything worthwhile accomplished. But what else is new?

THE IDIOT BOSS PERFORMANCE REVIEW

If the sample performance review in the HR manual looks identical to the review your Idiot Boss presents to you, it's because he copied it word for word. Unfortunately, the sample review has average rankings across the board. I-Bosses don't understand the concept behind performance reviews any more than they understand the concept behind inflatable tires. Bosses do performance reviews, people put air in their tires, and Idiots don't understand the need for either of them.

You can actually convince your I-Boss to improve your performance review rankings if you make a game out of it. Point out how your Idiot Boss can give you a larger raise if he elevates your rankings. Tell him how *he* can get a raise by suggesting the same thing to his boss. When he does and is slapped silly, he'll be too embarrassed to confess to his boss that he gave you a raise just because you asked for it. Play it smart and never mention the unfortunate incident again or point out the red handprint on his cheek. If your Idiot Boss tries to bring it up, develop instant amnesia. He'll drop it soon enough.

Throughout the year, always have your I-Boss's latest ridiculous project nearby in case he unexpectedly drops in on you. Pull the bogus papers over the real materials or football pool you're working on and fire a preemptive comment to cut off any project he's cooked up to amuse himself. Spout something about what a terrific idea it was to rewrite last year's medium-range plan and that you should have it finished for him in time for the Super Bowl...next year's Super Bowl.

Prepare all year long for a performance review from your Idiot Boss by:

☐ Keeping everything you do as overstated as possible. Take every opportunity to make all activities seem driven by your allegiance to the corporate philosophy as your Idiot Boss understands it. Without embarrassing yourself in front of your peers, arrange your workspace to reflect the type of corporate empire the Idiot imagines he's in charge of.

☐ Using body language that reflects the type of follower your Idiot Boss imagines his leadership style will attract. If he feels that "reengineering" means treating everyone like a piston rod, walk and talk like a piston rod. Hopefully, your Idiot Boss will fancy himself a leader of self-actualized, creative, and enthusiastic people. That way, you can be yourself and get credit for it.

☐ Using voice mail and e-mails to reassure him that his vision is being realized. Like the Machiavellian Boss, your Idiot Boss probably sees his role in the universe quite differently from the way the universe sees him. Your Idiot Boss needs the reinforcement that his imagination is reality.

☐ Explaining repeatedly how special projects are a way to accelerate his agenda (thereby shaping your workload more the way you want it). As always, you can create special projects or reframe your existing projects to give the appearance that his agenda is comprehensive and meaningful.

☐ Celebrating success openly with your peers and your Idiot Boss. The key here is to boast and brag that what you've accomplished is what your Idiot Boss imagines is important. You'll even want to make sure that the people who matter are appropriately informed of what you've done.

☐ Making wardrobe and workspace decorating choices based on the cultural mores of the empire in your Idiot Boss's imagination. This is like naming the softball or bowling team "The Cheese Movers," "The Saw Sharpeners," "The Blinkers," "The Tipping Points," "The Ice Sellers," or "The Outside-the-Box Bunch." Your Idiot Boss won't read these books any more than the Unprepared Boss will, but they're likely to be on his shelf because HR bought him copies. Regardless, he'll feel enlightened by association.

Consider doing these things for 12 months. If your diagnosis is correct and your boss truly is an Idiot, you will receive the best marks possible on your performance review. If you have convincingly created the illusion that his imaginative empire is alive and well, he can't help but feel important. You should want your Idiot Boss to feel important. While it's true he's not, any doubt he has about his importance will wind up as burdensome, unnecessary, and even ridiculous work on your desk. Again, preemption is key to applying these techniques to every boss type.

THE GOOD BOSS PERFORMANCE REVIEW

A Good Boss will have engaged you consistently throughout the year regarding organizational goals and objectives and your role in their attainment. She will have engaged you week-in and week-out in constructive confrontation. You will have nothing new to talk about at your performance review except how your Good Boss is scheming to get you more money and better working conditions. If she has truly been a Good Boss, she will have orchestrated an effective and well-balanced team approach to organizational performance objectives.

Many larger organizations appropriate a fixed amount of funds to be distributed as raises in each department. This is done independently of the performance review process. The performance review is simply a means to slice up the pie. I like the 360-degree feedback approach myself, and a Good Boss will attempt to gather and consider peer input to balance and validate her own, even if it's not the official approach of the HR department.

Your Good Boss knows that productivity and loyalty are tied to a sense of ownership, and a sense of ownership increases proportionately with participation. If team members can actually influence how salary and wage increases are distributed, they will feel empowered. The bond between Good Bosses and their team members is the strongest of any of the boss-employee pairings because the Good Boss has earned her team members' trust and confidence by sharing power.

Although Good Bosses share power, they remain ultimately accountable, to the point of taking the heat when team members screw up. As leadership author and lecturer Danny (*Seize the Day*) Cox says: "If the team hits a home run, a true leader points to them and says, 'They did it.' If the wheels come off the project, a true leader says: 'I'm responsible.'" If you have a Good Boss, rejoice, thank your Higher Power, be grateful, and pay it forward. Give her your best 12 months every year, and your Good

Boss will do the same. It's a beautiful thing. Even if you don't do your best, your Good Boss probably will anyway. Part of your Good Boss being at her best might involve her reminding you that you're not at yours. A performance review from a Good Boss is probably the only one you'll feel truly good about signing.

LIKE LIKES LIKE

Whether we're right or wrong, hard workers or lazy, smart or intellectually challenged, the fact remains that most bosses won't give raises to people they don't like. It's human nature, and I don't advise betting against it. Observe and determine what boss type you're working for and start developing your plan from there. Reflect to your boss what makes your boss happy. Spend your energy making your boss feel comfortable. Get all you can from the cards you were dealt and only then think about getting more. Sure, you can ignore the nature of the beast, ignore boss typology, work diligently with a sense of integrity despite your boss, and hope you will be recognized and rewarded. I tried that for most of my working life with only partial success. The fact that I kept frustrating myself long after I should have known better means I clung to at least some of my stupidity after I had asked my Higher Power to remove it.

IDIOTS BEWARE

Ambitious, creative, innovative, and enthusiastic team members can still draw enough attention to be executed or banished by status quo preservationists. Many people do a good job and make tremendous contributions to the achievement of organizational goals, only to have those achievements and contributions minimized, marginalized, and maligned. Such people often buy into the mythical belief they can take their hard work and enthusiasm to another organization where they will be better appreciated. That rarely works. Most of the time, they find the grass no greener in the new pasture, and all they have succeeded in doing is lowering their seniority. There are bad bosses everywhere. You might as well master the art of working with them right where you are. After a few such disappointing attempts to find greener pastures, some formerly enthusiastic people go numb, fall silent, blend into the woodwork, and manage to coast across the retirement finish line before anyone notices. They didn't set out to do it that way; the system merely knocked them unconscious, and that's how it all turned out. You could say they were slapped silly by Adam Smith's invisible hand, the one he claimed controls the economy. No one knows from whence it comes nor where it goes. But its impact is clearly felt.

STEP SIX FOR RECOVERING IDIOTS: "I'M ENTIRELY READY FOR GOD TO REMOVE

MY STUPIDITY."

Success and stupidity don't mix. My boss's stupidity is only half of the problem. My own stupidity can easily complete the disaster. With the help of my Higher Power, I'm counting on my recovery process to give me a chance to rise above my own intellectual challenges. Although your Idiot Boss's mental shortcomings remain beyond your control, you can anticipate I-Boss thinking and behavior and proceed accordingly. Becoming a subject-matter expert on your I-Boss can position you to reap huge dividends in terms of greater peace, serenity, and successful negotiation of working conditions and job expectations. The second but equally important part of that equation is becoming a subject-matter expert on your Inner Idiot to ensure that the little bugger doesn't pop out and sabotage you at the worst possible moment.

Throughout my career, I have done things I shouldn't have done, not done things I should have done, said things I shouldn't have said, and not said things that could have made things better. I'll wager that you have, too. I must choose every day not to waste precious time and energy dwelling on mistakes I've made in the past and wishing I could go back and try again. That would be idiotic. What's done is done. But to delete the past from my memory only to make the same mistakes again would be more idiotic.

The biggest demonstration of stupidity on my part, which I quickly blamed on my I-Boss's stupidity (even when there was no stupidity on his part—at least not at that moment), was feeling as if I were a victim of some great force dedicated to my destruction. I cast my boss in the role of that great and destructive force. Although there are times when any one of us can truly be victimized, it's just as likely that we're *volunteering* for failure by our own unwillingness to act wisely by gathering and applying critical data that could help us plot a more successful course of action. I became so accomplished at victimhood that I could re-engineer a good boss into a bad boss just to give myself a place to fall whenever I failed at anything.

STOP PURSUING PERFECTION

Professional growth, like personal growth, is a process of refinement. As we say in the church basement every Wednesday night, *progress—not perfection*. Honoring the process is more important than achieving perfection. Even if you achieve perfection, others in your organization (starting with your boss) will get their hands on your work and screw it up, and you'll wind up aggravated, agitated, and alienated all over again. Letting go of the notion you or anyone else can somehow achieve perfection will be one of the most liberating experiences of your life.

One way of replacing the stupidity of expecting perfection with something better is to observe how other people do things. You can emulate behaviors that appear to work well for them and avoid the ones that make them look like Idiots. Although I recommend adopting the thought processes of successful people, thoughts are much harder to observe than actions. That's why it's always safer and more sensible to lead off with the behaviors of successful people. The thoughts associated with successful behaviors will follow.

STEP SIX EXERCISE: "I'M ENTIRELY READY FOR GOD TO

REMOVE MY STUPIDITY."

Be neither victim or volunteer. You don't want to be a victim of anything you can avoid, nor do you want to volunteer for anything except greater success in dealing with difficult people, especially those who possess greater institutional authority than you. It comes back to accepting what you can't change, but changing what you can. And that can be quite a lot.

Make a list of five life situations that didn't go your way. Keep the items on the list reasonably relevant. Don't include the time you weren't chosen to be on the team you wanted to be on in fifth grade. A job loss is a good example. So is not receiving a promotion or a raise you felt you deserved. Each situation that you list should have been the result of someone else's decision.

Under each item on your list, describe five things that you did or didn't do that led to the decision that disappointed you. Reflect. Were those contributing factors something that you could have or should have known about if you had been paying attention to your boss's agenda and priorities? Were those contributing factors things that you would do differently now if given another chance? The good news is that whatever you're doing now, whether it's looking for a new job or trying to survive the one you're in, you are getting another chance. It might not be an exact replica of the one that got away, but remember Teddy Roosevelt's philosophy: Start where you are, use what you have, and do what you can. Unless you're ready to call it quits and say this is as good as it gets, flip the exercise.

Next, list five goals that you want to achieve. You can't undo what has happened, so don't waste your time trying to relive the past. If finding a way to survive and thrive without killing your boss is something you failed to do in the past but would like to do in the future, then it becomes a new target. For each of the five desired goals you want to achieve, list five new or adapted behaviors that will lead to the success. It should be quickly apparent that whatever roles luck and circumstance have in disappointment versus success, we can decrease the odds of disappointment and increase the odds of happiness by being better students of the game and of the players themselves.

I'm committed to succeeding in spite of stupidity. I want to stop allowing my own stupidity to keep ruining my best plans. Because we can't control the degree to which our boss's stupidity or nefarious agenda might be stifling our greatest hopes and dreams, we can at least shift the odds in our favor by no longer volunteering for abuse. A spinning airplane propeller probably won't affect your day one way or the other unless you walk into it.

7

Idiot-Think:
The Great Disguise

Sometimes the distinctions between the 12 steps for recovering Idiots are subtle. In Chapter 6, I prepared myself for my Higher Power to remove my stupidity. Now, I'm wondering why it's taking so long. I'm formulating numerous plans for replacing stupidity with something useful, which is what the preparation for stupidity extraction is all about. My fear is that once my stupidity is removed, the resulting vacuum will suck something far more dangerous in to take its place. We must quickly fill the void where stupidity once lived to prevent another, more profoundly stupid idea, notion, or behavior from replacing it.

STEP SEVEN FOR RECOVERING IDIOTS: "PLEASE, PLEASE, GOD—

REMOVE MY STUPIDITY."

The plan I suggest in this chapter is the old false identity ploy. If you can't beat 'em, join 'em. Or make it appear as if you're joining 'em. Sometimes it's just no use fighting the system. According to Laura Crawshaw, author and founder of the Boss Whispering Institute, we limit ourselves by choosing between fighting or flighting. Dr. Crawshaw suggests a third option: fraternizing. My false identity ploy is a form of fraternization.

Burn your personal fuel cells on things you have some control over and might even enjoy. If you're trapped in a culture of Idiots with no possibility for improvement in your lifetime, you might as well blend in. Why burn yourself out? By adopting the appearance of an Idiot—by thinking like an Idiot—you can move up in the organization without threatening anyone. Changing identities is not a clever maneuver to trick your I-Boss into liking you. That would be difficult to sustain over the long haul. As "honest Abe" Lincoln once said, "You can fool some of the people all of the time and all of the people some of the time. But you can't fool all of the people all of the time," or words to that effect. Attempting to fool all of the people all of the time requires operating against your essential nature. This is like struggling against gravity. You're better off being real and finding ways to use your essential nature to your advantage. Pretending that you like your I-Boss when "despise" is the more accurate term is like trying to hold a fully inflated beach ball underwater. It's easy to do at first. Then it becomes tedious. You start to wonder why it's so important to hold the ball under the water. *Oh, yeah*, you remind yourself. *I'm fooling everybody by keeping my true feelings beneath the surface.* As time goes on, it becomes increasingly difficult and inconvenient. You'll eventually need to eat and perform other essential functions of the species. What seemed at first like a small expenditure of energy starts to add up. Every now and then, the ball starts to slip. You catch yourself just in time to shove it back under the water again. *Whew*, you think. *That was close.*

BEACH BALL NIGHTMARES

As you read this, there are more people around your office holding big beach balls under the water than you might think. They're the ones that have that funny expression on their faces. You know the expression I'm talking about—the look of constipation or of suffocation. They appear to be holding their breath a lot. The truth is they're in constant fear the beach ball will pop to the surface and their true feelings regarding their I-Boss will be exposed.

The lucky ones really are constipated. The only thing between them and relief is an effective laxative. Unfortunately there is no off-the-shelf remedy for unresolved malice toward your I-Boss. You must find a way to simultaneously be real and peacefully coexist with her. Stoking your conflict boilers won't bring you relief. Constant fear of exposure will cause you to toss and turn all night, raise your blood pressure, and can give you ulcers. I've often bolted upright out of a dead sleep in a cold sweat, after dreaming that my beach ball popped out of the water in the middle of a staff meeting. To make matters worse, sleep deprivation makes it even more difficult to concentrate on keeping the thing submerged.

You know you're in trouble when your I-Boss wanders by unexpectedly and catches you off guard. "Whatcha doin' there?" he asks. Taken by surprise, you frantically scan the office for telltale signs of your beach ball and instinctively countermove with a response you learned in childhood. "Nothing," you say with all of the energy and innocence you can muster.

"Aw, come on now," your I-Boss cajoles. "You're up to something. You jumped when I snuck up on you."

"You snuck up on me?" Surprised indignation might turn the blame around onto the I-Boss. If he really was trying to catch you in some sort of subversive or insubordinate behavior, you might be able to invoke an entrapment defense. The entrapment defense is brilliant way to claim that doing something bad isn't bad if someone deliberately catches you doing it. A.C.L.U. lawyers use it to defend criminals against what they believe to be crooked and conspiratorial police officers all the time. To these lawyers, there are no criminals, just victims. To the culpable employee, there are no subversive or insubordinate behaviors, only Idiot Bosses and entrapment.

You may consider yourself above such deleterious abuse of the legal process—until your I-Boss sneaks up and surprises you. Instantly, your number-one priority is to get off the hook at any price and by any means possible—ethical or unethical—before you know if you're even on the hook. You instantly turn into a trial lawyer. The guilty human mind is an amazing thing. Once you determine there is no smoking gun lying around, you do your best to regain control of the situation.

"What makes you think I'm up to something?" you retort with confidence, returning to your normal voice as you realize the beach ball is safely stowed out of sight. This is remarkably similar to a mother catching her child with his hand in the cookie jar. Once the evidence is swallowed, he can deny it until the cows come home.

"You practically jumped out of your chair when I opened my mouth," your I-Boss presses. "Are you sure you weren't trying to sneak in some real work instead of working on the rewrite of our medium-range plan?"

"Yeah, that's what I was doing," you blurt out, seizing the opportunity. "Nothing gets by you, boss. I was trying to do something productive and you caught me red-handed."

"Well," he says proudly. "We do what is important to me in this department and not what's important to anybody else."

"I forgot for a minute," you apologize. "But, you brought it to my attention just in time."

"I'm not as dumb as I look," your I-Boss chuckles as he continues down the hallway. "You have to get up pretty early in the morning to be more awake than me."

You sit for a moment, trying to figure out what he thought he meant by that last comment. Then, as always, you just shake it off. The important thing was your Idiot Boss didn't see your beach ball. You're safe for now. But he noticed you were hiding something, and that's troubling. Your façade is getting more and more difficult to maintain.

Don't bank on cluelessness

I-Bosses rarely make such transparent comments, except in the fiction I write. But they can see a beach ball if one pops up right under their nose. They might not recognize the beach ball as a simile for your loathing and resentment, at least not right away. But if they see enough beach balls popping up around the office, their suspicions will eventually be aroused. I-Bosses don't understand the concept of hidden feelings as much as they understand you might be hiding a candy bar in your desk when you're supposed to be on a diet. That's big news to them. Any feelings you might be harboring are of no great consequence to an I-Boss. But the very fact you're hiding something is enough to set off his sensors. If you insist on keeping your real feelings under wraps, always have a candy bar in your desk that you can pull out when your I-Boss sneaks up and accuses you of hiding something.

IDIOT-THINK

This business about nearly everyone in the office holding his or her beach ball underwater partially explains the phenomenon I like to call Idiot-think. Idiot-think is remarkably similar to groupthink. Truthfully, I merely borrowed the idea from Irving Janis and gave it a new coat of paint. Just because you haven't experienced groupthink for yourself doesn't mean you haven't been exposed to the virus. As with groupthink, most people participating in Idiot-think do so without realizing it.

Idiot-think occurs because nobody wants to be a patsy. W.C. Fields put it this way: "If you're in a poker game for 30 minutes and you haven't figured out who the patsy is, you're the patsy," or words to that effect. Groupthink occurs when members of a group disguise anonymity as unanimity at the expense of quality. Idiot-think occurs when nobody wants to stick his or her neck out and risk being criticized or ostracized. A group of codependents can drive you insane when they try to make a decision. Nobody wants to offend anyone else or give anyone a reason to not like them. At the same time, they're all trying to control the outcome. It's enough to drive you bonkers. There is safety in unanimity. That's why it's so popular. With a group decision, the blame is spread out over many people should something go wrong. Nobody wants to ruffle feathers, even in their own imagination. That includes your I-Boss.

Be careful not to underestimate the degree of cluelessness your Idiot Boss is capable of. Most people have enough dignity and self-regard to avoid being exposed by a bogus unilateral decision—hence the groupthink phenomenon. Remember that I-Bosses are capable of *groupthink solitaire*. They'll go bogus all by themselves, not realizing there is safety in numbers. Worse, an I-Boss might be bolstered by the mistaken belief that she is safely inside her protective cocoon of sycophants—only to discover after boldly blurting out an incendiary remark that there is nobody from her tribe around for miles.

Be your I-Boss's new best friend. Never leave her alone like that. The more bizarre and incredibly stupid a superior's idea is, the more over-the-top your support should be. As you blend into I-Crowd you need to be prepared for anything that comes out of your I-Boss's mouth. When your I-Boss suggests the solution to your firm's filing for bankruptcy is to have all of the fire extinguishers in the building serviced, throw down your pen and say, "Brilliant. Why didn't I think of that?" (This is a good line to have at the tip of your tongue any time your I-Boss opens her mouth.) The scary part is when you realize that you've actually begun to believe your own flattery.

The great disguise, reversed

Every time the name of this book is mentioned, somebody says, "I have a great Idiot Boss story for you." I'm convinced working for an Idiot Boss is one of the most common experiences on earth. I'm also convinced that Idiot-think is the second-most-common phenomenon. Everywhere I turn, individual acts of stupidity are being eclipsed by acts of group stupidity. Being out of touch with the pulse of an organization is characteristic of an I-Boss; executives knowing the state their organization and pretending that they don't, is something else entirely.

The best intentions, the worst results

Idiot-think will come up and bite you just when you think everything has been resolved and people are truly committed to positive and productive change. It's a pervasive and insidious problem. When a group of well-intentioned people tries to accomplish something, their first order of business should be to check their stupidity at the door. Idiot-think in the form of group denial is a difficult problem to overcome. Innocent communication problems can be repaired like dilapidated bridges. However, people have strong reasons to deny reality. Overcoming denial can be practically impossible. To help people admit they are engaging in denial is like reaching the first base camp on Mount Everest. It can be done, but only about one in 10 or 20 million people ever try. There are probably better odds for winning the lottery. Of those who reach base camp, even fewer ever reach the summit.

I have learned from my mistakes and have become a much more effective coach, consultant, and facilitator over the years, ever since I packed away my need to impose my interpretation of justice on an unwilling audience. Now I try to start where I am, use what I have, and do the best I can—as opposed to pounding square pegs into round holes. By trusting more in my Higher Power and the inherent resourcefulness of my clients,

I find myself acting a lot less stupid and helping people find more meaningful solutions. I wouldn't know any of this unless I had screwed up with all the best intentions of saving the day.

BLEND INTO THE CROWD WITHOUT LOSING YOUR GOALS

If everyone holding a beach ball underwater for no good reason would just let it go, beach balls would be popping up all over the place. The office would look like the ball crawl at IKEA. You can get rid of your beach ball by simply deflating it and throwing it away. No one needs to know except you. Just because you're blending in doesn't mean you've lost sight of your goals. Denial is one of the most powerful defense mechanisms known to the human race because it protects us from reality. People avoid goal-setting for similar reasons. Setting goals places a demand on performance: If you want to avoid the pressure to perform, don't set goals. If the challenge of problem-solving frightens you, deny that there are any problems. Take heart in the fact that goal-setting can be a private matter, and you can adopt healthy ways to keep yourself accountable without becoming excessively punitive. Start by refocusing your energy away from your contempt for your Idiot Boss and toward personal growth and satisfaction.

We can all make our own lives easier by purging as much resentment and pent-up hostility toward our Idiot Bosses as possible and replacing it with healthy alternatives. It sounds Pollyannaish, but it's true. Just because you are no longer in denial about your feelings doesn't mean you can't find more productive ways to relate to your I-Boss. It's never too soon to get started, and even small attempts to tune in to the I-Boss frequency can pay off.

Start by facing some facts:

☐ Your I-Boss has more power inside the office than you do.

☐ You have more power outside the office than your I-Boss does.

☐ Assuming you work 60 hours per week and sleep eight hours per night, you still have a net gain of two hours per week in non-work waking time. Feel the power.

☐ You probably wish you were getting paid more.

☐ You either (a) like your I-Boss, (b) don't like your I-Boss, or (c) couldn't care less.

☐ Your I-Boss can't control your thoughts or emotions. How you think and feel is up to you.

☐ As an at-will employee, you have the choice to stay or leave and can set up the emotional scenario to make staying as appealing as possible.

Wardrobe

The following wacky ideas have worked well for some people. Try dressing outside of fashion guidelines. I-Bosses are clueless creatures. This is often reflected in wardrobe choices made by male Idiots. There are occasions, albeit fewer of them, when female I-Bosses dress in shocking and inappropriate ways. You can always tell when an I-Boss has been to the mall. A male I-Boss will show up for work in a coordinated wardrobe the day after he goes shopping and the sales clerk has selected his clothing. But give him a few days to get the matched clothing intermingled with the rest of his wardrobe, and color coordination is a thing of the past. Your window of opportunity to compliment the I-Boss on his coordinated outfit is narrow.

Don't be afraid to dress like an Idiot. Unless the male I-Boss has a wife or girlfriend who asks the rhetorical question, "Are you planning to wear that tie with that shirt?" he will. Bizarre ties usually amuse I-Bosses and will show the rest of the world you're a pillar of self-confidence. Be bold.

It's hard for people with taste to dress poorly. It usually requires some intense planning, both in terms of your emotions and in selecting your outfit. Take your cues from observing your I-Boss's wardrobe habits over time. You should be able to catalogue everything he is willing to wear in a week or two. Then try to mirror his wardrobe choices as closely as possible. He probably won't realize what you're doing, but he'll feel strangely more comfortable around you. Reflecting your I-Boss's horrific fashion sense will make him far more receptive to your ideas and suggestions.

If a male I-Boss wears a blue sock on his left foot and a black sock on his right foot, and he spots a male team member with a black sock on his left foot and a blue sock on his right foot, the I-Boss will probably compliment the team member on how sharp he looks. If your I-Boss wears a plastic pocket protector in the breast pocket of his short-sleeved oxford shirt, guess what you should be wearing. If you can't bring yourself to do it, at least compliment him on his stylish and sensible pocket protector. The condition of your shoes also affects your I-Boss's comfort level. If he wears old beaters, keep an old pair in your file drawer.

Hopefully it goes without saying that females should not attempt to imitate the bad wardrobe choices made by their male I-Bosses. In that rare case where a female I-Boss dresses strangely, female team members must walk a fine line between demonstrating a similar attitude about fashion and actually mimicking what the female I-Boss wears. Female coworkers with male I-Bosses should dress as professionally as possible. The male I-Boss might not have a clue how he looks in the big picture, but he's seen enough IBM commercials to know what the vertically mobile woman should look like. That is a potentially sexist thing to say, but sexism might be the least of your problems with an I-Boss.

Okay, I admit I'm exaggerating for effect. But it's not about feeling comfortable, here. If you want to be a fashion plate to enhance your dating life or simply stroke your own ego, that's your business. But if you're making your Idiot Boss look like a bigger Idiot in comparison, calculate your net gain or loss carefully. All of this is important only if you want your I-Boss to be more comfortable around you. Not every bad dresser is an I-Boss, and not every I-Boss is a bad dresser. Some extremely intelligent and gifted people dress like clowns, while some clueless Idiots dress like George Clooney. God Bosses, Machiavellian Bosses, many Sadistic Bosses, and some Unprepared Bosses are typically good dressers. In fact, the meaner or more insane the boss, the more likely it is that he or she will resemble an Armani model.

Some Good Bosses, most Buddy Bosses, Paranoid Bosses, Masochistic Bosses, Reluctant Bosses, and of course I-Bosses are notoriously bad dressers. Intentionally dressing down around a Good Boss won't be necessary. A Good Boss sees the person, not the clothes, and she will appreciate your style even if her own is less than ideal. Good bosses don't usually wear mismatched clothes as much as outdated ones. Good bosses don't feel any urgency to dress for success. To them, success is an inside job.

Buddy Bosses might prefer you to dress well so they can have a cool friend. Paranoid Bosses will think your sloppy wardrobe is a critical statement about them and an indictment of their taste. (It's tough to win with a Paranoid Boss.) A Masochistic Boss will turn anything you wear into a source of personal pain and anguish, as the Masochistic Boss will be sure to feel humiliated by comparison— that is, if a Masochistic Boss even notices what you're wearing. You could show up buck naked at the office, and your Masochistic Boss would probably be too busy repeatedly punching herself to notice.

If your I-Boss's boss is a fashion hound, you have a potential problem. Try to determine how your I-Boss is affected by his boss's wardrobe habits. You'll need to calculate if you'll make your boss more comfortable by imitating him or his boss. It never hurts to compli-ment those higher on the food chain as long as you re-main aware of how your wardrobe choices and groom-ing will affect your most immediate relationships. It can be a tough call.

Hair and humor

Wardrobe is not the only fashion issue with an I-Boss. Many I-Bosses missed the memo from HR informing the staff that crew cuts went out of style during the Nixon administration. Recent fashion trends suggest that you might want to consider cutting your hair with a hedge trimmer. In-terestingly, many people pay a lot of money these days to make their hair look like it was cut with a power tool.

You can make I-Bosses feel more comfortable around you by tell-ing insipid jokes and stories about the time your dog barfed on the neighbor's morning newspaper. I chose this subject because many of the I-Bosses I've known are particularly fond of barf jokes. Make sure to start laughing about three-quarters of the way through your joke or story. I-Bosses always start laughing at their own jokes long before the punch line arrives. Although longitudinal research on the subject is minimal, I-Bosses don't seem concerned about whether anyone else will find their jokes or stories funny. They just assume that everyone will.

The most plausible explanation for why I-Bosses laugh at their own material is because they are telling the joke or story primarily for their own amusement. This is consistent with my theory that I-Bosses are usually bored. You can also resonate with your I-Boss's mood by always appearing to be in good spirits. I-Bosses are rarely tuned in to the emotions of other people and will remain jolly long after the ship hits the iceberg. Although I-Bosses are capable of a wide range of emotions themselves, they don't easily pick up on emotional indicators from others, such as weeping, screaming, throwing furniture, firing small weapons, and other demonstrative acts probably instigated by the Idiot's behavior.

Go legit

One of the first signs that your Higher Power has removed your stupidity is when you've accepted your powerlessness over your boss's stupidity. That's when you'll be able to abandon your futile struggle to control the uncontrollable. You can then begin to change the things in yourself that have kept you on the merry-go-round of madness for so long. If swallowing your pride to advance your agenda with an I-Boss is too difficult, however, take the legitimate approach. Disguising yourself as one of the Idiots might not be so bad, especially when you discover how much you have in common. You and your I-Boss might agree on more than you think. It will be up to you to do the research and inquiry, but the results can be positive. A little office anthropology on your part might reveal that your I-Boss likes to play golf but never has the time. You may be in the same dilemma. It's up to you to take the initiative and organize the office golf outings. Several good things can happen. You might get to play golf on company time and/or the company dime. You can at least be sanctioned to spend work time organizing golf activities for team members. If you have golf in common with your I-Boss, you've opened up a new topic and forum that's actually pleasant for you both. If you don't play golf and hate golf-speak, at least you can get your I-Boss out of the office for half a day per week by encouraging and facilitating his hobby.

Shared interests can have a positive effect and hold potential for activities or conversation—love of movies, literature, photography, fine dining, greasy spoon dining, expensive wine, cheap wine, animals, hiking, motorcycles, sports of any kind, you name it. Even if your initiative to organize vocational interests around the office doesn't include anything that's appealing to your I-Boss, the fact that you're contributing to a relaxed and pleasant working environment will probably give you an positive image in his eyes.

Idiot Bosses, unlike their Machiavellian, Sadistic, Masochistic, Paranoid, and Reluctant counterparts, like it when everyone seems to get along and enjoy each other. Being a part of making that happen is not fake or phony, even if it starts out that way for you. Helping to bring out the true interests and passions of your I-Boss and fellow team members, and then exerting some leadership to establish avenues to share the joy, will pay dividends for everyone—most importantly *you*.

Putting on the great disguise might seem like a cheesy, manipulative ploy in the beginning. But it can be a way to test the waters and see if you really wouldn't be happier and more content at work using some imagination to expand your horizons. Using your energy to organize activities offensive or displeasing to your I-Boss is counterproductive. The whole point of the great disguise is to set your feet on a path to workplace serenity, even if the direction is not one your instincts initially tell you to follow. If you prefer not to fight and find no honor in flight, try a dose of fraternization. It might work. As the folks at the New York Lottery like to say, you never know.

Break out. Push back your boundaries. Be crazy. Put on the disguise and make your workplace more you-friendly. What do you have to lose except long nights of tortured slumber and teeth grinding while your I-Boss sleeps like a log? You can always return to your current state if being happier and less resentful doesn't appeal to you. What are you planning to replace your stupidity with anyway?

Step Seven Exercise: "Please, please, God—remove

my stupidity."

Imagine there's no stupid. Instead of making yet another list, engage in some ideation. Draw a hot bath, head for the spa, or just isolate yourself in a quiet place for an hour or two without distractions. If you're a parent of one or more youngsters, you might as well skip to the next chapter and blow off this exercise. For those of you who are still with the program, exploit your peace and quiet by considering what your plan is for your next workday, perhaps just the morning.

Consider whether there is a more intelligent and impactful way you could go about your business than your usual MO, even it's just for that morning. Then act *as if*. It's difficult for me to act as if I were smarter, not because I can't be any smarter, but because I'm so invested in my habitual customs and practices. I think I would create a better work scenario for myself if I went into the office with a more upbeat, can-do attitude. I think I could make better choices if I did a better job of prioritizing my tasks. I always respond to my CEO's requests immediately, but I don't always rank other priorities according to more subtle distinctions on the organizational food chain. Paying closer attention to who has unspoken, non-structural influence—popular authority—wouldn't hurt me a bit and might make me feel less bollixed up when I'm drafting a to-do list.

I think I'll get at least two medium-difficulty yet annoying tasks completed and out of the way before lunch. Instead of getting tangled in the underbrush that is my in-box, I'm taking out a couple of big things first. As Danny Cox (*Leadership When the Heat's On* and *Seize the Day*) once said, "If you have a frog to swallow, don't look at it too long. If you have more than one frog to swallow, swallow the biggest one first."

Hmm. I'm feeling smarter already.

8

A Strategic Partnership

It's important to understand the antics of organizational Kahunas because they establish and maintain the atmosphere in which you work. The shenanigans taking place in the C-suite flow downstream to the rest of the organizational population, sometimes in a trickle, other times in a tsunami. How successful you are in tapping your Idiot Boss's power will depend on how savvy you can become with the unwritten, unspoken, and publicly disavowed rules of engagement that actually govern life in your organization.

HOW TO HARNESS THE IDIOT'S POWER

Let's begin with some high-level issues and work our way down. Non-Idiot senior executives who find themselves saddled with Idiots in management positions below them on the organizational food chain are faced with a complex problem: How do they make the company work in spite of these clowns? Isn't that similar to what you're asking as you look at the same people up the organizational food chain: *How do I succeed in spite of these people?* This was not such a difficult question back when everyone knew each other. In my father's day, you joined a company right out of college and stayed there until you retired. Among other things, that meant that you got to know people. You came up through the ranks together. If certain people were Idiots, you had 40 years to figure out what to do with them, 15 years if they were new hires.

Today, fewer and fewer executives at the top worked their way up through the ranks. Now, both for-profit and nonprofit organizations recruit most of their top brass and middle brass from outside. The single-employer career that many of our parents knew has all but faded into history. In today's rapidly changing and unstable corporate landscape, top executives must deal with how to organize, motivate, and lead the Idiots in their workforce in such a way as to maintain a productive working environment for the non-Idiots. The dynamic nature of upper management presents a series of new problems, not the least of which is what happens when the newly recruited top executive turns out to be an Idiot. Surprise, surprise.

Recruiting and hiring top executives is a dicey business. If you stop and think about it, why would executives who are wildly successful in their present situations want to pull up stakes, fold their tents, and move to another organization? Why would effective leaders who have cleaned up messes, turned losses into profits, fine-tuned their present organizations until they're firing on all cylinders, and built confidence and morale to the highest levels ever, want to leave Nirvana behind and move to an ailing organization? We've all heard the legendary stories about empire builders who get bored after they've done it all and long to roll up their sleeves, find some raw material, and build another empire, brick by brick. That happens more often in the movies than in real life. It's far more common to find chief executives on the move who aren't getting much accomplished despite an incredible salary, bonus, and benefits package. Why are they so eager to leave? Why are their boards not more intent on keeping them?

If a top executive does for her company what Jack Welch did for General Electric, she will retire from General Electric, as did Welch. If a top executive does for a company what Michael Eisner did for Disney, you won't see another entertainment firm hiring him away—unless people inside have had enough of him or he has had enough of them, which foreshadows the "happy executives don't leave" point below. Executives sometimes hop from one firm to the next if they're vertically blocked; when this happens, the jump opens the ceiling again. What about those executives making essentially lateral moves for a compensation increase that their current employers could easily match? Methinks the executive with suitcases packed is either unhappy where she is, has a family or lifestyle need to consider, or is not doing a very good job, and is smart enough to get out while the getting is good. I've known them all. You probably have, too.

In the latter example, it makes sense why the present employer doesn't fight to keep her. So what does the new employer get? Someone with all of the right credentials, for sure. Someone who can look and sound the role she's been hired to play, definitely. But what else? Could the new firm be hiring the former employer's problems? Is it possible the unsuspecting new firm has just taken on an Idiot? As an executive, I have unloaded Idiots on unsuspecting employers and had Idiots unloaded on me. Truth be told, it might save everyone money (and a ride up and down the great expectations/major disappointment roller coaster) if these companies would just build people movers to shuttle Idiots from one office building to the next.

ARE JOB-HOPPERS HAPPY?

Are super-mobile executives happy in their present positions? Apparently not. Are they people who are prone to loyalty and who revel in healthy, long-term relationships with their coworkers? Definitely not. Are they willing to wave goodbye to their team members and say, "Have a good life. I was just offered a bigger payday"? Apparently so.

In many cases, the hot new executive was available and anxious to make the move because a.) he failed to move the previous organization purposefully forward, b.) he was starting to worry about when the non-standard accounting practices making things appear better than they were would be exposed, and c.) he knew it was just a matter of time before someone pointed out that the emperor had no clothes. I knew one fellow who was in his fifth or sixth corporate presidency; each one lasted approximately two years before he was canned. He was disemployed from every presidency after proving himself completely incompetent. Yet there always seemed to be another firm eager to hand him the key to the president's office.

At the first sign his new firm was onto him and his rationalizations wouldn't hold up any longer, he returned the headhunters' calls, let them know he was back on the market, and wound up stepping straight out of one executive tower into another without ever touching terra firma in the process. I doubt seriously if the headhunters even asked why he was available again so soon. Hear no evil, see no evil, speak no evil. Collect commission.

Power

Many companies produce eloquent mission statements, manifestos, and mantras. Would you believe me if I told you most of them don't operate by those principles? Very few organizational value systems are primarily about serving the customer, the community, or the corporate population—unless, of course, serving the customer, the community, and/or the corporate population is profitable. Then, and only then, will such things be popular in the C-suite. Even so, don't be surprised if even profitable service to the customer, the community, and/or the corporate population doesn't get the type of support you might expect from the Kahunas, despite your cynicism about the profit motive always trumping the altruism motive. At the end of the day, it's not primarily about profits, it's about power. The occupants of the C-suite are preoccupied with power, and power is more than mere money: it's the ability to make or influence major decisions that make or break careers, build or lose fortunes, install or overthrow governments. In Las Vegas, the C-suite would be called the high stakes room, and the first order of business is always to ensure the house wins.

There are several reasons why power brokers become power brokers. By power brokers, I mean board members or anyone with the authority to negotiate high-level positions and commit significant portions of the organization's treasury. It's human nature to want someone else to fix things. Wealthy Southerners say it like this: "If you don't want to do it yourself, hire it done." Board members do that with the leadership of the organizations they govern. They hire it done. There's nothing wrong with hiring it done until they abdicate their role in leading the leader. But that's human nature, too.

As children, when we had a boo-boo, we wanted Mommy to kiss it and make it all better. As adults, when we have an ache or a pain, we want the doctor to prescribe a pill to make it go away. When our automobile stops running perfectly, we want the service technician to make it run like new again. As children, we didn't pay Mommy for her loving ministrations. Our tears were sufficient motivation for her. As adults, crying doesn't get us very far. We expect to pay people to make our problems go away.

Other factors

Board members are also impatient. They look primarily to short-term financial performance to justify their actions. Serving the long-term interests of their organizational populations is well down the list of priorities. They will claim that external stakeholders demand the financial performance. However, most external stakeholders, as well as employees with ownership interest in the firm, are in it for the long haul. This means that the people who the board members are claiming to appease would prefer to see long-term growth, not knee-jerk, expensive quick fixes. Historically, organizations that invest first and foremost in the growth and development of their team members perform better on their bottom line than those that don't.

THE SOFT SPOT BETWEEN THE ROCK AND THE HARD PLACE

If you look at all the impatience, denial, avoidance, and outright lying going on at the highest levels of American enterprise, you can easily become cynical and resentful. Or you can join Aunt Eller and say, "Well, alright then," to all of it. Whether you fully understand it or not, it is what it is. In the church basement on Wednesday nights we define resentment as drinking poison then waiting for the other person to die. Same thing with throwing your cell phone in the toilet to punish the person you're arguing with. Your challenge is what to do in spite of the impatience, denial, avoidance, and outright lying going on in your organization. Oh, it's there—maybe to a greater degree in some companies than in others, but it's there. And scenarios played out in the executive suite are replicated in smaller scenarios in managers' offices everywhere. "Joining 'em" doesn't mean adopting their values; it means learning how to operate effectively in their environment. As long as you swim in the same aquarium there is no avoiding the water.

MAKE YOUR MOVE—POSITIVELY

Being obsessed with justice is being all about you and your unresolved childhood fairness issues. Justice is great, fairness is wonderful, and being right is always a treat. But put on your own oxygen mask first before you go helping other people with theirs. You'll be of no use to yourself or others if you pass out. Your first calling is to position yourself for maximum effectiveness within the organization you have chosen to work for.

Let's assume that a people-centered executive has made it to the top of your company or the board managed to hire one in spite of itself. It can happen. What does the new executive do with the Idiots she inherited? It's a problem. I-Bosses seldom do enough of anything to get them in trouble with HR. Nor do they usually accomplish anything beneficial to the organization overall. But doing nothing particularly good or bad is not sufficient cause for termination in today's litigious labor market. Entropy and inertia are not causes for dismissal.

If you use the techniques I've discussed in this book to tap into your I-Boss's power cell, in an organization led by a person-centered executive, the woman at the top might be extremely grateful. The I-Boss under the leadership of an effective executive is a potentially positive force because the top person wants to boost productivity in a culture of encouragement. If you contribute to that, your efforts are likely to be recognized and rewarded. You can be a part of the solution the big boss wants and do yourself some political favors in the process.

This can happen several ways. An ambitious person studies what successful people do and tries to get the same results from a similar effort. A clever person studies what successful people do and then attempts to get the same results through someone else's effort. Your job is to make your I-Boss look clever. Make peace with contributing good work that your I-Boss will take credit for. It's a technique similar to passing credit due to you along to the Machiavellian just as you would pass a gravy boat at Thanksgiving dinner. If you have an intelligent, person-centered big boss, she will be quick to recognize that the good work coming out of the Idiot's department is likely the result of his talented and hardworking team members.

If the big boss doesn't recognize this right away, drop some hints. Do this in the form of a compliment. Say to her, "I sure do appreciate how my boss gives me the encouragement and support to complete these projects on time and under budget." If the big boss has half a brain, she will recognize that your I-Boss didn't have anything whatsoever to do with your successful efforts, and in fact was probably more like a millstone around your neck as you tried to swim the channel.

The big boss wants the department to run smoothly, so she will appreciate your contributions in that regard. If the big boss doesn't notice such subtleties, keep at it subtly yet consistently. If she still doesn't catch the drift over time, you might not have the well-meaning ally you thought you did. If you don't get recognized despite your best efforts, it's time to pursue another avenue. Meanwhile, because you've kept things positive by framing your comments as compliments to your I-Boss, you haven't hurt yourself or left a bad taste in anyone's mouth.

By framing all of your propaganda in a positive context, you open up the possibility that a truly intelligent big boss will begin to like having you around. Even a less-than-intelligent big boss will appreciate your presence, even if she doesn't quite understand why. That could mean a promotion. Positive people like to be around other positive people. In the best of all possible worlds, the big boss might recognize that you are being strategically positive and affirming. Seeing your advanced political shrewdness, the big boss might think, *Hmm, that's the kind of person I need on my A-Team*.

Being positive never hurts, unless your boss is a God, Masochistic, Sadistic, or Machiavellian Boss. In those cases, it's best to just disappear, literally and figuratively. Being negative doesn't help with those types, either, unless you're attacking the nice people. Being a constant irritant won't put you on anybody's A-Team. But, as you've already learned, varying boss types define "irritant" in different ways, so craft your strategy accordingly.

360-Degree Snooping

Pay attention to your Idiot Boss's superiors and carefully study how they: (a) insult him when he's not around, and (b) humor him when he is around. In this way you will learn how useful he is to them. If they insult him whether he's present or not, don't waste your time coming to his rescue; he's toast. If your I-Boss is treated respectfully by his superiors, whether he is present or absent, you know his superiors are decent folks and will probably give you a fair shake, too. The worst place to openly criticize your I-Boss is in the presence of those who can and choose not to.

Next, pay attention to how your peers: (a) insult your Idiot Boss when he's not around, and (b) insult your I-Boss when he is around. In this way you will learn how cognizant he is of reality. Most I-Bosses don't know when they are the brunt of a joke. In these cases, the budding Sadists around the office have a field day with the poor, unsuspecting I-Boss. It's always a good idea to avoid the cynical I-Boss bashing, no matter how tempting it is. Should the I-Boss ever be in a situation to help you, it's advisable to keep a good face on your relationship. More than that, you don't want to be observed bashing your I-Boss by his superiors. That will not score points for any plans they might have to enhance your future prospects.

When the Big Boss Is Not Friendly

I took the easy scenario first, the one in which the top executive is enlightened, friendly, and supportive of dedicated, hardworking people. As you might have guessed from the bleak picture I painted of hiring practices within many organizations, you're more likely to encounter a top executive who sees you as little more than a piston rod in the big engine of the firm—if she sees you at all. In these cases, your I-Boss is not going to receive much personal coaching and nurturing attention, either.

It's sink or swim for everyone. Because terminating employees is such a tricky business, many executives allow the bottom of the pool to fill with the bodies of those who sank and then hire new bodies to swim in their place in increasingly shallow water. You can exercise your prerogative to become disgusted, get angry, feel disenfranchised, and resent the heck out of the new administration. Or you can put your newly acquired skills to good use and exploit the situation to your advantage.

As I mentioned previously, everyone has an agenda, even new top executives—or, perhaps, *especially* top executives—with ice water in their veins. Put your research and inquiry spectacles on and spy what the big boss most desires; then, determine if your Idiot Boss can fit into that scheme. It's dangerous for you to make an end run, even on an I-Boss. He may not get upset, but those above him will see someone out of his silo, and that makes the Kahunas uncomfortable. The keepers of hierarchical power charts like everybody to stay under their bosses in neat, straight columns. Being spotted outside your silo without a hall pass is likely to get both you and your I-Boss into trouble.

Try to engineer schemes and plans that will resonate with the bigger boss's ambitions and then feed them to your I-Boss for presentation. He might not understand what it is you want him to do, so the operation must be approached delicately. If you can put together good stuff and make sure it makes its way into your I-Boss's office, you can then "leak" word to the higher-ups that your I-Boss has some exciting new stuff coming along.

You can also do a drive-by with the big boss's clerical assistant: "Ever since your boss came, my boss has been acting like a new man. He even has three plans for trimming costs and increasing production based on your boss's last speech to the stockholders," or words to that effect. Make sure you add something like "These must be exciting times around the C-suite." The clerical assistant will feel important, and you might have set the wheels in motion for your I-Boss to receive an invitation to the top floor.

He won't want to go alone because he knows he can't explain your plans. This is a great opportunity to assure him of his capabilities, pump up his ego, and offer to go with him as backup. Comfort, support, and encouragement will get you much further with your I-Boss than resentment and cynicism. Building a partnership with your I-Boss requires you to take the initiative and do all the work. The research, strategizing, planning, and patient execution of each step are all on your shoulders. But this is the closest thing to control you'll ever have. If you care enough to invest in your career in spite of the Idiots in your path, you must take this approach.

Facing criticism

The cynical and negative people in your area will resent you for no longer joining them in bashing the I-Boss. They may even distrust you for actually initiating contact with him. That's okay. This is your opportunity to point out how the work you're doing is moving the organization, or at least your small part of it, in a worthwhile direction. The alternative is to continue going around in circles, which is characteristic of an I-Boss–led department, or, worse, rewriting the medium-range plan again.

Handled properly, you could even become a champion for your coworkers. Unless they are terribly misguided, which is always a possibility, they would probably prefer to set their working agenda rather than haplessly jump and fetch with every changing whim of the I-Boss. If you can forge a strategic partnership with your I-Boss, in which you can actually influence departmental priorities, you will be your coworkers' new best friend.

WHO ARE YOU, REALLY?

Where and when did you stand at your crossroads and etch your worldview on the inside of your forehead? When did you make the decisions that now inform your attitudes about fairness and meaning in the workplace? Many people never wax nostalgic for the days when their personal context was framed and their professional foundation was laid. Yet that's where your current attitudes toward work and play, duty and destiny, family and career are anchored. Arrested development means unfinished business. If we don't successfully complete our developmental phases, we won't fully mature. More specifically, people who do not successfully fill glass number one before filing glass number two can develop nasty habits rooted in their half-empty glasses. Those nasty habits will drive others bonkers.

It's never too late to finish unfinished business, and the world will be forever grateful. It is therefore a good idea to poke around and learn what really makes you tick. Once that's done, you will know how to become an asset rather than a liability, a friend rather than a foe, and a truly strategic partner to your Idiot Boss rather than just another spoke in the wheel. By now you should be resigned to the fact that you go through this exercise because your I-Boss won't.

Stuck in adolescent rebellion

Engaging in denial and avoidance of real issues, which is the cultural paradigm of far too many working environments, creates a population living in a state of ignorant dysfunction. Lacking the knowledge or courage to adopt a better plan, many of us resist and even refuse to replace denial and avoidance with healthier thinking and behavior. Among the first things middle-aged Idiots realize when entering recovery is that they're stuck in adolescent rebellion. To become unstuck, we must first realize and accept the fact that we're developmentally arrested in a stage akin to that of the adolescent (a child's mind stuck in an emerging adult's body). No matter how old we are, it's childish to believe that the answer to every problem or discomfort is to blame authority. Back in adolescence we blamed our parents, teachers, the police, and the president. Now, we've either forgiven or stopped talking to our parents, still blame George W. Bush for the state of the economy, and project responsibility for the rest of our grievances on our boss.

Now for the bad news: Your Idiot Boss won't accept the responsibility for getting you unstuck. Not because she has a highly actualized respect for relational boundaries (after all, she's still an Idiot); she just won't know what you're talking about if you bring the subject up. Just as well. You shouldn't be shopping around to find a host for a parasitic sense of responsibility anyway, no matter how available and enticing a host your Idiot Boss is.

We enter adolescence still expecting the labor and sacrifice of others to sustain our leisure activities and abundance (read: living off of Mom and Dad). Then, abandoning logic altogether, we rebel against the authority figures who have invested the labor and sacrifice to get us to where we are today. While still in the throes of adolescent rebellion, we haven't yet given up the notion that somebody else is responsible for our happiness and well-being. Therefore, as adolescent reasoning goes, it is someone else's fault if we're not feeling as happy and well cared for as we think we should be. Sound like your office? The experience of working for an Idiot might have inspired you to buy this book. Hopefully, however, you'll finish it with a strong sense that you're really working for yourself and that how content (or contentious) you are is up to you.

Beware of your associates

You don't need to be an active practitioner of adolescent rebellion to be sucked into its backdraft. Have you ever found yourself involved in a grievance meeting at work, wondered how you got there, and wished you weren't there? It amazes me how many rebels without a cause or common sense I still encounter in organizations all over the country. They exist at all levels. Sometimes they're union stewards; sometimes they're vice presidents. Like anyone else, the more power they wield, the more damage they can do. These types of people exist everywhere—people who don't put into the system, but claim the right to complain about it and make demands on it.

If I resent everyone who I don't feel has earned the right to do what they do, say what they say, or receive what they receive, I'll become immobilized by my own anger and sense of injustice. Then who suffers? My cell phone winds up in the toilet. If you have earned the right to express yourself through the enormous contributions you've made, I applaud you. But guess what? Others who've made no such contributions are going to make themselves heard anyway, and they will be recognized. Get used to it. Better yet, for your own sanity, *get over it.* Shift your focus to ways you can contribute still more. That's being true to your nature. Blaming your I-Boss is not. Although many people do little to earn respect, nobody deserves to be treated disrespectfully. We need to be reminded from time to time that we contribute to the corporate cause because doing our part is part of the grand scheme, the scheme that benefits many people. Dealing with an I-Boss might cause you to bite your lip, take a deep breath, count to 10, and let the air out slowly. But getting over it doesn't mean giving up. There is no reason to accept your lot without proactively doing something about it.

If you choose to remain passive, blindly accept what your I-Boss hands you, and then gripe about it, I can only assume that griping lights your wick. Meanwhile, you're not truly helping yourself or anyone around you. You've read too far and have too much information now to merely accept an I-Boss relationship strictly on his terms. You're not stepping up and becoming more involved for his sake, unless you choose to. You're doing it for yourself and those around you who are willing to share your attitude.

THE EIGHTH STEP: "MAKE A LIST OF ALL PERSONS I MIGHT HAVE HARMED WITH MY STUPIDITY AND PREPARE TO MAKE AMENDS TO THEM ALL."

Does anybody have the white pages for the Western Hemisphere? At first glance, these recovery steps seem to be pulling me in the opposite direction from my emerging coexistence with my I-Boss. However, as my understanding grows, it all weaves itself together in a sort of cosmic tapestry. The stupidity I've been describing so far didn't just hurt me; it also made life difficult for others. Don't you wish your I-Boss had such an epiphany? Will you choose "me for the sake of me" or "me first, who wants to follow"? The steps helped me learn the difference.

I used to dwell on the injustice of office politics. Things I felt were unfair could keep me up for several nights in a row. There were times I felt it was my moral obligation to expose my I-Boss as a moron. But none of my bitching and moaning hurt my I-Boss. And none of it helped me. Again, I was the one drinking the poison, not him. As much as I feel compelled to expose things for the way they really are and force the hand of justice, I've learned it's more important to keep my composure. Discretion truly is the better part of valor. Positioning ourselves properly relative to our I-Bosses, requires constant positioning radar. If we stay between the navigational beacons, we will not only survive life with an I-Boss, but arrive at the right destination and thrive.

Because we can't change our I-Bosses directly, examining how we might have foisted I-Boss–like injury and inconvenience upon others will help us to keep perspective and develop a strategy to survive and prosper, in spite of our situation. Making a list of people to whom we should make amends—even if we don't actually follow through—can be a real eye-opener. If you genuinely want to transform your attitude toward your Idiot Boss and develop a strategic (albeit understated) partnership with him, start by becoming the kind of partner you would want to have.

EIGHTH STEP EXERCISE: "MAKE A LIST OF ALL PERSONS I MIGHT HAVE HARMED WITH MY STUPIDITY AND PREPARE TO MAKE AMENDS TO THEM ALL."

This step calls for a list. Listing the names of people you have harmed in some way, anything from impugning their capability, character, and competence around the office to getting them fired. "It's just another stupid list," you might say. True, but if you still believe that everything that has ever gone wrong in your career is someone else's fault, and that everything you have ever done has had a positive impact, guess again. If this is you, you *need* to make this list. Come up with the names of 12 people to whom you could legitimately apologize for something you did, directly or indirectly, to cause them problems. I, for example, have rebelled passive-aggressively against ideas various bosses have tried to advance over the years. That hurt them and it hurt me even more, no matter how smug and justified I felt (being the smartest person on the planet, after all).

That first name will be the tough one, and the offense might be ever so slight, but it's a start. The names will come more quickly and the offenses will become more egregious as you get into it. It's like digging in a landfill: The deeper you dig, the more nastiness you uncover. Don't waste time arguing with me or with your Inner Idiot about whether there is anyone out there to whom you can legitimately apologize. Trust me, there is and you can.

Next comes the miracle—and I do mean *miracle*. Note which people you could make amends to without hurting or offending them in the process. Ponder it. Reflect on it. Pray about it. Then pick one, perhaps the most innocuous one, and script a brief and eloquent apology. Then at the appropriate moment, you will take that person aside and tell them you owe them an apology, which is part of the next step. Before you know it, you'll be looking for people to whom you can make amends and, better yet, recognizing how to silence your Inner Idiot before you do something that will require an apology. That's how recovery works. That's how strategic partnerships are built. On trust.

9

Idiot-Speak:
How to Talk to
Your Idiot Boss

STEP NINE FOR RECOVERING IDIOTS: "MAKE AMENDS TO EVERYONE I MIGHT HAVE HARMED WITH MY STUPIDITY, EXCEPT WHEN CONTACTING THEM MIGHT PLACE MY LIFE IN JEOPARDY."

Hopefully you didn't waste time arguing with me or your Inner Idiot at the end of the previous chapter about whether you needed to apologize to anyone. When you get to the Step Nine exercise at the end of this chapter and make amends, you will set off a chain of positive events that will take up the space in the universe that your Inner Idiot would have otherwise used to embarrass and humiliate you. Making amends puts matters in perspective. It forces you to consider the other person's needs and point of view. It establishes a whole new platform from which you can relate more positively to people you didn't think you could get along with. It can help explode the myth that you can advance your career by insulting your boss.

If I were coaching you right now, I might gently explore the concept of humbling yourself. Pride is such a destructive force and will nearly always lead to a fall. Don't point at Steve Jobs and say pride never befell him. Perhaps not. Jobs's achievements are remarkable and truly something to be proud of. Maybe his accomplishments left him plenty of headroom for pride. Maybe, with so much to be proud of, pride never reached critical mass and became destructive. For the rest of us, I think the best course is to be humble and helpful. I am not talking about false humility. Once you consider another person's feelings and point of view, the humility will be real and liberating. Pride can be a heavy burden if you need to keep propping it up. Humble, helpful, and happy. That's the ticket for me.

Quoting the classic country song "Take This Job and Shove It," even to an Idiot Boss who might not know exactly what it means, is not a career-enhancing move. It is pride-driven behavior. If you want to be relieved of the burdens that working for an Idiot can place on you, if you want to be liberated from the oppressive weight of hating your I-Boss, and if you would like to restore the energy and enthusiasm you once brought to your work, I have some good news and some bad news. The good news is you can change your entire relationship with your I-Boss. The bad news is you need to make some amends in your I-Boss's direction. Not to worry. He will probably never realize what you're doing unless you come right out and say, "I'm sorry. I thought you were an Idiot." Just applying the methods and techniques contained in this book will make him feel better around you and better in general. Accordingly, he'll start treating you much better once your strategy is executed.

Making amends has much to do with language. If the words we choose to include in or omit from a conversation speak volumes about who we are and our attitudes and beliefs, then our actions could fill libraries. Research conducted by UCLA psychology professor emeritus Albert Mehrabian determined that words account for only 7 percent of a face-to-face message. Vocal inflection accounts for 38 percent, and facial expression accounts for 55 percent. Dr. Mehrabian's analysis didn't include arm gestures or freeway rush hour hand gestures when words are unnecessary, but his point is pretty well made. It's not the words we say—it's how we say them. If you scowl while telling your I-Boss you're about to throw his computer monitor out the window, he'll dive under his desk. If you say the same thing with a smile, he'll open the window for you.

CONTENT

You can't make proper amends unless you understand the basic components of communication. What you say or don't say and what you do or don't do, says it all. That's how it is with your Idiot Boss. You can make your relationship with your I-Boss work for or against you depending on what you communicate and how you choose to communicate it. I've already advised you to listen carefully when your I-Boss speaks. What does he tend to talk about: work or hockey?

If he likes to talk about hockey, you'll just annoy him if you try to steer the puck toward work-related issues. You can cleverly maneuver around this impasse by using hockey metaphors when describing the work issues you find important. Speak in terms of "taking the gloves off," reach organizational objectives by "scoring goals," put problems in the "penalty box," and make corporate history by turning a "hat trick."

I don't know what those things mean, either. But if my I-Boss was a hockey fan, you'd better believe I'd Google "hat trick," and I would have hockey magazines on my desk, a hockey stick standing in the corner of my cubicle, a puck as a paperweight, and a picture of Mario Lemieux on my screensaver. (Men can have pictures of other men on their screensavers as long as they're toothless athletes who play contact sports.)

Wayne Gretsky reportedly said, "I don't skate to where the puck is, I skate to where the puck is going to be," or something to that effect. That's a great line if your I-Boss is a hockey fan. If he's a basketball fan, use your imagination and reframe the quote, assigning it to whoever his favorite player is. Be careful not to mix your metaphors and expose your true ignorance by saying "Michael Jordan said, 'I don't shoot where the basket is, I shoot where the basket is going to be.'" Enter hockey quotations or whatever his favorite topic is into your search engine and watch future conversations with your I-Boss ripple across your monitor.

If you want to win over the hearts and minds of other people in the office, especially your Idiot Boss, help them live out their fantasies—within reason. What extracurricular activities does your I-Boss engage in away from work or at work? I won't go so far as to invoke the "Teach a Pig to Sing" analogy, but you'll live a happier, healthier, more productive life if you develop methods and techniques to visit your I-Boss's world when appropriate rather than trying to get him to visit yours. If your Idiot Boss has frustrated you to the point of distraction, it is very possible that you've done the same to him. You've probably been spending an excessive amount of time and energy trying to get him to think and act the way you think and act. That would wear anybody out.

Humbling yourself can be a healthy exercise. Putting other people's interests ahead of your own is the best way to ensure you're not being manipulative. In a world of perpetual self-actualization and pursuit of inner enlightenment, this humility business might cross you up with your life coach who is urging you to grab your share of the gusto. As your executive coach, I say take the high road of selflessness in the organization. Be a true team player. Stay classy. You will feel much better about yourself and less annoyed by your I-Boss if you remain on high ground. It's all that time in the gutter, wallowing in resentment, that makes you feel crappy.

IDIOT-SPEAK

Remember the metaphorical languages mentioned in the previous chapters: the power versus accomplishment versus relationship orientations? The auditory versus visual versus kinesthetic frames of reference? Idiot-speak is like learning a foreign language. Berlitz has yet to offer CDs and multiple-platform digital applications on Idiot-speak, but I'm sure they're not far away. Idiot-speak is not hard to learn. For example, Idiot Bosses are particularly fond of quoting the latest business best-sellers. "We're going to *Switch* this department into shape. I don't want any *Outliers* putting in *Four Hour Workweeks* when our *Our Iceberg Is Melting*. We can still shift this department into *Drive* and *Deliver Happiness*. If that doesn't get it done, we'll *Rework* our way into profitability."

Communicate your way to happiness

Idiot Bosses truly want to communicate with their employees because it makes them feel as though they've been invited to their own birthday party—in addition to making them feel powerful and understood. Unfortunately, of all the interpersonal skills they lack, Idiot Bosses are most lacking in effective communication. Communicating requires a meeting of the minds at some level. That leaves it up to you because your boss has no clue what level you are operating on. Making your I-Boss feel like every day is her birthday can yield big dividends.

The Internet has made it much easier to engage in Idiot-speak. Listen carefully to her pontifications and identify the books she's quoting. Search them by author or title, order a copy, and then leave it lying conspicuously on your desk. Better yet, carry it around with you—to meetings, to lunch, to the restroom. Read it while you wait for her to putt on the golf course. Refer to the book often, using her name in the sentence: "What you said this morning made it sound like you're in search of *A Whole New Mind*, Mildred." Hearing her name mentioned in the same sentence as an author she idolizes will bring on the warm fuzzies, and all the credit will go to you. "I think that is exactly what Daniel Pink had in mind, Mildred." Try to mention these things in e-mails to minimize the kiss-up factor in front of your peers. I know we've already prepared a heartfelt response for them, but why dangle a red cape in front of them if you don't have to?

If you choose to improve your relationship with your I-Boss rather than constantly challenging him or engaging him in a battle of wits, well-crafted communication will be your best tool. And knowing your I-Boss's choice of literature is a big part of it. If he doesn't leave any books or magazines lying around the office, it could be because he doesn't read. In that case, note key terms and phrases he uses in conversation, enter the terms on Google, and see what pops up. You might be able to turn your I-Boss on to a few Websites that will interest him. This is another good way to get your I-Boss distracted long enough for you to get some real work done. The stickier the Websites you recommend to your I-Boss, the more quality time you will buy for yourself.

Remember, if you're not resonating with the I-Boss's interests and obsessions, you could be annoying him. Making amends to your I-Boss doesn't mean truly being contrite for wrongs you've committed, as would be the case with family members or someone you truly care about; it means using the amends model to help keep a functional sense of humility in play for your own good. When you are allowed to operate freely, you do good things, don't you? This is about positioning yourself vis-à-vis your I-Boss so you can operate freely and do those good things.

Take your campaign viral

Another way to use language to ensure your I-Boss is comfortable around you is to send circuitous messages (otherwise known as the classic third-party compliment made famous by leadership expert Danny Cox). The third-party compliment is simple. Instead of complimenting your I-Boss to his face, which might be too over the top even for an I-Boss, compliment your I-Boss to someone who is likely to tote the tale back to him. If your I-Boss has a clumsy and obvious system of moles throughout the department, third-party compliments are even easier to execute. Just speak in glowing terms about him when a mole is within earshot. Bathroom stalls provide good covert operations opportunities. If you know the mole is in the next stall, act like you're talking on your cell phone and extol your I-Boss's latest triumph. Mention how proud you are to work for such a genius.

If the mole catches up with you at the sinks, wash your hands and act as if nothing happened. If the mole brings up the conversation, act embarrassed and say you sometimes just can't contain your enthusiasm. If the opportunity presents itself, go ahead and lay a compliment on the mole, too. Mention how you heard your I-Boss saying something complimentary about him or her. The mole won't tell the I-Boss about the compliment you claimed the I-Boss made, but the mole will deliver an account of your phony cell phone conversation back to the I-Boss as proof of his or her mole-worthiness.

If the mole is a true Idiot, he or she might thank the I-Boss for the compliment you made up. Your I-Boss might be truly confused and say, "Gee, did I say that?" Or he might try to save face and say, "Well deserved praise, Mole." Of course, the rare I-Boss might be sharp enough to realize he never said any such thing because he considers the mole a bigger Idiot than he is. In that case, you might have raised unintended suspicion on the part of your I-Boss. Being that your I-Boss is essentially clueless, I wouldn't lose any sleep over it. Nevertheless, you must use finesse when sending compliments via messengers.

When there are no obvious moles, you can still send circuitous compliments to your I-Boss. Compliments about your I-Boss made to his superiors are also likely to get back to him. This is a more direct use of the third-party compliment. People like to pass on good news. When something positive is said about a boss, other bosses like to pretend that it's the start of a trend. If Boss A hears one of Boss B's team members saying something good about Boss B, Boss A will make it a priority to mention it to Boss B in hopes that Boss B will have similar good news to share.

You don't have to be as obvious as to tell your I-Boss's secretary directly, as I suggested previously, although this can be effective if the script is sufficiently believable. Positive statements about your I-Boss made within earshot of his clerical assistant will surely make their way to the intended ears. Keep your radar moving, and when the assistant is nearby, launch into a compliment about the boss. This might require a few attempts before the secretary believes you, so try to vary your locations and delivery. To make sure that the clerical assistant finds you credible, spend some time observing and making notes on the secretary's associations, habits, and behaviors. Adapt the third-party compliment to the secretary. Reporting to the assistant that the I-Boss has paid him a compliment will put you on the assistant's A-list and ensure you will be portrayed in a positive light whenever the secretary has input or influence on the I-Boss's decision-making process (which is always).

In its purest form, Danny Cox's third-party compliment is intended to make people feel good about one another without communicating directly. To help quell a dispute or smooth ruffled feathers and promote increased cooperation and collaboration, a good boss will purposefully tell Person A that Person B said something positive about Person A. It is manipulation, pure and simple. But in the right hands, it is an effective tool in the cause of truth, justice, and the One World way.

Forcing the issue

If you're too impatient to allow the third-party compliment to run its course, you can be more direct. If you suspect someone around the office is desperate to score points with the I-Boss, that person just became your personal messenger for positive and affirming messages. Say positive things about your I-Boss in the kiss-up's presence because he will no doubt take the information straight to the I-Boss as a ploy to gain entrée into the I-Boss's inner circle. Anyone who wants to gain access to an I-Boss's inner circle for anything but mercenary reasons is likely to be an even bigger Idiot.

If you don't have a willing and able kiss-up available, you might need to take the bull by the horns and be the messenger yourself. Tell your I-Boss that you overheard his boss saying complementary things about him. Everybody wants to think they are respected and admired. You didn't plant that need for acceptance in his psyche. There is no need to feel guilty if you make use of it to bring about a positive outcome. The increased regard your I-Boss will have for you as a result of your machinations will make it easier for you to do work that is more fulfilling. Where is the vice in that?

Your I- Boss's humor is your humor

Smile and nod knowingly whenever your I-Boss laughs, even if you weren't paying attention to her joke or story. The true definition of terror is to be caught daydreaming when your I-Boss is talking, especially if she is telling a joke or making what she thinks is an earth-shattering point. If you wake from a sound sleep to hear your chuckling I-Boss asking you if you thought her remark was funny, grin and say, "Gee, boss, I don't know how we manage to get any work done with you around." Be careful not to say this if your I-Boss was making a serious, earth-shattering point, however. Look around the room before you answer and see if anyone else is faking a laugh at what she just said. If others are rolling their eyes, your I-Boss was probably trying to be funny. If everyone else is dead serious and is looking at you with piercing eyes, as if to say, "Danger, Will Robinson," then you say, "Working under you helps me keep my career in perspective." Your I-Boss will think you're paying her a compliment. She won't pick up on the sarcasm and realize her comments serve as a constant reminder that you are wasting your youth and energy working for an Idiot. In this day and age, when providing for yourself and the needs of your family are paramount and not always easy in an employers' market, you might want to consider putting away your resentment and being more appreciative of the employment opportunities you have, even if it requires suffering fools with a smile plastered on your face. In times of uncertain economics, Idiot-speak can serve you well as a second language. Learn it. Speak it. Use it well.

You Can't Avoid Gossip

Hopefully you know better than to believe gossip, much less pass it on, but many people do just that. Gossiping is a natural inclination for many and a tremendous temptation for almost everyone. Whether we gossip because we're Sadists or because we just want to scratch a dysfunctional itch and make everybody else feel as bad as we feel, gossip doesn't help anyone—not the gossiper and especially not the gossipee. Skilled Idiot-speak doesn't include gossip because the most effective messages are positive, even if they are calculated. The third-party compliment is not gossip. When gossiping, you tell Person A that Person B said something critical about Person A with the intention of causing a rift, hurting Person A's feelings, creating general hostility, or all of the above. A true third-party compliment will spread positive vibes by playing to the inherent desire for appreciation.

Of course, a true third-party compliment requires finding something genuinely positive and affirming to say. It's not as hard as you would think, though. As I've already mentioned, a broken clock is right twice per day. You can say to Person A that Person B is spot on with her timing at least twice per day because that's true. The value to you, oh humble one (and to Person B, when you point out the minor positive), is that you are leading the way up from the gutter to the high places where the air is fresh. People are eager to put forth their best effort when they feel recognized, respected, and appreciated.

Gossip not

People will gossip for a variety of reasons, none of which is positive or productive. I don't call the viral spreading of good news or positive information gossip—just so you know. People resort to pettiness because they lack the imagination or reinforcement to believe they can play at a more appreciative level. When people believe they are doomed to a lifetime of hard labor in the salt mines, they feel no compunction about taking others down with them. The gossiper's thinking is similar to a convict with three life sentences without possibility of parole: There's not much more to lose.

Some people deal with pain, disappointment, and discouragement by doing everything they can to cause pain, disappointment, and discouragement to others. In a workplace setting, effort, loyalty, and results are supposed to count for something. Nobody knows better than a gossiper that all of those qualities can be washed away with the ingestion of a little negativity into the equation. You have probably been victimized more than once by negative statements that diminished or eliminated the goodwill your positive efforts should have produced. I know I have. Others, especially Machiavellians and Sadists, use gossip as anything from a surgical instrument to slice open the jugular veins of their opponents and victims to a weapon of mass destruction. Whether gossip is used for amusement, payback, or premeditated injury, it can be a destructive force. Worse, it is unavoidable. Know how to deal with it or be destroyed by it.

There is no way to avoid gossip entirely. You might as well try to walk between the raindrops during a cloudburst. There will always be bored slackers, injured egos, and calculating career climbers. Nothing guarantees complete protection against gossip, any more than drinking diet soda guarantees you'll lose weight. Hiding in a closet won't get it done, either. Gossip can bend around corners, crawl under doors, travel through cyberspace, and penetrate the thickest walls.

The trench coat approach

Depending on how much gossip you deal with at work, you might need a bio-hazard suit. Creating a barrier to protect yourself from words is best done with actions. If you try and shield yourself with anti-gossip (mere words), you are at the mercy of a superior foe. Gossipers are much better wordsmiths than you. I ordinarily reserve the moniker "wordsmith" for eloquent endeavors such as writing books about Idiots. In truth, skilled gossipers have forgotten more about the power of language than I'll ever know.

Doing positive things—meaning things your boss finds impressive—will counteract a ton of negative words, unless you keep your good deeds a secret. This is yet another good reason to make your activities and accomplishments as visible as possible, in the context your boss finds most pleasing. To digress from your I-Boss for a moment, if a Machiavellian knows you've accomplished something worthwhile and have attached her name to it in such a way as to advance her career, she'll value you. People can say what they will about you, but as long as the Machiavellian thinks you're propping her up, the gossip will fall on deaf ears.

The same goes for all boss types. If you've done a good job of convincing your boss that you're providing what he or she wants, gossip flung in your direction will roll off your back. At least it won't damage your reputation as far as your boss is concerned. Whether you are a faithful servant to a God Boss, an anguished victim of a Sadistic Boss, an enabler of punishment for a Masochistic Boss, a mole for a Paranoid Boss (to confirm the conspiracy), a best friend to a Buddy Boss, or a mirror for an Idiot Boss's inflated self-image, you are reasonably indemnified against the damage gossip can cause.

This is not a one-time deal, but an ongoing effort. Your anti-gossip campaign is only as successful as your last action. Gossip is not only as ubiquitous as the air you breathe, it is relentless. It will never back off, and as soon as you do, it will nail you. If you've allowed your gossip insurance to lapse, it will be too late to bring up all of the premiums you've paid in the past with positive actions. Keep your gossip insurance current.

The reverse-osmosis approach

In yet another application of the third-party compliment, a little intelligence doesn't hurt. Not the kind of intelligence you lose when the doctor drops you on your head as a newborn, but the espionage, cloak-and-dagger stuff. You know there is gossip going on out there, so try to monitor it. This doesn't mean becoming a gossiper yourself. It means becoming a good listener. I took pride for many years that I didn't engage in workplace gossip and paid no attention to it—until it bit me on the backside. Pay attention to who huddles at the water cooler, who makes subtle hand gestures at meetings, who walks to the parking lot together, and, most of all, who goes to lunch together. What informal network of people e-mail each other constantly? Do major rumors ripple north to south, south to north, east to west, or west to east in your office? Who is in the office when gossiping seems the most active, and who is conspicuously absent when it seems to die down?

By identifying the sources of the gossip, you will know from whom you need protection. Most importantly, you'll know who to compliment to your boss. If you are complimenting the gossip(s) to your boss on a regular basis, when some of that gossip hits the fan, your boss will take it with a grain of salt. You want your boss to say "How can it be that so-and-so says such derogatory things about my loyal employee, especially when my loyal employee is constantly complimenting so-and-so? What's wrong with this picture?" Of course, there's always the chance that your boss will assume you're a gullible Idiot. But that's a chance you have to take.

THE OFFICE BULLY

Adult work environments, including white-collar offices, are often as susceptible to pranksters and bullies as the schoolyard. Gossip is an effective weapon in the arsenal of the emotionally wounded. Sadists are entertained by observing pain in others. It's like the blood-thirst of those who enjoy dogfights or cockfights. They could wander around hoping to see two dogs fight or two roosters rip into one another, but they're too impatient. So they breed dogs and roosters to do combat and stage the matches.

If your boss uses intimidation tactics, you have a choice to make. If it's a Machiavellian, God, Sadistic, or Paranoid Boss, standing up to her might only bring down more fire and brimstone on your head. Like my obsession with justice and being right, your proud defiance might hurt you more than it's worth. Career advancement is more about who has the power than who is right. Bullies don't have any power except that which is given to them. Bosses have functional authority over you. There's a big difference. If the office bully is also the boss, however, shrugging your shoulders, grinning, and bearing it will probably serve your long-term prospects better than battling back from a position of diminished power. If the bully is a peer, cut him off at the knees. I don't recommend doing anything that will leave a mark or trace evidence, but you need to let the bully know you're not intimidated.

If kindness is truly not your style, leave a copy of *How to Work for an Idiot* lying on the bully's desk where the boss is sure to see it while the bully is out to lunch. Once the bully is convinced you're more dangerous than he is, he'll be off to find another, more cooperative victim. Your best weapon against the bully? Confident humility and compliments. The bully just won't be able to overpower your kindness if it's rooted in confidence.

Finally, never brag or boast about defeating bullies. Never go whining to an I-Boss, or any boss, about a bully. Bosses who lack skills to resolve conflict will just bury their heads, and the bully will be emboldened. Meanwhile the boss will label you a complainer. Bosses who like blood sports will egg on the conflict for their amusement. Good Bosses are so tuned in to their team members, they will sense a problem quickly and deal with it long before you end up fighting a lonely battle.

TIPS TO AVOID AND DEFLECT GOSSIP

☐ Keep your radar active to determine who is congregating for potential gossip sessions.

☐ Make a mental note of who could benefit from your diminished status.

☐ When in doubt, don't speak your mind. Use discretion.

☐ Don't get suckered into criticizing other people, no matter how tempting it is.

☐ Politely ask the person who seems so interested in your opinion about someone else to explain why the information is so important.

☐ If she won't talk but insists that you do—don't.

☐ If she blasts the other party, simply say it's too bad she feels that way.

☐ Suggest that she contact an intermediary from HR to work the problem out.

☐ Keep your comments positive. There's nothing to be gained from bad-mouthing a coworker.

☐ Use the third-party compliment. It works.

SHAMU ON TRUST

No matter how you choose to communicate with your Idiot Boss, or anyone else on your team for that matter, make sure there is a subtext to your message that says "I'm your friend. I'm not going to hurt you. If push comes to shove, I'll take a bullet for you." You want your I-Boss and your peers to consider you a stand-up person. The only way you're going to convince them to trust you is to jump in the tank, swim with them, and speak their language. Most of all, consistently demonstrate your willingness to admit to and make amends for your mistakes. That will send the unmistakable message: "Big Person Here."

Step Nine Exercise: "Make amends to everyone I might have harmed with my stupidity, except when contacting them might place my life in jeopardy."

"Boss, I owe you an apology," you say at the appropriate moment, when you don't run the risk of embarrassing the boss or anyone else should this not go well.

"For what?" your boss asks, shocked that the word *apology* is in your vocabulary.

"When you were proposing to get the Kabul office included in the global safety initiative, I didn't speak up in support. I didn't see the wisdom in what you were proposing at the time. I do now. Just want you to know that I'll try to be more on top of such things in the future."

Then shut up. Don't speak again until your boss does. After your boss gathers himself, which might take a week, he'll respond. He might grunt and walk away. He might say, "Gee, thanks," and walk away. Don't worry about the response. The miracle is that you will be on your boss's radar to determine if you're legit. How good is that? You now have the opportunity to reopen your case where your boss is concerned and demonstrate your sincere desire to be a true business partner. You can reinvent yourself in his eyes. If that is important and helpful to you and your career, your boss's new opinion of you could pay huge dividends.

Then pat yourself on the back. By being open and transparent you have neutralized your Inner Idiot (at least temporarily) and positioned yourself to make some miraculous progress in your power relationships. Prepare to feel a fabulous, liberating feeling. Then repeat the process with number two on your list, and so on down the list until you're done.

10

Idiot-Eat: How to Break Bread With Your Idiot Boss

Eating is the great American pastime and fairly popular as a business activity in other parts of the world, as well. As far as metaphorical languages go, food and dining are among the most universal. Following are some practical tips you can use to improve relations with your boss. For example, always reconnoiter restaurants carefully when you enter. If you spot your I-Boss eating at a table with your associates, position yourself with your back to him, but try to stay within earshot. This is always a hoot because anyone trying to schmooze the boss will know you can hear what's going on, and will get all bollixed up trying to save face with you as a peer while scoring points with the boss. This is actually an art form you need to master. Some would describe this duality as speaking out of both sides of your mouth. You, on the other hand, are a new creature and see the wisdom in forging a stronger and more productive working relationship with your I-Boss. Any influence you exert on those with more authority than you is a testimony to your growth and development as an emerging leader.

It sometimes boils down to which is more important to you: the ability to manage up and show positive results, or staying in the good graces of your coworkers, who may or may not have any genuine interest in seeing you succeed. The more your coworkers understand what's in it for them if you win, the more they will step out of the way and refrain from criticizing you for doing what it takes to forge and sustain better relationships with those in power.

This restaurant relationship-building with your I-Boss is one reason why you carefully index the key points your I-Boss makes back at the office. When you're at the table with your I-Boss and coworkers, you can proclaim to your table companions how these very ideas will revolutionize the industry. If you're at a nearby table, as in the original scenario, proclaim such things just loud enough for your I-Boss to hear. With you quoting your I-Boss chapter and verse, he won't hear a word the person at the table with him is saying.

Maneuver yourself at parties and receptions to do the same thing. Always position yourself so your I-Boss will "overhear" you singing his praises. If praising your I-Boss in these social situations feels too obvious to you, praise his ideas. Say to your cocktail companions, "I don't remember who said [fill in I-Boss's idea here], but it's a fabulous idea." Your I-Boss will probably excuse himself from his present conversation and join your group to take credit.

Parties and receptions are also good opportunities to work over the moles and kiss-ups and plant valuable messages in their puny brains to carry back to your I-Boss. They might not have many social opportunities outside of these parties, so make them feel welcome even if it's not your party. Your I-Boss across the room will be pleased if he observes you treating his moles well.

WORKING THE MEAL

A one-on-one meal is a rich opportunity to tell your I-Boss everything he wants to hear without your being labeled a turkey around the office. Just make sure the waiter is not a recently downsized colleague who still has your associates' e-mail addresses. I could have and perhaps should have used the off-site coffee meetings to work with Big Bill, find the common ground we shared, and extend an honest effort to understand and appreciate where he was coming from. But I had that demon resentment gnawing away inside me and I didn't take advantage of my opportunities. Back then I lived a one-dimensional victimhood in which everything I did was right and everything Bill did was wrong. In that twisted mindset, everything I did was virtuous and everything he did was evil. Even the way he put four creamers in his coffee annoyed me. How dumb to let that get to me. I never stopped to consider that he was a human being, too, trying to sort out his mess of a life as I was trying to sort out mine, and probably having the same amount of success. Looking at the bright side, Big Bill always picked up the tab. If you've been resisting lunch invitations from your I-Boss, try accepting once in a while. He might pay for it. Since the economic meltdown of 2008, however, eating on the company tab has been curtailed in most firms while requirements for receipts have escalated. I heard that even Google has stopped the free food. The belt tightening is real and appears to be the new rule rather than the exception. Nevertheless, your I-Boss might be willing to take you to lunch and expense it because he's brash or stupid enough to do so. Your I-Boss's boss might expense her lunches with peers and subordinates and doesn't want to rock the boat by enforcing a prohibition. Who knows? If a free meal is available, eat. *Eat.*

Even if your I-Boss insists on going Dutch, it could be worse. He could be a regular prankster and think it's a cute trick to ask you to lunch and then stick you with the bill. This is more likely to occur with a Sadistic or a God Boss, the latter of which considers your picking up the tab a form of tithing.

MAKING THE MOST OUT OF BUSINESS MEALS BEGINS WITH

FOLLOWING A FEW SIMPLE RULES:

- ☐ Understand what a business meal means to your boss. Some think meals are work time; others think they're opportunities to talk about everything but work. Whichever the case, your boss sets the agenda, not you.

- ☐ Are business meals a cover for your boss's desire to slam back a few before returning to the office? If so, use the designated driver or doctor's orders excuses to not join in the

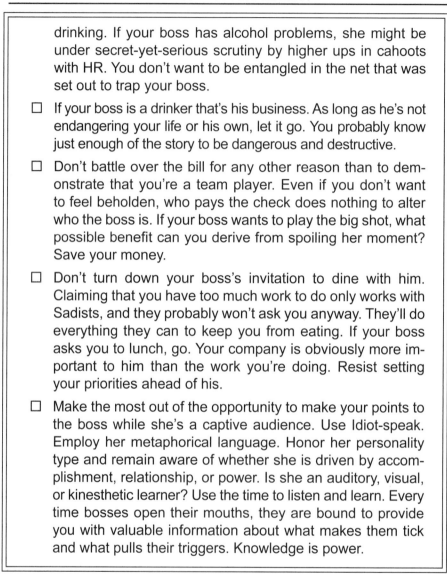

drinking. If your boss has alcohol problems, she might be under secret-yet-serious scrutiny by higher ups in cahoots with HR. You don't want to be entangled in the net that was set out to trap your boss.

☐ If your boss is a drinker that's his business. As long as he's not endangering your life or his own, let it go. You probably know just enough of the story to be dangerous and destructive.

☐ Don't battle over the bill for any other reason than to demonstrate that you're a team player. Even if you don't want to feel beholden, who pays the check does nothing to alter who the boss is. If your boss wants to play the big shot, what possible benefit can you derive from spoiling her moment? Save your money.

☐ Don't turn down your boss's invitation to dine with him. Claiming that you have too much work to do only works with Sadists, and they probably won't ask you anyway. They'll do everything they can to keep you from eating. If your boss asks you to lunch, go. Your company is obviously more important to him than the work you're doing. Resist setting your priorities ahead of his.

☐ Make the most out of the opportunity to make your points to the boss while she's a captive audience. Use Idiot-speak. Employ her metaphorical language. Honor her personality type and remain aware of whether she is driven by accomplishment, relationship, or power. Is she an auditory, visual, or kinesthetic learner? Use the time to listen and learn. Every time bosses open their mouths, they are bound to provide you with valuable information about what makes them tick and what pulls their triggers. Knowledge is power.

Vacation requests

Meeting off-site has some practical applications, especially in dealing with I-Bosses. If your I-Boss gives you grief about requesting your vacation time, take her off-site. During your meal together, lead your I-Boss into a conversation about her vacation. Milk it for all it's worth. Encourage her, *beg* her not to leave out a single detail. Pay attention to the adjectives she uses to describe the landscape, the wind, the waves, the smell of fresh pine forests, whatever. If she says two weeks just didn't seem long enough, make a mental note. After she has worked herself into a euphoric state, tell her you want to take the same amount of time she did, go where she went, and, using her adjectives, have the same experience she had. Once the time off is granted, go wherever you want to go.

Her nostalgia, combined with that full tummy feeling, will be the best possible moment for you to ask. Nothing back at the office can match it. Hopefully you're eating alone with her. If that's not possible, take your shot anyway. You just gave your peers a lesson well worth the price of admission. Being away from the office tends to make people forget deadlines, pressures, and problems of all kinds. Get your boss to commit to your time off before you finish dessert.

Food works well with most every boss type. Even Masochists and Paranoids feel cheerier with a blood sugar rush. Asking a God Boss for your vacation over an off-site meal, especially if you're paying for it, exponentially increases the probability of success. Your God Boss's kingdom will be a little less familiar. His omnipotence will seem a little less omnipotent. Overall, he's more vulnerable. Back at the office, you'll need to do much more penance to get the dates you want. Picking up the tab might be enough to put him over the edge. It's an offering, after all.

Machiavellian Bosses can be handled the same way. Using her descriptions, tell her you think the head of the company should require all employees to take vacations exactly like hers. Promise her you'll tell everyone at your vacation destination that your boss, [insert her name here], sent you. She'll be most cooperative if she thinks your vacation will help expand her sphere of influence.

Sadistic Bosses are a complex challenge when it comes to vacation requests. In a restaurant situation, poke at your food but don't eat. Lay your fork down and sigh. When he smiles that serpent-like smile and asks what's wrong, tell him you have vacation time coming and you just hate to go on vacation. He'll be suspicious at first, but stick with the program. Explain that all you ever do on vacations is worry about the work back at the office. No matter where you go, you can't get your mind off the pile on your desk. Describe how you always fret about the money you spent traveling to an exotic place only to sit on a wind-swept beach in complete misery.

Plead with him not to make you go. Tell him if he forces you to take vacation time you'll insist on taking work with you. Slam dunk.

Promise your Masochistic Boss that you'll take lots of pictures, and tell her every detail of the fun you had as soon as you get back. You'll even call in and let her listen to the surf once in a while to help her die of envy. Mention how you'll leave travel brochures on your desk while you're gone and download a picture of paradise for a screensaver so she can be miserable every day you're away. She might even extend your time off.

Asking a Buddy Boss for vacation time is dangerous. He'll readily grant you the time off. But he'll want to come with you. Offer to organize an office vacation slide-show party when you return. He might go for that. If he still insists on accompanying you, hang tough. Try telling him you're meeting a stranger you met on a blog site, your mother is coming along, or there's a typhoid outbreak where you're going. If nothing dissuades him, you might need to include him in your travel plans. But all is not lost. Insist on booking the tickets and accommodations. Send him to another continent while you wing your way to an undisclosed destination, blaming the faux pas on the travel agency after the fact.

A one-on-one lunch with a Paranoid Boss is best for a vacation request for the same blood sugar advantage as with the others. A Paranoid Boss will suspect you are going to use your time off to further the global conspiracy against him. Win his temporary trust over lunch by offering to test his food. If he still resists granting time off because you're involved in a plot, invite him to go along. You might need to purchase a companion ticket and actually hand it to him. Make sure it's fully refundable if you want to get your money back when he refuses to go. Lean over the table slightly and whisper that you'll carry a sealed envelope on your person at all times containing the names of all the conspirators to be mailed to him in the event of your untimely death. If you live through your vacation and don't mysteriously lose the envelope, you'll present it to him upon your return. Hopefully he'll buy into enough of your nonsense and grant you the time off before he figures out the only way you would know if his lunch was safe to taste is if you were part of the conspiracy to poison him.

A Reluctant Boss is pretty easy to maneuver when it comes to time off. Just fill out all of the paperwork in advance. Have all of the details attended to and present her with a document to sign. So adverse to managing people is she that she'll likely just sign whatever you stick in front of her. "Just sign the vacation request beside the X and I'll be out of your hair." Some Reluctant Bosses might not even notice you're gone. That's how much they avoid paying attention and engaging those who report to them. This is all to your advantage when it comes time to recharge your batteries. Don't over-state your vacation time or otherwise unethically exploit your Reluctant Boss's lack of attentiveness. If you're busted by HR, you'll drag your Reluctant Boss into a series of investigative activities and demands for explanations that she will never forgive you for. In other words, getting greedy and getting caught will backfire with your Reluctant Boss because you will wind up dragging her precisely where she has no desire to go: into management bureaucracy.

Your Unprepared Boss is the opposite in that he very much wants to be treated as the boss. He won't want to be tangled up in bureaucracy any more than the Reluctant Boss, but he wants to be the one to pull the trigger on your request. If you make it seem as though you're trying to sneak one past him, he's likely to deny your request just to establish his bosshood. Go ahead and do all the prerequisite paperwork and minimize any real work your Unprepared Boss is likely not going to know how to do anyway. But when you present the request to him, make sure you are asking his permission in such a way as to honor the aforementioned boss-hood. "Hi boss," you chirp with vacation request in hand. "Can I get your approval on a vacation request?" He'll likely want to think it over and ask you to leave it with him. Each time you go back to check on it, make sure to ask if he has "made his decision" about your request. Unless he has a legit reason to deny it, chances are he'll approve it just to get you off of his back—as long as you never try to wrestle control of the situation away from him.

Of course, a Good Boss will not need to be in that full-tummy, high-blood-sugar place to consider the value of granting you time off. She'll bug you to make sure you take all the time you have coming to you because she's truly concerned about your personal and professional health and well-being. When you return, she'll probably take you to lunch to hear all about your time away. Don't forget the pictures.

I-Boss Bonding Specifics

As I mentioned earlier, schmoozing over coffee, drinks, and meals is part of business cultures everywhere. Use these opportunities to bond with your I-Boss in ways that will make life easier for you back at the office. Remember to talk about what the I-Boss wants to talk about. Laugh at the I-Boss's jokes and funny stories, even if it's the fifth time you've heard the one about how his dog vomited on his neighbor's newspaper. "Gee, boss," you chuckle. "I never get tired of hearing about your dog's editorial opinions." Your I-Boss is probably in search of an audience. Many people eventually just stop listening to I-Bosses. Take advantage of the fact that he wants to be heard.

Your jokes and great ideas are not on his agenda. You need to respond to the image he sees in his foggy mirror. The last thing you want to do is clean his looking glass. Mealtime is a terrific opportunity for you to play detective and study the image your I-Boss sees in that foggy mirror. *Be* the mirror. Whenever humanly possible, order whatever your I-Boss orders. Eat at the same pace at which your I-Boss eats so you finish your meal at the same time. With your I-Boss talking so much, you'll need to be patient. Don't shovel food into your mouth while he's talking; pause, and then take a bite when he does. Draw your fork or spoon toward your mouth the same way he does.

Maintain this culinary discipline to make him feel as though you were an extension of him. When your I-Boss pauses to take a bite, you'll be biting, too, and won't be tempted to add anything to the conversation. Let there be silence. He will break it soon enough. As you chew your food, your Idiot Boss will likely be talking with his mouth full. Concentrating on eye contact will help you fight back the nausea. Idiot Bosses reveal some of their innermost thoughts while they are chewing. If your I-Boss gets some food stuck on his face or between his teeth, politely point to that spot on your face or teeth. If he gets the message and removes the food, great. If not, forget it. You did your best. When he gets down to serious business, track his line of thinking, as difficult as that might be. Be an active listener. Continue to maintain eye contact, nod frequently, and repeat key words and phrases aloud while nodding your head. "Uh huh. Think outside the box!" "...the big dog on the street moved your cheese," "...to infinity and beyond," "...a whole new *Blink* at your *Tipping Point* and drive costs out of the business by executing against strategy...." Swallow.

Be careful not to outshine your I-Boss's dexterity with the cutlery. If he eats peas with a knife, you eat peas with a knife. If he eats salad with a spoon, you eat salad with a spoon. If he stirs coffee with his spoon handle, do the same, whether or not you've used your spoon to eat your salad. If mirroring your I-Boss means holding your fork in such a way that it protrudes from the end of your fist, get used to it. You want your I-Boss to feel comfortable and safe around you. His sense of ease and familiarity will pay dividends.

If you're spotted at the restaurant by your peers, acknowledge everyone graciously. If they are not already sold on the benefits of you having a stronger working relationship with your I-Boss, you can always claim later that you were there under duress or were pleading for better department-wide working conditions. If coworkers approach your table and ask how things are going, seize the opportunity, chuckle, and say, "Our boss was just telling me about the time his dog hurled chunks all over the Sunday *Times*." Horrified expressions will come over their faces and they will back away from the table slowly. Your I-Boss will appreciate what a good listener you are and you'll have your peers' sympathy for the rest of your life.

RAISING THE STEAKS

When your I-Boss invites you to lunch with an important client or someone higher up the corporate food chain, you'll need to do a bit of a balancing act. When the big cheese isn't looking, but your I-Boss is, imitate the I-Boss. When you think you can get away with it, imitate the big cheese. It's likely your I-Boss will hog the conversation, including his dog vomit story that "gets 'em every time." You have helped create that delusion, but nobody else has to know that. Fade into the woodwork at these multi-tier gatherings. Observe and learn. A drama will be played out in front of your eyes that may reveal why the big boss tolerates your Idiot Boss—and trust me, it won't be for his jokes and funny stories. While your I-Boss entertains, you and the Kahuna can chew your food. Your I-Boss isn't playing to you anymore, anyway.

This also gives you an opportunity to raise your level of table manners to match those of the person highest on the food chain. Laugh only when and if the big Kahuna or client laughs. If the client or mega-boss doesn't laugh at your I-Boss's humor, make eye contact with your I-Boss and wink as if to say, "You're really funny, boss. What does this Idiot know?"

Save Your I-Boss's Bacon

Meals are social events. If ever there were an opportunity to demonstrate how adept you are in the social graces, mealtime is your chance to shine. You can be a Miss Manners graduate with a specialization in silverware usage, memorize wine lists and cross-reference them to historical rainfall totals in various regions of France and the Rhine Valley—and still blow it if you forget who's boss. Your shining comes from helping your I-Boss shine, not in outshining him.

Your vastly superior knowledge of fine dining can score points with your Idiot Boss when you use that knowledge to spare him embarrassment. If you don't have vast knowledge of table etiquette, go to the library, go on-line, or go to charm school and get some. Even Idiot Bosses don't seem to mind gentle reminders about which fork to use for what. "I love a crisp salad," you croon on the way to the restaurant where you and your I-Boss will meet a big muckety-muck for a meal, "which I eat with that little fork way on the outside, of course." Your Idiot Boss will look at you and repeat, "Of course," as if he knew all along.

"Unless, of course, they offer me a chilled fork," you continue.

"Of course," your I-Boss agrees. "Chilled is always better."

He won't admit it, but your boss is willing, even anxious to take cues from you regarding table manners. That is, unless he's a completely clueless Idiot, in which case it's every diner for him- or herself. In the event your I-Boss is open to suggestions, make them. The more dependent you can make him regarding socially acceptable behavior, the more he owes you. If knowledge is power, knowing your way around a meal served with white gloves is an awesome power, indeed.

Put your superior intelligence-gathering skills to work and find out about the muckety-muck's proclivities. Usually, a big Kahuna's secretary will gladly divulge what his favorite wine is, whether he prefers well-done steak or raw tartare, and anything else that will help you make his dining experience pleasurable. Let your I-Boss know what you found out. Hopefully he's bright enough to realize how to use such information to his advantage. Even better, he'll appreciate that you are a veritable fount of career-enhancing data.

DINING INTERNATIONAL

Fortune 100 companies that until only recently still considered themselves to be deeply American, deigned to open foreign offices to conduct business offshore. As the first decade of the 21st century gave way to the second, these same companies, if they haven't been purchased outright by foreign interests, now find themselves employing as many, if not more employees in countries outside the United States as they employ stateside, and generate as much, if not more profit offshore.

In the old days, American companies shipped their unskilled labor jobs to lower-paying labor markets. The intellectual capability stayed home in the landscaped office parks and glass towers of Western industry. It is a rarity for a company of any appreciable size to be isolated to just North America. It seems as if everyone in business today is increasingly confronted with cross-cultural issues. When cross-cultural issues present themselves to your I-Boss, you have an opportunity opening wide enough to drive a truck through. You've always urged your Idiot Boss not to slip off his shoes under the dinner table. Now you can enlighten him on all kinds of foot etiquette, from removing his shoes at a fine Japanese restaurant to never showing the sole of his shoe to a Korean. (You might want to carry an extra pair of socks in case he has a hole in one of his.) The cultural mores of virtually any country are easily researchable on the Web. You can hire firms like Partners in Human Resources International to provide you with acculturation coaching, and you can commission cultural inventories and set up cultural sensitivity and acclimation training. Now more than ever, you need to stay ahead of the game, anticipate any faux pas your I-Boss is likely to commit, do your research, and coach him. In all likelihood, he'll appreciate your efforts.

THE TENTH STEP: "CONTINUE TO TAKE PERSONAL INVENTORY AND, WHEN I'M

WRONG, PROMPTLY ADMIT IT."

I'm glad the 12 steps leave a little wiggle room to conduct remedial work. My often-clumsy conduct at social gatherings is a constant opportunity for remedial work. If I had to get everything right the first time, I'd probably be a perpetual relapse statistic. To continue taking personal inventory is a good idea because the more layers of the onion I peel away, the more I seem to discover. The more I probe my personal Inner Idiot issues, the more I understand Idiot Bosses and how to deal with them. The personal inventory exercise is particularly helpful in the context of my career because I am forming a picture of how boneheadedness in my personal affairs is mirrored by boneheadedness in my professional affairs. Idiot Bosses are Idiots at home, too. As I mentioned in Chapter 1, I've been an Idiot employee, an Idiot Boss, an Idiot spouse, an Idiot student, an Idiot teacher, and an Idiot coach. I've been an equal opportunity aggravation to more people than I care to count. The more I see my boss's Idiot behavior at work, the more I suspect he demonstrates the same at home. The major epiphany for me is that whatever Idiot behavior I demonstrate outside the workplace (and there is quite a bit) is probably going to show up at work sooner or later.

If I remain seized up with anger and resentment toward Idiot Bosses, I'll keep trying to peel their onions to get at the core of their behavior instead of my own. Chopping their onions is a more appropriate way to put it. No, hacking them to itty-bitty pieces with a machete is the more honest way to put it. But as we agreed chapters ago, that kind of bitterness and revenge-seeking resentment only spoils our days; poisons us; and voids the warranties on our cell phones, not theirs—unless we bring a real machete to work, in which case we ruin two lives.

THE TENTH STEP EXERCISE: "CONTINUE TO TAKE PERSONAL INVENTORY AND, WHEN I'M WRONG, PROMPTLY ADMIT IT."

Making that list of everyone we have ever harmed and checking it twice is not enough. Making amends and apologizing whenever possible, as long as doing so will not cause serious emotional or physical injury to me or to you, is a great leap forward in humility and improved perspective. Mealtime and social gatherings often present good opportunities to admit wrongdoing. Bosses are more likely to be forgiving when in a festive mood or with a tummy full of yummy food. However, the whole concept of self-inventory is not static. The only time you can stop taking personal inventory is when you're dead or when you decide to stop investing in living, whichever comes first. The good news is that the Tenth Step Exercise is really just a natural progression from the make-the-list, get-ready-to-make-amends, and make-amends tasks in steps Eight and Nine. No need to plan ahead. No need to locate old flames, bosses, parents, friends, enemies, or shop clerks. Two things are important, however:

1. Continue taking a personal inventory by making it a habit to journal your experiences day-in and day-out. Create an on-line diary, or do it the old-fashioned way in a handwritten journal. But pay attention and document what you're thinking, saying, and doing. Are you breaking out of old patterns? Stuck in old patterns? Developing new and healthier patterns? Developing new and more destructive patterns? The point is to pay attention. We backslide when we don't pay attention. How can you know if you're moving forward if you don't track your progress? How often have you been told "If it can't be measured, it can't be managed?"

2. When you become aware that you've made a mistake, admit it promptly. Don't stew about it and build a mountain out of a mole hill. Confront sooner rather than later. Nip it in the bud before its roots run deep and spread far and wide. Enough colloquialisms. Make a personal inventory of your behavior over the next 24 hours in the workplace. Your choices of where to eat, what to eat, and with whom might give you ample opportunity to admit a mistake.

Beware of Idiots at mealtimes. What happens there can work for you or against you. Play your food wisely.

11

Idiocy: Some Theories

If Idiots didn't exist, would we create them?

THE ELEVENTH STEP: "THROUGH PRAYER AND MEDITATION, I SEEK TO INCREASE CONTACT WITH MY HIGHER POWER, AS I INTERPRET HIM, PRAYING FOR KNOWLEDGE OF HIS WILL AND THE COURAGE TO CARRY IT OUT."

The original (and wordier) eleventh step refers to God or our Higher Power "as we understand Him." This essentially means that your Higher Power is whatever you decide it will be. Some people are their own Higher Powers. God Bosses certainly are. For my Higher Power to be of any use to me, he must be larger and more encompassing than I am. I believe my Higher Power has a will and a plan far more advanced and potentially positive than anything I could devise. The secret is to get in touch with his will and his plan for how I should spend my time and energy. That will be the true fast track to success: surrender and succeed.

Maybe Idiot Bosses are not a mistake after all. Is it possible that I-Bosses are not the freaks of evolution we initially perceived them to be? Perhaps Idiot Bosses were created to keep us honest and humble. Do we need I-Bosses in our lives and we're just too proud to admit it? Who else can we blame for our continual career frustrations? Do we hate our Idiot Bosses because they deserve it, or because they can't defend themselves? Are we the bullies and are our I-Bosses the 98-pound weaklings? Are I-Bosses part of the same food chain that includes the rest of us? If one person's floor is another person's ceiling, is one person's I-Boss another person's hero? Although we sometimes go off on our customers, at the end of the day, we are all somebody else's customer.

I have sometimes invented Idiot Bosses in my life to evade capture and punishment for my own transgressions. Scapegoats are easier to conjure than solutions. Why spend energy planning for a better future when I can spend it all whining about the present and the past? We create Idiots so we can stand on someone's shoulders to keep our heads above the flood of stupidity to which we all contribute. The stories about Idiots are legion. They clog up cyberspace like hairs in the shower drain. I'm not so sure these people are all Idiots, however. They might merely be Idiots of convenience that we create to make ourselves feel better.

Among my esteemed colleagues is a great teacher and a terrible golfer, all rolled into one, a distinction I reserved for myself until we met. He is a scientist and I am a philosopher. His discipline is exact science. Behavioral science, despite its moniker, is an art form. In the precise world in which he operates, fools are easily quantifiable, and he snipes at them without a second thought. My friend sent me a collection of actual answers to test questions submitted to science and health teachers by students. These might have appeared in your cyber flotsam at some point:

1. H_2O is hot water and CO_2 is cold water.

2. When you smell an odorless gas, it is probably carbon monoxide.

3. Water is composed of two gins, Oxygen and Hydrogen. Oxygen is pure gin. Hydrogen is water and gin.

4. Momentum: What you give a person when they are going away.

5. Vacuum: A large empty space where the Pope lives.

6. Germinate: To become a naturalized German.

Sure, go ahead and laugh. I might have given some of those answers in desperate sweaty moments when I realized, too late, that studying might have been a good idea. It's easy for smart people, especially scientists, to think of the rest of us as Idiots. Their questions have only one correct answer. Look at these answers philosophically or artistically and you can appreciate the trend toward multiple intelligences, which is another way of saying that we're not all scientists. There is no single right answer when you're dealing with human beings.

IDIOTS: REAL OR NOT?

Idiots in the workplace can either be real or imagined. If they are real, we need to deal with them. If they are imagined, we need psychiatric help. As former Secretary of State Dean Acheson wrote, "A memorandum is written not to inform the reader, but to protect the writer." Not if you're an Idiot. Try some of these actual management directives on for size:

☐ "Teamwork is a lot of people doing what I say."

☐ "Doing it right is no excuse for not meeting the deadline."

☐ "My hope is that we can boil down these two documents and make three."

☐ "This project is so important, we can't let more important things interfere with it."

☐ "E-mail is not to be used to pass on information or data. It should be used only for company business."

☐ "We know communication is a problem, but the company is not going to discuss it with the employees."

There are two ways to ensure your words will be memorialized—say something exceptionally wise or exceptionally stupid. These managers thought their logic was as solid as Gibraltar. One even gleefully gave me a pamphlet a former employee had published, filled with his convoluted logic. He thought the publication was a tribute. I thanked him for the pamphlet and excused myself. I was late for a meeting back on Earth.

If you really want to know the answer to the question at the top of this chapter, "If Idiot Bosses didn't exist, would we create them?" you must first accept that it's a stupid question. Idiot Bosses by anyone's definition do exist. The better question is "How do you survive them?" A deeper and more ominous question is "Am *I* really the Idiot trying to live a life of denial and disguise?" Maybe I'm even projecting my own stupidity on an Idiot Boss, making him appear worse than he truly is.

It's in the blood

Genetics is yet another way we should be able to connect with our Idiot Bosses at some level. Some of us have Irish blood; others have German. Some people have Italian blood; some have French. For most of us, if we trace the roots of our family trees deep enough, there are bound to be Idiots somewhere in the woodpile.

Try looking at your I-Boss through a different lens for a change. The bloodlines are not in their favor. This explains their anemic comprehension skills. When you attempt to persuade an I-Boss to do something, your first task is to help him grasp the concept. Give him the benefit of the doubt. Idiot Bosses want to be liked despite the fact they are so unlikable. Keep saying to yourself, "He really means well." Not that saying it makes everything okay. But at least it lifts the shroud of evil intentions. Compare your I-Boss to other boss types with truly evil intentions and you'll appreciate him even more.

Good Bosses always mean well and generally have the intelligence to do well. Many Idiot Bosses would be Good Bosses if they could just hold a thought long enough without getting bored and trying to play manager. The line that separates Good Bosses from I-Bosses is sometimes as thin as a few points on the intelligence compass. Good Bosses are concerned primarily with the growth and development of their team members because they know that highly motivated people are highly productive people.

The intelligence factor separating a Good Boss from an I-Boss includes recognition that meaningless tasks I-Bosses force on their team members are counterproductive to growth and development of the individual and, subsequently, to the organization. I-Bosses don't intentionally set out to thwart the performance of their team members; they just come by it naturally. I-Bosses give lip service to reaching company goals as they parrot the mantras of motivational authors. But in the end, they muck up the works with irrelevant tasks, inappropriate performance "evaluations," and miscommunication. They don't grasp the notion that all of the minor chaos they create daily eventually adds up to major chaos. It's all in the blood analysis report.

Idiot procreation, as you'll recall from Chapter 4, is the result of Idiots adding more and more Idiots to the payroll in order to protect themselves from exposure as Idiots. When that many Idiots are added to the organizational blood supply, the overall intelligence of the organization is bound to be diminished through Idiot inbreeding. Fresh blood, in terms of new ideas and ways of looking at things, will reinvigorate the energy that the younger, more robust organization once had.

CONCEPT AVOIDANCE

Intelligence in the right hands makes a Good Boss effective. Stupidity in the wrong hands will turn an otherwise-effective organization into a circus. Good bosses know that the integrity of the 10th floor depends on the integrity of the nine below it. Imagine you're having a conversation with an Idiot Boss over lunch in the penthouse restaurant of a skyscraper he just helped complete. "We saved money by mixing substandard building materials with the good stuff," the I-Boss explains as he tries to pick a sesame seed out of his first molar. You stop your salad fork just short of your open mouth, blink twice, and set the loaded fork back on your plate.

"Did you just say this tall building we're sitting on top of is constructed with substandard building materials?"

"A memo came down to cut costs," the I-Boss says, flicking the sesame seed over his shoulder. "I figured that meant cutting labor or material expenses, and with the union and all, cutting labor would have been tough, so I bought some brand X items." The I-Boss slathers butter all over the rest of his sesame roll and crams it in his mouth. "Got some great-looking stuff from a guy named Freddie the Palm," he mumbles through a mouthful of roll and butter. "Really cheap, too."

"Aren't you worried?" you ask, trying to avoid looking at what he's chewing.

"Heck no." The I-Boss swallows and takes a big gulp of water. "We came in on budget and they gave me a big raise."

"I mean do you feel safe in a building made from inferior building materials?" you ask, scanning the walls and ceiling for cracks or other telltale signs of structural failure.

The I-Boss chuckles. "You must think I'm stupid."

"I didn't say that," you counter, hoping the thought, so present in your mind, didn't somehow slip out.

"I'll have you know," he assures you, "that I used the highest-quality steel and concrete here on the upper floors where the executive offices are located. The questionable concrete and steel more prone to structural failure were all used on the lower floors where the peons work."

"That was a stroke of genius," you say pleasantly as you get up from the table and exit the building as quickly as possible.

Education is probably lost on a person too blockheaded to realize that the health and well-being of the big picture depends on the health and well-being of its component parts. A Good Boss gets it and cares enough to do something about it. A Good Boss consistently demonstrates intelligence, character, and common sense. Common sense alone can cover a multitude of sins.

Much of the frustration we experience when dealing with Idiot Bosses comes from expecting them to demonstrate common sense. Idiots can do sensible things, but it won't necessarily be because something is sensible. It will more likely be the result of your efforts to lead them in that direction through Idiot-speak, Idiot-eat, Idiot-think, and other Idiot interventions.

BLOOD SACRIFICE

If God Bosses didn't exist, would we create them? Not likely. They are of no functional use to anyone. I-Bosses can be distinguished from other boss types by more than just the presence or absence of intelligence. Consider how intelligence is used. People in positions of power who truly believe they are gods combine delusional thinking with superior intelligence to produce the curious cognition cocktail that guides the behavior of God Bosses. The ability to focus and stay on task can be a God Boss's strongest suit, "as he understands himself." His primary task is not the achievement of organizational goals and objectives. A God Boss's behavior seldom relates to what he is actually being paid to do.

As an aside, I've noticed that leaders who actually believe they are deity tend to have underlying paranoid tendencies. That's the only way for a God Boss to stay in power. He must repress or eliminate anyone who might point out he's a mere mortal. My mom always left out the part in *The Emperor's New Clothes* where the child who exposed the ruse was arrested by secret police, imprisoned, and tortured before disappearing altogether. I know she was trying to protect me, but if she had left that part in, I would have been better prepared for corporate life.

As I mentioned previously, God Bosses can't allow reasonable people within their sphere of influence to have any voice or platform from which to expose them as frauds. But silencing people and disposing of their bodies without drawing attention requires the very same cunning and imagination that was required for them to believe that they were omnipotent in the first place. A God Boss will demonstrate his intelligence in clever-yet-diabolical schemes necessary to silence seekers and speakers of truth. A God Boss's work is never done because there is always someone with a natural desire to reveal the truth—except when filing income taxes, filling out job applications, or explaining to their spouse the real reason they arrived home late.

Machiavellian Bosses also often apply their superior intelligence to evil purposes. Unfortunately, to Machiavellians, success necessitates failure in others. Whereas a God Boss will take out someone he thinks is threatening to expose him, a Machiavellian will take people out for merely standing between her and what she wants. Machiavellian Bosses, intelligent and cunning as they are, strike with stealth and skill to surgically remove the offending party or parties. Whereas the God Boss prefers leaving a wide swath of destruction, a Machiavellian Boss will leave a small drop of blood left clearly visible on the victim's computer keyboard for the other team members to see as a compelling reminder of the price of interference.

Just as God Bosses have an underlying fear of being exposed, Machiavellian Bosses have underlying narcissism. And of course Idiot Bosses have underlying cluelessness, which I'm amazed is not a diagnostic category in the Diagnostic and Statistical Manuel of the American Psychological Association. The fact remains that all of these boss types exist, so we don't need to ponder if we would or would not create them in their absence.

An Exception to Everything

If there is no one around the office to inflict pain and suffering, a Masochist will do the honors herself—to herself. Even so, she need not look very far for someone to lend her a hand as long as there are Idiot, God, Machiavellian, and Sadistic Bosses around. Idiot Bosses usually cause pain and anguish unintentionally. God Bosses cause pain and anguish as a method of guaranteeing loyalty and support. Machiavellians cause pain and anguish in their ongoing struggle to transfer all that belongs to others into their offshore accounts. Sadists love to cause pain and anguish, period.

I find Sadistic Bosses more tolerable than Masochistic Bosses. Their behavior seems more natural in a demented sort of way. Masochistic Bosses are like Reluctant Bosses until they discover the dramatic opportunities for self-abuse that leadership offers. A department full of team members can be turned into an angry mob with pitchforks if you annoy and antagonize them enough. For a Masochistic Boss, it could be death by angry team members. Left to their own devices, Masochists love working for Sadists because the Sadist provides a steady and reliable dosage of pain and abuse. Sadists, on the other hand, can't stand anyone who actually enjoys pain. As a result, a Masochist will never last for very long in a Sadist's department.

Sadists want to be bosses from the get-go because it's the perfect setup in which to punish and abuse unwilling victims with complete impunity. It is a brilliant tactical maneuver and as close to the perfect crime as one can get. The inhuman workloads Sadistic Bosses enjoy foisting upon their team members can lead to sleep deprivation, malnutrition, and even institutionalization. In each case, a shrewdly intelligent Sadistic Boss can claim under oath that the team member was overly ambitious, which will only drive the team member deeper into despair and self-destructive behavior. If Sadistic Bosses didn't exist, would I create them? Definitely not. Give me an Idiot any day. If Sadistic Bosses aren't careful, HR can get involved. Then Sadists find themselves talking to coaches like Dr. Hoover and their lives are forever changed. No more fun pain, just the good pain of gain.

Vertical Mobility and Trial Lawyers

With HR departments hedging against runaway labor litigation, the safest way to get rid of undesirable parties in your department is to help them get promoted (see Chapter 4). Nobody sues for being promoted. With incompetent knuckleheads being herded up the management ladder in an effort to get them away from actual working departments with a minimum of paperwork and reduced out-of-court settlements, the real working folks in the mushroom stem are supporting a cap increasingly populated with nutty, unproductive, self-defeating bosses.

Defying Explanation

I know of no body of physical or biological evidence to explain the existence of the Paranoid Boss. Similar in many ways to their cousins the God Bosses, Paranoid Bosses exist in a theoretical or, more specifically, imaginative world of their own creation. Whether or not we ever develop the ability to explain them, Paranoid Bosses are insufferable. Nothing you can do will satisfy or please them, and it's hard to stay motivated when everything you think, say, and do is under constant suspicion. As with most negative energy in the universe, the cycle of paranoia feeds on itself, takes on a life of its own, and becomes self-perpetuating. The perpetual motion machine might be a myth, but a Paranoid Boss's imagination will go on forever. If Paranoid Bosses didn't exist, I see no reason to create them. They are a perpetual, equal-opportunity aggravation to everyone.

Extreme Measures...Like Reorganizing

I don't recommend dissolving your company as a strategy to get rid of a problem employee. That would be like burning down your house to get rid of termites. Unfortunately, organizations are constantly trying to deal with their organizational potholes (read: problem bosses) by reorganizing. Reluctant Bosses are often made bosses because the person with prior management responsibility for their area was such a screw-up that the area was reorganized to move the incompetent boss aside. In the process, the incompetent boss was relegated to another function with fewer harsh consequences for failure. It's confusing, I know. Why not just fire the incompetent boss? Litigation, as the new retirement plan, is yet another way to avoid confrontation by reshuffling the deck without appearing to have changed much.

Tell that to the Reluctant Boss who knows that she has been saddled with additional responsibility, albeit with higher compensation. The boss who doesn't want to be a boss is supposed to somehow step up and fill the void that her predecessor never filled—except, perhaps, with hot air. The Reluctant Boss flies under the radar by design, which will ultimately lead to another organizational redesign, and another, and another—all of which could have been avoided by constructively confronting the core leadership issues with sensitivity to organizational needs and boss typology to begin with. I wouldn't necessarily create Reluctant Bosses if they didn't already exist. I would hope to create more subject-matter-expert-friendly circumstances that could keep Reluctant Bosses contributing where they are most comfortable and productive.

FLIPPING A COIN TO MAKE THINGS WORSE

Sometimes the cure is worse than the disease. When a department is devoid of leadership or suffers from bad leadership, regardless of its form, and when the powers that be reorganize to solve the problem, an Unprepared Boss is sometimes slipped into the corner office. Whereas the Reluctant Boss might have been promoted based on demonstrated competence at conducting specialized work, an Unprepared Boss might be promoted because he throws himself in front of the Big Kahuna's car in the executive parking garage.

In the same way that Reluctant Bosses are oftentimes replaced with other Reluctant Bosses, Unprepared Bosses are often replaced with other Unprepared Bosses, at which point these new bosses fail. Lather, rinse, repeat, *ad nauseum*. If I were faced with the decision to create a Reluctant Boss or an Unprepared Boss, I'd go with the former. At least a Reluctant Boss would be happy if she were returned to the cave where she was writing code before being so abruptly thrust into the ranks of management. An Unprepared Boss will not be happy until he's a boss, whether that makes sense or not. Although ambition can be a positive driving force, if I wanted to create anything vis-à-vis an Unprepared Boss, it would be a powerful desire to grow and develop in what author and leadership expert Margaret Wheatley calls the New Management Science.

I CAN TAKE ONLY SO MUCH FRIENDSHIP

Buddy Bosses often resemble Idiot Bosses except they are not quite as clueless. Buddy Bosses can be quite intelligent. They're just lonely, which plays into the vulnerabilities of codependents like me. Although lonely people with intelligence can be really annoying, they rip at my heartstrings. I-Bosses, on the other hand, aren't sharp enough to realize that they're lonely. That's like being so poor you don't realize you're poor. If you have a Buddy Boss, take up a collection and buy him a dog. A cat won't work. Cats will just ignore him and not give a rip if he's home or not. Dogs are much higher maintenance and might keep your Buddy Boss occupied long enough for you to sneak away for a weekend with your spouse and kids. Your Buddy Boss will eventually need to get home and feed the dog, greatly reducing the number of requests to spend long evenings with you. If Buddy Bosses didn't exist, I would leave it that way.

SOMETIMES THE ANSWER IS RIGHTFUL TERMINATION

When someone is disruptive to departmental efficiency and cohesiveness, and that person will not respond to conflict resolution efforts or extensive attempts to construct workable solutions, it's time for the powers that be to separate the wayward sheep from the flock. As unpleasant as termination is, it is sometimes the best solution to this problem. An untenable situation with a problem employee hurts team members more than it hurts bosses. Bosses have the power and, indeed, the obligation to address personnel problems, whereas all team members can do is wait and hope.

One of the worst workplace scenarios imaginable is a disruptive and abrasive team member left to terrorize his peers and a boss who refuses to do anything about it. Chances are you've been in that situation. It's rough. Your boss is probably aware of the problem, although she might pretend she's not. To those who have never faced this situation as a boss, it's hard to explain. Part of you doesn't want to admit you lack the skills to work it out. Part of you doesn't want to open a can of worms by addressing the problem and setting off a stink bomb, only to find out that the in-house counsel won't allow you to dispose of it. You don't relish the thought of making an enemy out of this person. You hold out hope for some miraculous resolution and reconciliation to occur.

Going through the exhaustive and intricate process of terminating someone is about as pleasant as getting root canal. If you're one of the team members suffering while your boss wallows in indecision, you can do several things. Having studied what language your boss speaks and what drives her personality, you can approach her in the most diplomatic, well-thought-out manner possible and let her know how much the situation is thwarting the department's productivity and morale and damaging her reputation. Be prepared for your appeals to fall on deaf ears. And be prepared if the management solution is to reorganize rather than separate the bad influence from the organization. Finally, don't be surprised if the one whose job is dissolved in the reorganization is you. In terms of probabilities and Vegas odds, any one or a combination of the last three is far more probable than an honest and courageous constructive confrontation with a problem employee or workplace relationship.

Remember, I'm an executive coach to the C-Suite. I don't approach difficult issues with a glass-half-empty, pessimistic, cynical attitude. I think there is hope and potential in all things and in all people, and I'm willing to work hard in partnership with my clients to make it so. Having said that, I know the official and unofficial, the spoken and unspoken rules of engagement. And I've learned and earned a firm grasp on reality inside organizations. The last thing you need in an author, consultant, or coach is naïveté or a Pollyanna perspective. Things can turn out really well or they can turn out ugly. Sometimes a journey through the ugly places is necessary to reach the new day. As Zorba the Greek observed, "It's the mud that makes the roses grow," or words to that effect. As leaders, we can't be afraid to get covered in mud once in a while.

YOU CAN'T BE TOO CAREFUL

Always remember that when you bring a problem to someone up the organizational food chain, you're creating an expectation that the person will act on the information you provide, which might be the last thing that person wants to do. Assume you're on your own until you can find reasonable assurance you will be supported. Don't assume you will be supported, even if your organization's Standard Operating Procedures say you will. And remember that any executive with sufficient power to assist you in the event you need to go over your boss's head will himself be one of the major boss types. Know with whom you're working before you expose yourself to retribution. Information is power. Nothing is stopping you from gathering as much of it as you can.

BE THANKFUL

If your I-Boss is not allowing an annoying and unresolved problem to abscess, rejoice. Regardless of any theoretical, theological, or biological explanations for Idiot Bosses, be grateful. Be glad they are unconscious of the havoc they create and that nothing keeps them awake at night. Let them snooze. If we lose sleep hating them, it's nobody's fault but our own. I'm not saying I would create I-Bosses if they didn't exist. Let's not get carried away. But I would gladly substitute an I-Boss for a God, Machiavellian, Sadistic, Masochistic, Paranoid, or Buddy Boss any day. Reluctant and Unprepared Bosses, on the other hand, might be redeemable, given sufficient time and effort.

Think of the poor souls who haven't read this book. They're still blaming their Idiot Bosses for their career frustrations and plotting a coup. You, on the other hand, are an enlightened creature, realizing that without your I-Boss, things could be much worse. Remember that next Thanksgiving when your I-Boss doesn't invite himself over to your house.

ELEVENTH STEP EXERCISE: "THROUGH PRAYER AND MEDITATION, I SEEK TO INCREASE CONTACT WITH MY HIGHER POWER, AS I INTERPRET HIM, PRAYING FOR KNOWLEDGE OF HIS WILL AND THE COURAGE TO CARRY IT OUT."

Consult your Higher Power. When I entered the ranks of management in the Entertainment Division at Disneyland, Walt Disney had been dead for more than 11 years, but he was still running the company. I had the privilege of working with people who had worked for Walt for enough years to truly know the man. To some, Walt *was* a Higher Power. He was certainly a visionary. The company really didn't do much of anything he hadn't thought of himself until nearly a quarter of a century after his death. That's how far ahead of the curve he was.

I vividly recall design and production meetings where many approaches and techniques were discussed. After several plausible solutions were identified, someone would invariably ask, as if on cue, "What would Walt do?" There was always a minute or so of silence as those who knew and worked with him (as well as those of us who studied him) pondered the question. Each time, reflection on Walt's "Disney Way" produced yet another alternative solution or enhanced the solutions on the table.

Your Eleventh Step Exercise is to ponder deeply the nature of what you're trying to accomplish, consider how an intelligence far greater than your own would approach it, and then formulate a plan that resonates with the greatest source of wisdom you can access. The actions you take will make more sense at a deep level and produce better and more sustainable results over time if you have taken the time (meaning real time, at least 30 minutes of silent reflection to start with) to prayerfully consider how a power greater than you might add to, mitigate, enhance, or radically change your original plans. Then pray for the serenity to accept the things you can't change and the courage to do the things that will truly energize your life and your work. I predict that your wisdom, together with the wisdom of your Higher Power, will know the difference. Pray or meditate for 30 minutes per day, day or night, for seven days and tell me if nothing changes for you, if bad bosses don't become more manageable, and/or if problems that once seemed insurmountable aren't whittled down to doable proportions. This will all start in your "incubator," your inner idea machine from which fabulous solutions pop up when you least expect them.

12

Recalibrating Expectations, Repurposing Anger

Pretend for a moment you've just marched into your Idiot Boss's office in a righteous rage. You plant yourself directly in front of his desk with your feet shoulder-width apart. You clench your fist, shake it in his face, and say, "You miserable so-and-so. I'm smarter and more talented than you. I work harder and get more accomplished in one day than you do in a month. If you had half a brain you would treat me with the respect I deserve, double my vacation time, give me a raise, and beg me not to quit." Just the thought of it feels good, doesn't it? Dream on.

Do you want to thrive or just survive at work? If thriving sounds good, open your fist and let go of the anger, frustration, and resentment. "But, Dr. Hoover," you say, "I'm familiar and comfortable with anger, frustration, and resentment."

"Sure, you are," I agree. "But, do they make you happy?"

Didn't think so. Open your fist and let them go.

If you think living with open hands instead of fists is for the birds, remember that birds don't have hands. Most creatures don't need opposable thumbs because they don't reflect on their circumstances and calculate how miserable and angry they are. Therefore, they don't need to clench fists full of anger, frustration, and resentment. Animals don't resent what they don't have. Anger, frustration, and resentment are not what make humans a higher life form. The ability to transcend what our essential natures prompt us to do in favor of a healthier behavior is the unique value proposition of being a human among all carbon-based life forms.

Anger Is the Issue

What is so important about anger that I'm devoting a whole chapter to it? For one thing, as my dear friend Danny Cox says, "Anger is self cannibalizing. It eats you up inside," or words to that effect. Anger is the engine that spews vitriol against bosses out of its tailpipe or, perhaps, it's the poison we drink as we hope someone else will die. Anger is the emotion that boils up when we discover we have no control over something that we never had any control over to begin with. Back to my rhetorical question from Chapter 1. Once we know better than to blame our bosses for all of our unresolved adolescent rebellion issues, but blame them anyway, who's the Idiot?

Q: What causes anger?

A: *Unfulfilled expectations.*

Q: What do we tend to expect of our bosses?

A: *Everything.*

Q: What expectation can you hold your boss accountable for?

A: *None.*

There is an exception to everything, even expectations. You can expect your boss not to harass you sexually. You can expect your boss not to create an actionable hostile work environment by impugning your ethnicity, faith, race, sexual orientation, or any number of issues that will have you speed dialing your attorney. When your boss crosses the line from Idiotic behavior to dial-a-lawsuit behavior, these exceptions fall into a new category called your new retirement plan. I am going to assume that a lucrative out-of-court settlement on a grievance against your boss will mitigate much, if not all, of the anger you might feel toward him for not fulfilling your expectations.

The anger that you and I need to repurpose at work is based on expectations that our bosses fail to meet when we have no choice but to accept their failure or find another job (and another boss). If we choose to stay, our only hope of achieving true serenity and peace comes from turning our expectations and everything else we can change over to our Higher Power. To that end, let's review the 12 Steps for Recovering Idiots through the lens of repurposing anger.

The phrase *repurposing anger* implies that we'll wait until we get angry at our bosses and then do something with that anger other than bash, blame, bicker, or bait. Perhaps we can take the anger we feel toward our bosses and kill bacteria with it. Maybe we can figure out a way to use boss-fueled rage to end the world's dependence on fossil fuels. I'm not suggesting that we take existing anger and do something new with it. I am suggesting we adopt alternative behaviors that will preclude anger, such as repurposing expectations. The phrase *an expectation is a resentment waiting to happen* echoes through the church basement every Wednesday night. Once our expectations are under control, the anger thing is solved. Make expectations reasonable, realistic, and responsible and there will be no anger.

STEP BY STEP

The whole notion of repurposing expectations brings us back to the 12 Steps for Recovering Idiots. All the behaviors necessary to transform one's substance addiction (unless you're a codependent like me who is addicted to the addict and/or an Idiot addicted to cluelessness) and modify the destructive behavior are found in the 12 Steps. Idiot-syncracies can be very addictive, and it requires complete surrender to a Power greater than us to repurpose our expectations and really mean it—not just go through the motions and give the exercise lip service.

> STEP ONE: "I ADMIT THAT I AM POWERLESS OVER THE STUPIDITY OF OTHERS
>
> AND MY LIFE HAS BECOME TOO STUPID TO MANAGE."

It should be clear by now that our own stupidity and the stupidity of others can really bollix us up. When we stupidly sign over control of our happiness to someone else, that's stupid. When our happiness or sadness is contingent on other people fulfilling expectations that we can't enforce, or perhaps weren't realistic or reasonable to begin with, we've turned our lives into a giant game of Russian roulette. To think, *Maybe my boss will meet my expectations or maybe she won't, and I'll sure be angry if she doesn't* is a silly way to live and completely abdicates what little power we actually have in this world—the power to set expectations.

An overriding issue vis-à-vis expectations is whether the expectations were discussed and/or negotiated with the boss in advance and vice versa. That's why the art of constructive confrontation makes it explicitly clear that a boss must not hold a direct report or vendor accountable for failing to meet an expectation that was not clearly articulated and agreed to in writing by the direct report or vendor. But even if expectations are discussed and negotiated between the boss and the bossed (with documented expectations for and from both parties, as the art of constructive confrontation calls for), the boss can still fail to meet those expectations with impunity. If you fail to meet them, it is much more likely that there will be consequences. So your expectation must take into account that failure on your boss's part to meet expectations, whether deliberate or accidental, conscious or unconscious, is a distinct possibility.

Knowing that such failure can occur positions you to respond not with anger, but with serenity. Are you pleased with the failure? Of course not! But to allow something that was likely to happen anyway to cause you anger is self-destructive behavior. I don't mean that you throw up your hands and quote the wall plaque that reads "Blessed are those who expect nothing for they shall not be disappointed." No matter how true that might be, you can continually learn new and better ways to help your boss (a) remember that he has an expectation to fulfill, (b) find the resources necessary to fulfill the expectation, and/or (c) provide whatever is in your control to motivate her to complete what she committed to completing.

Reasonable and realistic expectations will serve a much more pleasant purpose than expectations that are tripwires for an emotional explosion. If your boss accuses you of not meeting her expectations when you clearly think you did, you can respond by saying that (a) her perception is wrong, (b) she wouldn't know a fulfilled expectation if it bit her on the heel, or (c) you need to get up earlier in the morning and better anticipate her needs and desires such that you'll improve at making her feel better with each boss/employee encounter.

> STEP TWO: "I REALIZE THAT THE CHALLENGE OF AN I-BOSS IS TOO BIG FOR ME TO HANDLE BY MYSELF AND I NEED A POWER BIGGER THAN ALL THE JARGON-SPEWING BOSSES IN THE UNIVERSE—GOOD, BAD, OR OTHERWISE—TO KEEP ME FROM GOING *COMPLETELY* CRAZY."

Recalibrating your expectations vis-à-vis your boss is tricky. It requires adult supervision to succeed with consistency. That's where your Higher Power comes in. The resentment virus is too pervasive to be overcome simply by using willpower. Resentment can unleash your Inner Idiot without warning, and before you know it, you might be babbling ludicrous thoughts and ideas in front of an astonished roomful of your peers, employees, and bosses. (Maybe they wouldn't be so astonished, actually.) Regardless, call on your Higher Power to help. One thing your Higher Power does better than you is maintain perspective. If it is your boss babbling incoherently, let your Higher Power repurpose your expectations to make better use of his ramblings, or to distinguish between what you need to pay close attention to and what you don't.

I call on my Higher Power not just daily, but many times throughout the day to keep my expectations reasonable and realistic. I need a perspective higher and an intelligence greater than my own to set expectations for myself, my boss, and everyone else around me so as not to set me up for self-cannibalizing anger. In a world where perception is reality and perspective can get distorted through various lenses, we all need a way to repurpose our expectations in a way that will position us and everyone around us for the best possible outcome. That outcome might force us to fall back and regroup. But that is preferable to consuming a few more internal organs every time something or someone fails to meet expectations. I can't think of a better way to maintain what little sanity I have left or perhaps revive a little of the sanity I've lost.

> STEP THREE: "WE DECIDED TO TURN OVER OUR WILL AND OUR LIVES TO OUR HIGHER POWER—AS WE UNDERSTAND HIM."

I'm either going to do this my way, which is how I screwed things up in the first place, or I'm going to walk the walk and conduct myself as if my Higher Power truly were in charge. There is a huge difference between talking the talk and walking the walk when it comes to setting expectations and dealing with failure—others' and your own. Just paying lip service to the concept of setting expectations from the perspective of a higher intelligence can just add fuel to the fire of disappointment, resentment, and anger.

Redesigning expectations that are truly new and different can produce a remarkable feeling of liberation. Shedding the disappointment, resentment, and anger that stem from failed expectations can make you feel as though a tremendous weight has been lifted from your shoulders. In extreme cases, it's like awakening to a sunny morning following 40 days and 40 nights of rain. In my case, and in the case of some of my clients, 40 *years* is more like it.

The "as we understand him" thing is included in steps Three and Eleven to help us avoid trying to *be* the Higher Power. Behaving as if we were the Higher Power is what causes us to have unreasonable and unrealistic expectations, resentment, and anger. Our Higher Power is separate from us. If not, "turning my will and my life over to my Higher Power" is the same thing as "turning my will and my life over to myself." It won't work, unless you're a God Boss, and we all know how realistic a God Boss's expectations are.

STEP FOUR: "WE MUST INVENTORY OUR OWN IDIOTIC BEHAVIOR."

If I don't take what the folks in the church basement call a "searching and fearless" inventory of my behavior, I might skip lightly over this step and thereby lose the tremendous benefit I could be deriving from the other steps. This is where a 360-degree feedback exercise comes in handy for anyone engaged in leadership, much less leadership coaching. Am I in fact doing the things I believe I am doing? More importantly, do the important stakeholders around me believe I'm really doing the things I believe I'm doing?

It's easy to see how we can get tangled up if our self-perception is not consistent with the perception of others. Unless you are an individual contributor (whose boss pays no attention whatsoever) or a robot, measuring your perception of your behavior against the consensus perception of your behavior is essential to keeping expectations reasonable and realistic.

I have watched, sometimes helplessly, as executives, sometimes C-suite occupants, steadfastly ignored their 360-degree feedback, even refusing to share it with their bosses and critical stakeholders—people with enormous influence over their career success who are usually among the 360-degree feedback providers. I've never seen a case with little or no transparency or disclosure on the part of a coaching client end happily. Take the inventory regularly, take it seriously, and acknowledge your need for continuous improvement.

STEP FIVE: "ADMIT TO MY HIGHER POWER, TO MYSELF, AND TO OTHERS THE

NATURE OF MY WRONGS."

This is the part that deals with sharing the results of your 360-degree analysis. If you have no formal 360-degree assessment, solicit feedback from your critical constituency—the people who have the most influence on your career success. These people can include customers, peers, vendors, and direct reports. First and foremost, include your boss. Regardless of the boss type, he or she is the 800-pound guerilla that you should be loath to ignore or wrestle with.

I'm not suggesting that you take up people's precious time talking about yourself or, when you tire of talking about yourself, asking them to talk about you. It is important, however, to develop the skill of soliciting feedback and receiving it well. Receiving it well means accepting a realistic perspective from your critical constituency about the things that challenge you most as well as how you can improve on the things you do well. The latter is the *appreciative inquiry* approach. Always look for the good things as well as growth opportunities, and, as Aunt Eller advised her niece Laurie in *Oklahoma*, say, "Well alright, then" to both.

It's never just about your "wrongs," because the things you do extremely well might be things that you do *too* well (otherwise known as *overused strengths*). You might be a cool operator under fire, with ice water in your veins, capable of keeping your head when everyone around you is losing theirs. But if you diminish the urgency and magnitude of things to the point that others are not taking them seriously, it can hurt productivity and results. Talk about the important stuff and don't sweep the really important stuff about expectations and results under the rug.

STEP SIX: "I'M ENTIRELY READY FOR GOD TO REMOVE MY STUPIDITY."

Not so fast. It is easy to get all hyped up about getting a new lease on life and plunging into Idiot-free peace and serenity. And well you should. But this chapter is about recalibrating expectations so that you won't need to think about repurposing anger. True, "Idiot-free peace and serenity" doesn't mean you're free of Idiots. That will never happen, but (a) you won't be one of them, and (b) you will no longer give Idiots the power to make you angry because you will have reclaimed that power in the form of managing expectations.

So allow yourself to get excited at the prospect of having your stupidity exorcised. But be realistic and reasonable about your expectations. It took you a long time to become the way you are. It took your boss a long time to become the way she is. Nobody is going to change overnight, and nothing happens for no reason, remember? Whatever the reasons for your dysfunctional expectations management and that of your boss, those reasons are still around. Identifying those reasons (probably character defenses, a.k.a. character defects) and getting them out into the light of day will take some time, and will include multiple inventories and multiple conversations about what's working and what's not.

It's not a one-time thing; it's an all-the-time thing. In the same way that we are never not communicating, recovering Idiots and recovering Idiot Bosses are never not working the steps. Continuous improvement has no graduation date. Frequent celebrations, yes. Graduation, no. If you keep a ready attitude and continue working your steps, your readiness will become true willingness. Willing hearts are rewarded hearts, and rewarded behavior is repeated behavior. It's amazing how being realistic and reasonable about your own expectations tends to keep you fair and reasonable about other people's expectations, too.

STEP SEVEN: "PLEASE, PLEASE, GOD—REMOVE MY STUPIDITY."

Whether you or your boss (probably both) engage in intermittent situational stupidity or an unceasing fusillade of stupidity, your personal stupidity is the only stupidity you can do anything about, at least directly. Having prepared yourself for your Higher Power to excise the stupid gene from your body, you'll be ready for a more intelligent way of living when it arrives. But you won't know when it arrives. By the time you notice improvement in the form of greater serenity, peace, and simpatico with your boss (who'd have ever thought you could stomach such a thing?), it will already be happening. You'll start to see pleasing things in your rear-view mirror.

That's why you need Step Six. You will notice that you went through a day or perhaps a week without feeling as awful as you used to feel. You might notice that your boss hasn't been the incredible pain that he used to be, at least not in the last 24 hours or maybe the last five days. When I worked the steps, admitted my powerlessness over cluelessness, took the inventory, and turned my will and my life over to my Higher Authority, and so on, good stuff started to happen. I couldn't predict when or set my watch by it, but things really started to change.

I believe that when you make a deal with your Higher Power, he keeps his end of the bargain. When I realized that I didn't resent my boss as much as I used to and how much better I felt because of it, I didn't long to reclaim my resentment as much as I wanted to prolong the good feelings. I believe I not only felt good but began acting more intelligently. At least that's what people around me observed. My motivation to keep up my end of the bargain was strong. But I needed to stay with the program because there is no graduation date. As soon as I took my eyes off of the steps, I felt the atmosphere go toxic, slowly at first and then faster and faster. Knowing that I needed to quickly return to reasonable and realistic expectations and get back on track helped me take corrective action and return to the steps, which in turn hastened the return of good feelings. Be ready for success when your Higher Power grants it.

> STEP EIGHT: "MAKE A LIST OF ALL PERSONS I MIGHT HAVE HARMED WITH MY STUPIDITY AND PREPARE TO MAKE AMENDS TO THEM ALL."

If you're not ready to repurpose your anger in the form of repurposing your expectations, you will wind up re-*porpoising* your life. Without completely surrendering your will and your life to your Higher Power, you will be up one day and down the next; alternately flying through the air and diving under water. Up, down, up, down, like Flipper leading a cruise ship through the Bermuda Triangle. By leaving roots of doubt in place, you might be able to white-knuckle an improved relationship with your boss, but it won't last for long. Before you know it you'll be going under again.

If you and I only partially commit to recovery, it will show up when we make our amends list. We'll begin to write a name down on the legal pad, pressing harder with each letter until the lead on the pencil breaks. The fact that the resentment is still there proves that we still have unrealistic and unreasonable expectations in place. Getting that "over my dead body" feeling when you think of a person you need to apologize to is an indication that you need to move that person toward the top of the list. He or she is still not meeting your prior expectations and, more importantly, you haven't opened your fist and let it go.

Once you have recalibrated your expectations to more accurately reflect the real you and the real boss you work for, the current resentments will start to dissipate. And so will past resentments. Resentments can only find harbor in your mind as long as the expectations that birthed them remain intact. You will also be surprised at how the names that once made you see red have now become innocuous. Because I have recalibrated my expectations and made them a tool for balancing my life (instead of building walls too high to climb), I can now think of the most egregious enemies I ever had and truthfully think, *He/she really wasn't that bad.* Seriously, you can do it. Start making the list.

STEP NINE: "MAKE AMENDS TO EVERYONE I MIGHT HAVE HARMED WITH MY STUPIDITY, EXCEPT WHEN CONTACTING THEM MIGHT PLACE MY LIFE IN JEOPARDY."

There is no better way to prove you are a new creation than to completely get rid of the old you. The former person who would have never in a million lifetimes said a kind word to certain Idiots who made your life miserable (or so the former you thought) is displaced by a new person in the same body who can actually smile at that same Idiot and accept that we're all sharing the same oxygen. You might find yourself thinking: *This is me. I know me. But this doesn't feel like me. Whahappened?* By now you know what happened and you know how to keep it happening.

Making amends is more than gritting your teeth and trying to make nice with people you despise. If you're still in the despising business, you need to rework your program. When you get your expectations in order, you will discover that you no longer despise anyone. *Even evil villains have a mother who loves them*, you think to yourself. That doesn't make what they do okay, but you can see them more realistically as complex people, not as cartoon caricatures or one-dimensional cardboard cutouts. Making amends doesn't necessarily mean you actually utter the words *I'm sorry* in so many words. It is more powerfully done by saying "You could be right," which implies that you could have been wrong, which is yet more powerfully phrased as "I'll accept responsibility if I was wrong about that."

Some people make a big production out of apologizing and make it all about them. *Look at me! I'm making amends!* Stop acting like a Masochist. Focus on the other person—in this case, your boss. There are many ways to say you're sorry. Bringing those donuts to the boss's office on a regular basis, changing your tone (which will happen naturally when your expectations are straightened out), doing a better job meeting your boss's expectations, speaking your boss's language, and no longer expecting your boss to read your mind are all part of taking ownership of the new you and the new relationship.

Saying "I'm sorry," no matter how you express it, doesn't diminish you. Putting other people at least on the same level as you is liberating. It takes up a lot of energy and inner resources to resent people. Your Inner Idiot is a perpetually hungry, high-maintenance tapeworm who lives on unrealistic expectations and resentment and is constantly demanding more. By recalibrating your expectations, you can shrink your Inner Idiot to manageable proportions.

STEP TEN: "CONTINUE TO TAKE PERSONAL INVENTORY AND, WHEN I'M

WRONG, PROMPTLY ADMIT IT."

Confessing that you could be wrong and that your boss could be right is a big and difficult pill to swallow, but only if you harbor resentment based on unrealistic and unreasonable expectations. As I mentioned in Step Eight, if you find yourself partially out of the woods only to slip backward, if you begin to actually feel better about your relationship with your boss only to suffer a relapse, if you "porpoise" your way through your recovery, it is probably your Inner Idiot staying up all night rewriting the expectations you spent all day cleaning up. By continuing to put your motives, behaviors, and true feelings under the microscope, you can detect sooner rather than later when your Inner Idiot is taking your fresh new set of reasonable and realistic expectations and turning them into the emotional equivalent of junk bonds.

When you make amends, as discussed in Step Nine, you impeach anything your Inner Idiot is doing to sabotage the benefits of recovery. Because recovery is a process of continuous improvement, which invariably includes setbacks along the way, you need to be ready at all times to catch yourself reverting to old attitudes and behaviors. Admitting when we're wrong every time we're wrong is like a rolling amends. Monitoring ourselves and promptly confessing our mistakes, with the objective assistance of friends, bosses, coworkers, 360-degree feedback providers, and/ or fellow Recovering Idiots, creates a self-cleaning process that does not allow resentment to build up.

Remembering that it's not about you helps keep the focus where it will do you the most good, on adding value to the relationships you are in. At work, that means adding value first and foremost to the relationship with your boss. Having said that, every Wednesday night in the church basement we say, "It's not them; it's me." When there is blame to take, I'll take it rather than project it onto someone else. (At work, guess who that someone else would be?) If there is recognition to be given, I share it with others. It's my responsibility to keep myself focused on adding value. By doing so, everybody is a winner, especially me. I accomplish that by continuing to take my own inventory and not taking anyone else's. I admit my own mistakes instead of focusing on the mistakes made by others.

STEP ELEVEN: "THROUGH PRAYER AND MEDITATION, I SEEK TO INCREASE CONTACT WITH MY HIGHER POWER, AS I UNDERSTAND HIM, PRAYING FOR KNOWLEDGE OF HIS WILL AND THE COURAGE TO CARRY IT OUT."

Prayer is conversation. What good is a conversation with my Higher Power if I do all the talking? I don't learn anything more than I already know, and my Higher Power, who knows everything, is shut out of the conversation. I must listen in order to learn. Remaining open to the new perceptions that accompany new expectations requires that we follow the old "two ears, one mouth" formula. We should, at a bare minimum, listen twice as much as we speak. If nothing else, listening more makes us much more pleasant to be around and exponentially increases the likelihood that we'll learn something important.

Actively listening to my Higher Power is yet another way to keep my Inner Idiot from running amok with my imagination. I can be quiet on the outside and a chatterbox on the inside. My babbling like an Idiot on the outside is usually preceded by much babbling by my Inner Idiot. Just because I'm not speaking doesn't mean I'm listening to you. Just because people aren't fighting doesn't mean they're getting along with each other.

The more I engage my Higher Power to direct the repurposing of my expectations, the less opportunity my Inner Idiot has to author unreasonable, unrealistic, and downright false expectations. The healthier and more appropriate my expectations become, the better everything and everyone begins to appear. The more contact with my Higher Power I can maintain, the more my Higher Power's will dominates my life. If my will were such a great thing, I wouldn't be in the church basement every Wednesday night at 7 p.m. I might be in the sanctuary every Sunday giving thanks, but not in the basement sitting in a circle of metal folding chairs. Here's a prescription for sanity: contact, knowledge, courage. Repeat as necessary. That's the formula for every recovery program I've ever heard of. If you are your own Higher Power, it could be a lonely process.

Step Twelve: "These steps have me so jazzed, I want to share my joy with the world and apply them in all areas of my life."

The best way to learn something is to teach it. I wrote this book so you could learn how to really, truly, finally, once and for all get this boss-hating monkey off your back. But thinking that this monkey removal was a one-time fix, I managed to get that critter off my back only to have it crawl back on with a couple of his friends when I was focused elsewhere. I found myself in Dutch with my boss all over again, wondering *How could this happen to the guy who wrote the book?* If it can happen to me, it can happen to you. Once you feel the joy, hold onto it.

Keep yourself from backsliding by spreading the good news about better boss relationships. Remember that resentment has an unmistakable odor that indicates there is a rotten expectation not far away. The only way to stay fresh as a daisy in the expectation department is to keep your expectations reasonable and realistic and to inventory them regularly. Happily, the best way you can ensure you're doing this is by teaching others how to keep their expectations reasonable and realistic. Adopt a new language for your workplace discourse. Try saying things like "Let's try to put ourselves in the best position to succeed by keeping expectations of each other, our customers, and everyone involved in making this happen reasonable and realistic." You'll be amazed at how comments like that can help everybody around you feel more optimistic and less stressed.

Unless you just wanted a good laugh (and who wouldn't benefit from that?), anger is probably what led you to this book. Look at the cover. If that's not an angry illustration, I don't know what is. If you finish this book, take these principles and practices seriously, give them a good old college try, and you're still angry, I suggest taking an inventory of all the good that anger is doing for you and then starting over again at Chapter 1. You can repurpose anger, but whatever you do with it, you will still be angry. *To stop the anger, re-narrate your expectations.*

Your Step Twelve exercise is to faithfully do the first 11 exercises as often as needed to change how you feel about all the Idiots in your life. Never forget that an expectation is just a resentment waiting to happen, and that you cannot be happy as long as you harbor resentment. The longer you harbor resentment, the deeper the poison worms its way into your body. Frustration, anger, and resentment lead to depression. No more laughter. Give yourself the depression test: Watch a duck run. If you don't laugh, we'll save a seat for you in the church basement next Wednesday night at 7 p.m.

Index

About the Author

John Hoover, PhD, is a recovering Idiot Boss who successfully made the transition from angry employee to servant-leader by using the self-cleansing techniques in this book. He migrated from blue collar to white collar with the Disneyland Marketing/Entertainment Division and became way too white collar as an executive at McGraw-Hill. He is now a popular (and certified) executive coach and leadership and communications expert who knows the only hope for beleaguered executives is to laugh at themselves in the mirror. Dr. Hoover provides the mirror (having broken a few of his own over the years). He is passionate about creating win/win outcomes for talented men and women and the organizations they work for. Although Dr. Hoover enjoys combining learning and laughter, he is known for achieving serious results. As an executive coach, there is no stronger advocate for the alignment of what individuals do best with what organizations need most. As an expert in change, cultural design, cultural transformation, and interpersonal communications, Dr. Hoover is particularly effective at building and sustaining powerful and productive relationships between his coaching clients and their constituents. As the title suggests, Dr. Hoover is not afraid to facilitate difficult conversations and fully explore what people are really thinking and feeling. Dr. Hoover spent six years as a California Board of Behavioral Sciences–licensed marriage, family, and child counseling intern before moving into organization development and organizational behavior. He understands how organizations operate by unspoken and unpublished rules of engagement and now coaches CEOs and other chief executives in a wide variety of industries, including media, entertainment, education, fashion, financial services, manufacturing, retail, and government agencies. Dr. Hoover is the author or coauthor of 15 other books, including *How to Live with an Idiot*, and supervises the Executive Coaching practice at Partners International in New York City (*www.partners-international.com*). He also teaches for Fielding Graduate University, City University of New York, and the American Management Association.

After you have read the wisdom of Ken Blanchard, Marcus Buckingham, Dale Carnegie, Jim Collins, Malcolm Gladwell, Seth Godin, Marshall Goldsmith, Jon Gordon, Chip Heath, Scott Keller, Bob Nelson, Rick Patino, Colin Price, Tom Rath, and Jack Welch…introduce John Hoover to your Inner Idiot and enjoy a long and happy career.

You can follow Dr. Hoover's media and live appearances, workshops, commencement speeches, and publications, or simply rant, at *www.howtoworkforanidiot.com.*